KU-533-297

THE REBIRTH OF EAST EUROPE

third edition

Michael G. Roskin
Lycoming College

PRENTICE HALL, *Upper Saddle River, New Jersey 07458*

Library of Congress Cataloging-in-Publication Data

Roskin, Michael
The rebirth of East Europe/Michael G. Roskin.—3rd. ed.
p. cm.
Includes bibliographical references and index.
ISBN 0-13-613647-8
1. Europe, Eastern—Politics and government. I. Title.
DJK42.R67 1997
947'.0009'049—dc21 96-52810
CIP

Acquisitions editor: Michael Bickerstaff
Editorial assistant: Kathryn Sheehan
Buyer: Bob Anderson
Cover design: Patricia Kelly
Editorial/production supervision and interior design: Rob DeGeorge

This book was printed and bound by Courier Companies, Inc.
The cover was printed by Phoenix Color Corp.

© 1997 by Prentice-Hall, Inc.
Simon & Schuster/A Viacom Company
Upper Saddle River, New Jersey 07458

All rights reserved. No part of this book may be
reproduced, in any form or by any means,
without permission in writing from the publisher.

Printed in the United States of America

10 9 8 7 6 5 4 3 2 1

ISBN 0-13-613647-8

LEEDS METROPOLITAN UNIVERSITY LEARNING CENTRE
1702812943
KV-B
1137262 2-3-00
947 ROS

PRENTICE-HALL INTERNATIONAL (UK) LIMITED, *London*
PRENTICE-HALL OF AUSTRALIA PTY. LIMITED, *Sydney*
PRENTICE-HALL CANADA INC., *Toronto*
PRENTICE-HALL HISPANOAMERICANA, S.A., *Mexico*
PRENTICE-HALL OF INDIA PRIVATE LIMITED, *New Delhi*
PRENTICE-HALL OF JAPAN, INC., *Tokyo*
SIMON & SCHUSTER ASIA PTE. LTD., *Singapore*
EDITORA PRENTICE-HALL DO BRASIL, LTDA., *Rio de Janeiro*

CONTENTS

PREFACE

This book is not written by an expert on East Europe, nor is it intended for such experts. It grew out of my decision to include East Europe in an introductory comparative politics course. At the time, the upheaval in East Europe was making headlines every day; I could think of no way to make comparative politics more exciting or relevant. I looked for an introductory text and found nothing suitable. Existing works on East Europe tended to be overly specialized studies, sometimes of single countries, which have now been overtaken by events. Many of these studies, prepared with great diligence by careful scholars, are now irrelevant; some were based on mistaken assumptions. Furthermore, the leading edge of political science requires its practitioners to theorize too much. To read some studies, one might think East Europe was populated by theories rather than by humans.

The net package was a literature little accessible to undergraduates, especially to first-time students of East Europe. Many students have never been exposed to the basics that make something like East Europe intelligible. Especially lacking in the specialized literature are geography and twentieth-century history. How many students, for example, can locate Southern Dobrudja on a map? (Even worse, after they have been shown, a few still cannot locate Northern Dobrudja.) Accordingly, an introductory text must fill in many gaps in basic student knowledge.

For classroom instruction, East Europe and its recent upheavals provide some wonderful examples and case studies of legitimacy (or lack thereof), ideology (or lack thereof), the relation between politics and economics, international dependency, political culture, institution building, and party systems. Especially fascinating are the differences between East and West Europe and how rapidly the former will catch up with the latter. The project also gave me the opportunity to return to an area that was of great interest to me many years ago. From 1963 to

1964, I studied at the University of Belgrade, and I had authored an earlier book (*Other Governments of Europe*, Prentice-Hall, 1977) that had included Yugoslavia and East Germany. It was good to get back to an area that in recent years had not attracted the attention it deserves.

In the course of writing this book, it occurred to me that I was engaged in dialogues with three imaginary figures: one a leftist, one a rightist, and the third an optimistic political scientist. These figures are composites of people I have known over the years. The leftist, while uncomfortable about the actual workings of Communist East Europe, still thinks that Marx was basically right and that some type of socialism, perhaps the alleged "humanist" variety of the young Marx, is the progressive thing to aim for. But East Europe really was socialism in action: what you saw was what you got.

The rightist, on the other hand, is often little aware of how bad and backward East Europe was before the Communists took over and how difficult is the transition afterward. With the Communists out of power, rightists tended to think everything would be great. It is not that simple. The sources of instability are many in East Europe, and attitudes and institutions are not yet fully attuned to pluralist democracy and a market economy. Extreme and sometimes bloody nationalism erupted after the Communist blanket was removed. I still hope that after a long and difficult period of adjustment, most of East Europe will join West Europe as modern democracies and free economies.

The imaginary political scientist, steeped in theories of systems and stability, for some years thought East Europe was headed for a middle way of hybrid regimes in which the Communists shared power with others. After some decades of reflecting on middle ways or third paths between communism and democracy, controlled and market economies (the purpose of my year in Yugoslavia), I concluded that they do not exist, or, if attempted, have short life spans. Events in East Europe and the ex-Soviet Union, I think, bear me out. My imaginary scholar also closely analyzed party elites, too closely to notice that the whole system depended on the threat of Soviet intervention. Take away that threat and the game of musical chairs in some politburo is about as significant as arranging deck chairs on the *Titanic*.

This third edition has allowed me to get into the dynamics of building democracy and the violence of ex-Yugoslavia. Chapter 8 borrows from my article on party systems in the March 1993 *East European Quarterly*. My thanks to its editor, Stephen Fischer-Galati, for permission to use portions of this article. Chapter 9 includes portions of my article on the war in ex-Yugoslavia in the Autumn 1994 *Parameters*, the journal of the U.S. Army War College, where I served as a visiting professor from 1991 to 1994. This experience was a time of intellectual growth and challenge, during which I came to appreciate more sharply the security dilemmas of the region. Dr. Gary Guertner and retired Col. John Madigan, editor of *Parameters*, encouraged me to elaborate some of my ideas on ex-Yugoslavia. One of the highlights of the Army War College is working with

International Fellows, some of whom were directly relevant to this book. I must thank Col. Gunther Wolffframm of Austria; Lt. Col. Thadeusz Lesniowski, Col. Zdzislaw Wojcik, and Col. Kazimierz Sikorski of Poland; Col. Tibor Nagy and Maj. Gen. Ferenc Vegh of Hungary; and Lt. Col. Jiří Šedivý of the Czech Republic, from whom I learned so much.

Special thanks must also go to Zsuzsa Kelen, an economist and distant cousin in Budapest, who gave me many insights into the economic difficulties of the transition to a market system. Doctors Cestmir Konecny and Miloslav Had of the Institute of International Relations in Prague illuminated the factors underlying the Czech-Slovak split. Maj. Gen. Pavol Gavlas, director of the Institute for Strategic Studies in Prague, gave me a lucid, somber orientation on the security implications of Slovak separation, and Dr. Andrzej Karkoszka of the Polish Institute of International Affairs in Warsaw gave me a clear perspective on the various impacts of Poland's massive economic change. Dr. Anton Žabkar of the Slovenian Defense Ministry gave me an insider's view of the breakup of Yugoslavia and the role of the Yugoslav army in it. I also owe special thanks to my Lycoming colleagues. Historian Robert Larson, with whom I toured Central Europe in 1992, made important comments about and corrections in some of my historical chapters; he saved me from making several misstatements. Mathematician Andrzej Bucki gave me an insider's view of Solidarity and taught me how to pronounce Polish names. Robert Maples of our French department used his computer expertise to turn my electronic manuscript into camera-ready copy on the LaserJet. Sandra Rife prepared most of the maps. Additionally, I wish to thank Donald E. Pienkos of the University of Wisconsin-Milwaukee, Zachary T. Irwin of the Pennsylvania State University-Erie, The Behrend College, and Joan Serafin of Frostburg State University in Maryland for their conscientious and helpful remarks on the first edition.

Full responsibility, of course, is mine. I welcome all professional comments and corrections for a possible fourth edition. They can be sent directly to me at Lycoming College, Williamsport, PA 17701, or e-mail roskin@lycoming.edu.

MICHAEL G. ROSKIN

East Europe Today

INTRODUCTION

East Europe as a Unit of Study

The rebirth of East Europe was inevitable but unpredictable. Sooner or later East Europe was going to escape from the Soviet orbit and from communism, but precisely when no one could know. Upon coming to power in 1989 and 1990, every non-Communist leader of East Europe was stunned with disbelief. Only a few months before, many had been in prison or in the dissident underground. The speed of change was incredible because change was waiting to happen. The weak, unstable Communist regimes of East Europe were waiting for word from the Soviet Union that it no longer wished to retain them. When that word came, most Communist regimes were out of power in a matter of months. Communism in East Europe (or, for that matter, probably anywhere) is not a workable system. In East Europe, it lasted only as long as the Soviets were willing to prop it up. Most observers assumed this would be more or less forever.

In 1989, Soviet President Gorbachev pulled the props out and most of the Communist regimes of East Europe quickly collapsed: Transformed Balkan Communist regimes clung to power a little longer. Most Western observers greeted the changes with joy. Now, at last, the lands of East Europe would rejoin Europe and move quickly up to West European levels of prosperity and democracy. But things are not that simple, and East Europe will retain its distinctive characteristics for some time. East Europe has long been a backward area and has lagged behind most of West Europe for centuries. The Communists were not the sole culprits. The Communists, to be sure, took a backward area and kept it backward, but they did not invent its backwardness.

This book then is not a starry-eyed view of East Europe. It presents the region with all its problems, and with a few hopes. Ultimately, I am an optimist about East Europe. I am convinced that most East European countries are going to make

Is There Still a Second World?

For the last couple of decades, writers have used the shorthand expressions First, Second, and Third Worlds. The First World designated the market economies and democracies of West Europe and North America. The Second World was the centrally planned Communist economies of East Europe and the Soviet Union. The Third World was almost everything else, namely, Asia, Africa, and Latin America.

Now, suddenly, there seems to be no more Second World, certainly not in East Europe, which has abandoned Communist dictatorship and turned toward market economies. Should we promote them to the First World? There is no international tribunal to place countries in these simplified categories. This book is going to argue that East Europe is still quite different from the First World lands of West Europe. East Europe is poorer, less democratic, and is still experimenting with a market economy. If all goes well, East Europe may some day join the First World. In the meantime, it might qualify as either the Second World or World 1.5.

it, after much stress and strain, into a new, modern Europe. Not in my lifetime, but perhaps in my grandchildren's, East Europe may reach levels similar to those now found in West Europe. Until then, East Europe will be a fascinating place to study, for it resembles the West Europe of previous decades. Almost like taking a time machine back, in East Europe we can see firsthand the struggle to industrialize, to found stable democracies, and to calm the passions of political extremism. For political scientists, East Europe is a sort of laboratory of democracy, where we can witness in real time experiments we dare not try on our own political systems.

One problem in studying East Europe is that East Europeans do not think of themselves as East Europeans. They think of themselves as Poles, Czechs, Hungarians, and so on, and they do not like to see themselves as members of a broader regional entity. West Europeans, on the other hand, increasingly call themselves "Europeans" and think of themselves as members of the European Union, which is slowly turning into a supranational entity they are proud to belong to. There is no such pride of membership in East Europe, for the "East bloc" they were consigned to was not of their making. It was forced on them. And East Europeans, again in contrast to West Europeans, are still nationalistic. East Europeans of one country like to look down on East Europeans in neighboring countries.

When you ask East Europeans to generalize about what is happening in their region, it will strike them as an absurd question. They know and care, at most, only about what is happening in their own country. Comparisons among East European nations and generalizations about East Europe as a whole have rarely

What Did We Know and When Did We Know It?

Political scientists have some explaining to do. Some might be a little embarrassed. Most of us failed to anticipate or even conjecture about the collapse of communism in East Europe. Some specialists looked at the Communist regimes of the region as working, more or less permanent structures. Others argued that they would change but not totally; they would reform into "hybrid" regimes that mixed communism with democracy and centralized economies with market economies.

Why did we underanticipate change in East Europe? Do we tend to underanticipate change in general? Is political science inherently a status quo discipline, one focusing on what is, but incapable of detecting the forces for change? By trying too hard to sound scientific, some political scientists embraced formalistic theories of systems and stability that ignored the reality of contrived regimes imposed by foreign bayonets and secret police upon unwilling peoples. In these bloodless, abstract theories, hatred does not compute.

Some political scientists accurately foresaw major upheavals in Vietnam, South Africa, and Central America. These political scientists tend to be liberals or radicals, and they bring with them a critical intelligence that is skeptical of the existing state of affairs and capable of identifying the sources of change. Applied to East Europe, though, these same discerning eyes tended to dim, for they either paid little attention to the region or looked at it through leftist lenses. They liked to study revolution in the Third World, not revolution in the Second World. Some even refused to consider that socialism might be inherently flawed.

About the only people who accurately anticipated the impending collapse in East Europe were the emigrés, those who had fled their native lands to denounce the Communist regimes from exile. They understood the depth of hatred that many theorists missed. But they were often so angry, so nationalistic, and so immoderate in their views that many of us tended to write them off as fanatics. It turned out that many of them had a better handle on reality than some American specialists.

It may be unfair to expect political scientists to anticipate what few others anticipated. Practically no one saw what was coming, including the people making the decisions that made it happen. But political scientists really are supposed to have a handle on reality. If we cannot anticipate political upheavals, what good are we? I do not mean here that we need to make precise predictions about what will happen and when, but we should have a general sense that certain regimes may be headed for breakdown and others for success. "Early warning" is a worthwhile and feasible task for political scientists and one that would sharpen our analytic skills. A political scientist who accurately anticipates major change also demonstrates his or her mastery of data and of analytical tools. Prediction, or at least anticipation, should be considered important tests of political science.

occurred to them. They will tell you that comparisons and generalizations about East Europe are not valid, that each East European country is different. This book argues that generalizations about East Europe are not only possible but irresistible. East Europe, while far from uniform, can be profitably studied as a unit. The countries of East Europe share many historical experiences. Notice how one leads to the next.

1. All East European countries were parts of empires, most until this century. Once subjected to one empire, the East European victims usually soon fell into the clutches of another. The Ottoman Turks, the Habsburgs, the Prussians, and the tsarist Russians made East Europe their playground. This kept the countries of the region weak. In sharp contrast, in West Europe strong nation-states emerged early and were able to fight off conquerors and maintain their independence.

2. All East European countries got their independence late, some only at the close of World War I. With the French Revolution, nationalism rippled through Europe, waking up one nationality after another. During the nineteenth century, Romania, Bulgaria, and Serbia pushed out the Turks. By the beginning of the twentieth century, all the subject peoples of East Europe fairly ached to be free and independent. World War I gave them their chance. Their imperial masters, Austria-Hungary and Germany on one side and tsarist Russia on the other, bashed themselves until they collapsed. From the wreckage rose the subject peoples, the "successor states" to the old empires.

3. All the East European lands except Czechoslovakia flunked their first test of democracy during the interwar years. All were initially set up on a democratic premise, but by the 1930s military coups, royal dictatorships, and the growth of fascistic parties characterized the region. Communist parties, it should be noted, were small and scarcely a problem in the interwar years.

4. Weak and divided, East Europe was a pushover for the Nazis. Czechoslovakia, betrayed by Britain and France in 1938, was taken over without a shot in 1939. Hungary and Romania, under domestic fascistic pressure, joined Hitler's Axis, as did Bulgaria. Poland and Yugoslavia fought but were quickly crushed. By the time the war ended in 1945, the East European lands were weaker than ever and unable to resist becoming Soviet satellites.

5. All East European lands were conquered by Stalin's Red Army in World War II. As the Soviets pushed the Germans back through East Europe, Stalin set up obedient Communist puppets, most of whom had sat out the war in Moscow. Only Yugoslavia's Tito, head of the Partisan army that had liberated roughly half the country, had his own power base. Stalin didn't trust anyone who wasn't his puppet.

6. Stalin ordered all East Europe turned into Soviet satellites. Using his puppets and Communist control of the interior (police) and defense ministries, Stalin moved one step at a time to install Communist regimes modeled on the Soviet system. The

last country to fall was Czechoslovakia, taken over by a Communist coup early in 1948. No Communist regime came to or stayed in power by free elections.

7. The Communist regimes of East Europe, brutally inflicting the Soviet model on captive peoples, had almost no legitimacy. Most East Europeans resented and many actively hated their regimes. Over the decades, no Communist regime succeeded in rooting itself into the hearts of its people. Indeed, legitimacy grew weaker over time. In several East European lands mass discontent erupted in anger

The Study of East Europe's Politics

Until recently, East European politics was studied by relatively few specialists. They were trained not only in the languages and histories of their areas but also in the curious logic of Communist systems. To study Communist systems, one had to understand the Marxist-Leninist theory, the importance of party structure and of key party personnel, and the controlled, secretive nature of Communist regimes. Specialists, unable to interview decision makers, developed indirect methods to study East Europe's politics, including a lot of reading between the lines of party and state publications, carefully analyzing speeches for clues about policy, and noting who got fired, retired, or promoted. Using these indirect methods plus some sophisticated intuitions and insights, specialists on East Europe were able to come up with important and accurate analyses. For example, the split of East Europe's Communist parties into conservative and reformist factions was studied well and early by specialists.

Some specialized studies of East Europe, however, have quickly become irrelevant, for things have changed drastically. Closed politics has given way to mass politics. The indirect methods and reading between the lines are no longer particularly worthwhile. Now most of the region's politicians give interviews with reasonable candor. Lesser officials are no longer afraid to talk with visiting Western scholars and journalists. (Under the Communists, officials having any contact, including exchange of letters, with foreigners were subjected to scrutiny and were interviewed by security police.) Free and fair elections can now be studied and analyzed. Election and survey data show a rich political life that was earlier buried under Communist glop.

The study of dictatorships requires a special set of skills, the study of democracies another set. The skills needed to study East Europe are now in large measure the skills long used to study West Europe. This is not to say that the old East Europe specialists are no longer needed. What we need is "cross-training" between East Europe and West Europe specialists. The former must add such approaches as public opinion, interest groups, elections, and legislative behavior, while the latter must add language, historical, and geographic expertise. East European politics has not suddenly become the same as West European politics, but it has started to resemble it, lagging behind it by several decades.

and violence against Communist regimes.

8. All the Communist economies of East Europe performed poorly. The socialist economic systems that were to bring a material paradise on earth fell farther behind the capitalist systems of West Europe and Japan. By the 1980s, the gaps were glaring and embarrassing, and this produced even more mass discontent.

9. All the Communist parties of East Europe split into liberal and conservative factions. Their confidence shaken by economic failure, the Communists groped for economic answers. The conservative gerontocracies, fearing (accurately) for their jobs and for system stability, offered only the most minor of reforms, which changed nothing. Liberals, generally younger, acutely aware that their economies were becoming laughingstocks, urged major reforms, including large elements of a market system. The liberals sought "middle ways" between socialism and capitalism, between Communist party control and pluralism. They did not realize that a middle way did not exist for them.

10. Amid growing mass clamor, the relatively liberal Communists wrested control away from conservatives and promised major reform. But major reform of a bad, unloved system is not what most people of East Europe had in mind. They wanted an end to communism of any stripe and its replacement by genuine democracy. With their newly won freedom of speech, press, and assembly, they demanded free, multiparty elections. The Communist liberals had unleashed a tiger.

11. Free elections, all with Gorbachev's approval, ousted most Communist regimes in East Europe. The renamed liberal wings of the old ruling Communist parties—they now called themselves Socialists and probably were—got clobbered in these elections, with the exceptions of Romania and Bulgaria. Gorbachev was content with the results.

12. The catchall parties that ousted the Communists soon split, producing instable governments and the politics of outbidding, some of it exploited by extreme nationalists.

13. Such politics ripped apart the two federal systems of the region, Czechoslovakia and Yugoslavia.

14. In several countries the strain of economic transition was such that the left, in the form of ex-Communist socialist parties, returned to governing power in free and fair elections.

These fourteen points, and there are others, demonstrate that East Europe indeed forms a unit of study. Let us now consider these points more fully.

CHAPTER ONE

Caught between Empires

IS GEOGRAPHY DESTINY?

East Europe was dealt a poor hand and played it even worse. Geography has been unkind to East Europe, but what the political leadership of the region did over the centuries deepened the problems of geography. Human decisions compounded an unfortunate geographic situation into one of weakness, resulting in foreign conquest until most East European lands were reduced to backwater provinces of empires.

East Europe's first geographical problem is its proximity to Asia. Whatever tribes thundered out of Asia, they hit East Europe first and hardest. East Europe can be seen as West Europe's buffer zone and protective barrier, a role East Europe plays to this day. Particularly destructive were the Mongols in the thirteenth century, who left a gigantic swath of destruction that pushed East Europe backward at the very time West Europe was starting to stir culturally, economically, and politically. Then came the Ottoman Turks starting in the late fourteenth century. Unlike the Mongols, they did not destroy for joy, but they implanted a backward system that snuffed out budding kingdoms and cultures and retarded Southeast Europe for centuries.

Consider this: The last invasion of West Europe by non-Europeans began when the Moors crossed into Spain in 711. They reached Poitiers, France, where, in 732, they were beaten by Charles Martel. Thereafter, they were slowly pushed back until finally dislodged from Andalusia in 1492. Two peninsulas to the east, at this same time, the Turks were pushing into the Balkans, beating the Serbs in 1389 and the Hungarians in 1526. Three years after that, they were besieging Vienna. While West Europe, free of Muslim invasion or occupation, could develop its states and economies, East Europe (with the exception of Bohemia and Poland) suffered for centuries under the Turkish yoke, a yoke that started to lift only in 1699. The Turks were not fully out of East Europe until 1913. West Europe had a head start in nation building of several centuries over East Europe.

Central Europe is mostly a broad plain with few geographical barriers to invasion. The only significant mountains of the region are the Carpathians, forming a Slovak spine between Poland and Hungary until, in Romania, they curve south and join the Transylvanian Alps. They are cut by several passes that permit invasion. The Balkans, to be sure, are mountainous; *balkan* is Turkish for mountain. But the river valleys in the Balkans generally run from north to south, one of them straight to Belgrade, the gateway to the Pannonian Basin for the Turks in the fifteenth century.

The region has also been shortchanged on navigable rivers. West Europe has the Rhine, an important trading corridor connecting Switzerland, France, Germany, Belgium, and Holland and emptying into the Atlantic. The magnificent Danube, which flows through Bavaria, Austria, Hungary, Yugoslavia, and Romania, could not play an analogous role. For centuries, the lower reaches of the Danube were in Turkish hands, and it empties into the Black Sea, long a Turkish lake, so its utility for trade was limited by the hostility of the Ottoman Empire. If the Danube had somehow flowed in the opposite direction and emptied into the Atlantic, the history of East Europe would have been quite different.

Trade is an extremely important factor in the growth of national power. Access to the open sea enabled the modernizing regimes of France, Spain, Holland, and England to collect revenues from trade and colonization. Access to the sea was limited for East Europe. Polish access to the Baltic was impeded by the Teutonic knights and then by Prussia. The Dinaric Alps of Yugoslavia cut the Dalmatian coast off from the Balkan hinterland; most of Dalmatia was simply a Venetian colony. The Black Sea, relatively speaking, led nowhere, and for centuries it was Turkish. Compared with West Europe, East Europe was largely landlocked and isolated.

But is geography destiny? Did these geographic disadvantages doom East Europe to slow development compared with West Europe? A cohesive empire running the length of the Danube and able to beat back the Turks might have brought modernization and progess much earlier to the region. Much of the problem has been political. East Europe's curse has been its fragmentation, a problem that continues to this day.

EAST EUROPE'S ETHNIC GROUPS

The formation of a strong empire or kingdom in East Europe was retarded by the multiplicity of the region's very distinct ethnic groups. To this day, most of these groups retain a spiky sense of their uniqueness and resist being amalgamated into larger units. West Europe, in contrast, was generally able to meld smaller peoples into national entities, turning Frisians into Germans, Burgundians into Frenchmen, and so on. The disunity of East Europe's peoples left them vulnerable to conquest and foreign domination.

Let us be careful in what we mean by "ethnic group" here. We do not mean genes or bloodlines. Biologically, the peoples of all Europe, East or West, are so mixed that it is impossible to untangle their genetic origins. Contrary to Nazi (and sometimes more recent) demagogues, there is no "pure-blooded" nation anywhere in Europe. Typically, Europeans are the descendants of peoples who came in waves of immigration that washed into Europe, often from the east.

"Ethnic group" in our context means language, not blood. For example, at one point there were Slavic settlements as far west as Hanover in Germany; these people were soon assimilated into the German language. Many Germans, if you could trace their bloodlines back, are simply German-speaking Slavs. In the early eighteenth century, after the Turks were expelled from Hungary, the Habsburgs settled large numbers of Germans in the depopulated countryside. Their descendants are now Hungarian.

Most East Europeans are of Slavic origin. Like most Europeans, the Slavs originated as tribes on the borders of Europe and Asia and pushed their way west in the early centuries of the Christian era. Their languages are rather closely related, closer than the Romance languages of West Europe. A Slovak peasant, it is said, can converse with any other Slavic peasant. Slovakia is roughly the hub of the Slavic lands, and peasant speech has not changed that much over the centuries. I found decades ago that I could make myself understood with Serbian in Slovakia, but not in Bohemia (the Czech lands), for Czech has evolved more than Slovak.

Religion deepened the divergences among the Slavic tribes. The western Slavs were Christianized from Rome. Poles, Czechs, Slovaks, Slovenes, and Croats became Catholic and wrote with the Latin alphabet, with some extra marks for peculiarly Slavic sounds. They looked westward and are generally western in outlook. The eastern and southern Slavs were Christianized from Constantinople and became Eastern Orthodox. Their alphabet is Cyrillic, a variation of the Greek alphabet that was developed by the Greek monks who converted them to Christianity. Russians, Ukrainians, Bulgars, Macedonians, and Serbs thus developed a more eastward-looking orientation. This was especially a problem when Constantinople (now called Istanbul), the headquarters of Eastern Orthodox Christianity, was conquered by the Turks in 1453 and could no longer serve as a fountainhead of learning and innovation, as Rome served for Catholic Europe.

Splitting the Slavs of East Europe into north and south are the Hungarians. Not to be confused with the Huns who thundered out of Central Asia in the fifth century, the Magyars (as the Hungarians call themselves) drifted from the Volga region of Russia and settled in the fertile Pannonian basin in the ninth century. Although they accepted Catholicism about the year 1000, Hungarians still stand out for their strange language, which shares few cognates with neighboring tongues. Knowing a Slavic language or German will not help you understand Hungarian, which is distantly related to Finnish.

To the southeast of the Hungarians are the Romanians, descendants of the ancient Dacians and of the Roman soldiers who occupied the area. Romanian is very much a Romance language, and if you know French, Spanish, or Italian, you can read some Romanian. Romanians, though, were Christianized from Constantinople and most are Eastern Orthodox, although they returned to the Latin alphabet in the nineteenth century.

Albanians, descendants of the ancient Illyrians, with a Turkish overlay, have a tiny country between Yugoslavia and Greece. Their language is all their own, and they are divided in religion between a Muslim (but largely nonpracticing) majority and both Catholic and Orthodox Christian minorities. They are further divided tribally between the Tosks of the south and Ghegs of the north.

Complicating matters, East European borders do not neatly demarcate its peoples. Some ethnic groups are settled among other groups, what geographers call "interdigitized." The biggest single example now is Transylvania, part of Romania but with a Hungarian minority. They are so interspersed that Transylvania cannot be fairly partitioned into Hungarian and Romanian areas. Additionally, there are Hungarian minorities in Serbia and Slovakia. In the south of Serbia, ethnic Albanians form a big majority in the once-Serbian province of Kosovo, now the scene of violent ethnic clashes. The large Serbian communities deep in Bosnia and Croatia formed three centuries ago as Serbs fleeing the Turkish occupation were welcomed in Habsburg lands as settler-soldiers on the Military Frontier between the two empires. This is where bloody ethnic strife raged in the early 1990s.

Dispersed peoples add to the region's complexity. Jews, gypsies, and Germans at one point formed important minorities scattered throughout the region. The Holocaust reduced the Jewish population to a fraction of its prewar numbers. After the war, most Holocaust survivors emigrated. Now there is a significant Jewish community only in Budapest. Gypsies were also victims of the Nazis, but they are still found throughout East Europe. Sizable German colonies, some deliberately planted by the Habsburgs to secure their empire, have greatly shrunk. Millions of Germans fled westward from Poland and Czechoslovakia at the close of World War II. Many of the remaining ethnic Germans of East Europe emigrated over the decades to the jobs and prosperity of Germany, which by law has to take them in.

Is the ethnic complexity of East Europe really that different from West Europe? If you go back far enough in West Europe, you find all kinds of ethnic groups. The difference is that most West European monarchies had the political, military, economic, and cultural power to turn divergent ethnic groups into subordinate parts of their kingdoms, in time assimilating them and erasing their languages and cultures. France is the model for this kind of modernizing and centralizing monarchy. Neighboring Spain, unable to turn its Basques and Catalans into Spaniards, exhibits some of the problems of East Europe, especially of Yugoslavia. The point is that almost every country starts with or acquires ethnic groups. The stronger nation-states are able to control, dominate, and sometimes assimilate

East or Central Europe?

Before World War II, the region we are talking about was called Central Europe and the Balkans. After the war, it was called East Europe. There is no tribunal to settle geographic names. Names change over time in response to the political situation. Between the two world wars, Central Europe and the Balkans were the middle area between West Europe (countries that generally touch the Atlantic) and the vast Eurasian mass of the Soviet Union. With the Cold War and the division of Europe in two, it seemed more natural to call this middle ground East Europe, to distinguish it from West Europe. During the Cold War, there was no "middle," and the term Central Europe fell into disuse.

Some emphasize the religious grounds for distinguishing between Central and East Europe. Central Europe encompasses the Catholic countries of the former Habsburg (Austro-Hungarian) Empire plus Poland, also Catholic. East Europe, on the other hand, includes the lands of Eastern Orthodox Christianity—Russia, Ukraine, Serbia, Bulgaria, and Romania. Catholic countries looked to Rome for spiritual guidance and with this came a more western outlook, one still apparent today in art, architecture, and attitudes. For example, Lviv, in present-day Ukraine, was for centuries Polish-ruled Lwow, Austrian-ruled Lemberg, and Russian-ruled Lvov. It clearly looks different from most Russian cities. The streets are laid out in square grids, and the churches and many other buildings are western in style. Lviv feels European.

Eastern Orthodox countries, with the fall of the center of their faith, Constantinople, to the Turks in 1453, had no single spiritual capital to look to for guidance and modernization. Moscow claimed to be the spiritual capital of Eastern Orthodoxy, but most branches of the faith paid Moscow no special attention. Cut off by Tatar and Turkish occupation, the Eastern Orthodox countries were bypassed by the invigorating currents that rippled out of Italy with the Renaissance. Whether this was a matter of religious differences or Tatar and Turkish occupation can be disputed.

With the end of Communist regimes in East Europe, the term Central Europe quickly revived, and Hungarians, Czechs, and Poles started calling themselves Central Europeans. We will use East Europe here to designate the broad band of countries to the west of the ex-Soviet Union that were Communist. We will also find it useful to split the region into Central Europe (from Hungary north), which faces west, and the Balkans (lands to the south of Hungary), which doesn't know quite where to face. Central Europe turned quickly to democracy and market economics; it has plausible claims to join to NATO and the European Union. The changes that led to the ouster of Communist regimes in Central Europe came slower and later in the Balkans. Many Balkan lands never really ousted their Communist rulers and only pretended to establish democracy and market. The gap between two cultural areas remains alive to this day.

minority groups. The key is political power, and in this the East European states have historically been much weaker than their West European counterparts.

WEAK STATES

During the Middle Ages, there were kingdoms in East Europe as developed as any in West Europe at the time. Medieval Poland, Bohemia, Serbia, and Bulgaria attained great strength and respect in their day. Around half a millenium ago, at about the time much of East Europe fell under the Ottomans, a series of changes hit West Europe that moved it to modernity. These changes were generally weaker and occurred later in East Europe and left it relatively backward. The "strong state" developed in West Europe first. Exactly what caused the strong state and which changes came first is disputed, and the changes did not necessarily occur in the following order:

1. *The economy expanded* with trade, new industries, and the opening of the New World. With their access to the Atlantic, most West European monarchs eagerly promoted economic growth and expansion. Relatively isolated, East Europe had slower economic growth.

2. *Monarchs turned absolutist* and developed unquenchable thirsts for national power, both political and economic. Often at war, the ambitious monarchs developed standing armies and navies whose costs escalated. This forced them to modernize their kingdoms and improve administration (especially tax collections), commerce, communication, and education.

3. *The absolutist monarchs thus founded the modern nation-state.* Bypassing the conservative feudal system in which king was balanced by nobles, the new monarchs defined themselves as the last word in law. This gave rise to the notions of sovereignty and nationality. Loyalty to nation became more important than loyalty to locality or to feudal counts and dukes.

4. *The class structure changed as the economy modernized.* Middle classes developed, based on the growth of commerce and industry, in West Europe. They provided a more stable and enthusiastic basis of support for the new nation-state. Better educated, they also made better military officers in time of war. East Europe, still agrarian, stayed feudal, with a class structure composed of few nobles and many peasants. Serfdom lasted much longer in East Europe than in West Europe.

Changes such as these added up to what some call the "strong state" or "modern nation-state." East Europe lagged, in part for reasons of geography, but in large measure because it had already been incorporated into empires. Could the East Europeans have avoided it? Only if they had been able to unify, federate, or form alliances among themselves. This they could not—and still cannot—do.

FOUR EMPIRES

At least five distinct empires have dominated parts of East Europe. We will consider four here and save the fifth, the Soviet, for longer consideration in subsequent chapters. Once caught between empires, East Europe tended to stay caught.

The Ottoman (Turkish) Empire

This vast and long-lived, but ramshackle, empire exploded in the fourteenth century as the Ottoman Turks took Anatolia and the Balkans. The Muslim Ottomans beat the Bulgarians at Adrianople in 1361 and the Serbians at Kosovo in 1389, a victory that opened their way into the rich Pannonian basin of Hungary and on to Vienna, which they besieged twice, in 1529 and again in 1683. All Europe trembled until Polish cavalry under Jan Sobieski drove the Turks back from Vienna in 1683 in what is considered one of the most decisive battles of history. At about the same time, the Ottomans took the Arab lands of the Middle East and North Africa. In 1453, the Ottomans cracked the walls of Constantinople, which they had earlier bypassed, with their new cannons and took it over as their capital, Istanbul.

The Ottomans were compelled to keep expanding because much of their revenue was from booty. If they stopped expanding they would have little with which to pay the army. Meritorious soldiers were rewarded on the spot after battles by grants of lands in the newly conquered domain. This gave them a keen edge to fight well. In this way, the Ottomans built up a loyal, landowning class that they could count on to defend both the empire and their individual estates.

Ottoman Empire at Its Height

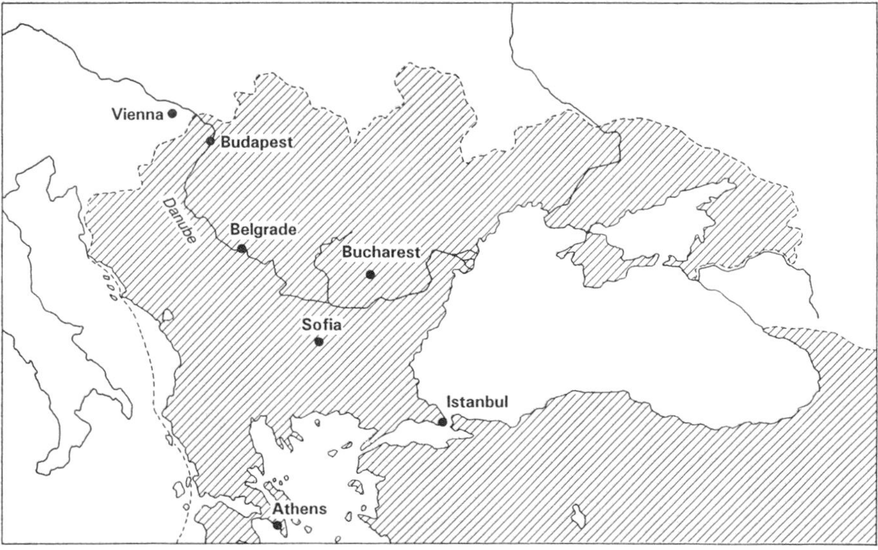

How did this gigantic empire, rarely well administered, hold together? There was a kind of Ottoman genius in running their empire: they didn't try to do too much. The sultan in Istanbul rarely tried to control the whole thing, which, considering the distances involved and poor communications of the time, might have been impossible. Many sultans were assisted by *viziers*, roughly prime ministers, who were able and vigorous men, many of non-Turkish origin. The Ottomans imposed a "blood tax" on their subject peoples and every few years collected it in the form of young boys plucked from their mothers and packed off to Istanbul to become *janissaries*, the administrators and police of the Ottoman Empire. Forbidden to marry and having no blood ties to the peoples they administered, the janissaries impartially and sometimes brutally imposed order.

Furthermore, in keeping with the hands-off Ottoman governing style, non-Muslim subject peoples of the empire were permitted to largely govern themselves as far as their internal matters were concerned. In what was called the *milyet* (nations) system, Christians and Jews had their own courts and customs. Non-Muslim religions were rarely persecuted; the Turks were tolerant.

The whole empire was loose and sloppy. Hugely corrupt and poorly run, it went into economic decline and slowly fell apart. As the economy and technology of its European Christian foes accelerated, the Ottomans found themselves getting beaten more frequently. In 1687, the Austrians defeated them at Mohács in Hungary. With the Treaty of Karlowitz in 1699, the Ottomans agreed to turn over Hungary and Transylvania to the Habsburgs, Dalmatia to Venice, and Podolia to Poland. They had occupied (and decimated) Hungary for a century and a half. Karlowitz marks the beginning of the slow Ottoman retreat in Europe, as Russia and Austria pushed them back and native Balkan nationalities revolted.

By the early nineteenth century, the Ottomans had lost most of the Balkans. They left behind several small states (see "Balkanization" box) and instability. North Africa and Egypt were only nominally part of the empire; powerful local chiefs actually ran them as independent countries. By the late nineteenth century, the Ottoman Empire was widely regarded as "the sick man of Europe." In 1913, the Ottomans were finally expelled from Europe except for the little corner of European Turkey that still exists. Allied with Germany in World War I, the

Balkanization

The small countries left as the Turks were pushed out of the Balkan Peninsula gave rise to the derisive term "balkanization," the breaking apart of an empire into small, weak countries. These lands included Serbia and Macedonia (which later became parts of Yugoslavia) and Moldavia and Wallachia (which later became Romania). The word *Balkan* connoted comic-opera countries (such as "Marsovia" in Franz Lehar's *Merry Widow*) that constantly squabbled among themselves.

> ***The Last Ottoman Problem: Palestine***
>
> In case you think the problems of the decline of the Ottoman Empire belong to another century, consider present-day Israel. Its conflict with its Arab neighbors and Palestinian inhabitants is also a leftover problem from the Ottoman Empire, for Palestine was a Turkish province for six centuries. As in the Balkans, the Turks were pushed back by a combination of local unrest and great-power intervention, in this case chiefly British.
>
> During World War I, Turkey allied with Germany, and Britain conquered Ottoman holdings in the Middle East, setting up "mandates" from the League of Nations to govern Palestine, Jordan, and Iraq. Britain also permitted large-scale Jewish immigration to Palestine, which increasingly awoke Arab fears that Palestine would be taken from them for a Jewish state. The Holocaust spurred Zionists into pushing Britain out of Palestine, and in 1948 the state of Israel was founded. Arabs and Israelis have been fighting ever since, backed, as in the Balkans, by major outside powers.

Ottoman Empire finally collapsed.

Bear in mind that the Ottoman Empire dominated much of the Balkans for four and even five centuries. This put a distinct stamp on the region that one still notices in foods, architecture, and attitudes. It gives the region a certain Middle East charm, but it retarded economic and political development. Left behind after the Turks were nationalistic rivalries that started World War I and that continue to this day. Worst of all, the Ottoman Empire prevented the rise of the sort of "strong state" that grew in West Europe. Without such strong states, East Europe was easy pickings for other empires.

The Habsburg (later Austro-Hungarian) Empire

This major dynasty, of German origin, ruled Austria from 1278 to 1918 and Spain from 1516 to 1700. This meant it had numerous other holdings—most of Latin America, the Netherlands, Hungary, Czechoslovakia, and parts of Poland, Italy, Romania, and Yugoslavia. At one point in the sixteenth century, under Charles V, Habsburg military might and New World gold, fighting on the Catholic side, came close to dominating Europe.

It is the eastern Habsburgs that chiefly interest us, for they formed the preeminent East European empire. Every country we are studying in this book (except Albania and Bulgaria) was for centuries, in whole or in part, under the Habsburgs. In large measure, we are studying the Austro-Hungarian "successor states."

In 1620 the Catholic Habsburgs beat the Protestant Czechs and incorporated their lands (known as Bohemia) into the Empire. Late in that century the Habsburgs pushed the Turks out of Hungary and likewise incorporated it into the empire. Hungarian nationalists note that the Habsburgs took their sweet time liberating Hungary from the ravages of Turkish rule. Hungary included Slovakia, Transylvania, and northern Yugoslavia, so all these areas came under the Habsburgs. From 1772 to 1795, with the partitioning of Poland, Maria Theresa of Austria, reluctant to dismember a sister Catholic country, "wept but took her share," the southern part of Poland, known as Galicia. Maria Theresa also began administrative and military reforms that turned the Austrian Empire into a reasonably efficient and rational unit.

Could it have survived? This gigantic and diverse empire was a natural trading zone centered on the Danube. (Vienna, Bratislava, and Budapest are all near each other on the Danube.) One wonders whether, if Habsburg policy had been more flexible and clever, they would have succeeded in building a cohesive empire in which German, Slavic, and Hungarian speakers would be proud and prosperous citizens. As a trade bloc, the Austro-Hungarian Empire could have become a major economic player and developed all its provinces. If it had stayed together, it would probably have rivaled Germany as an economic power. Broken into weak, small countries after World War I, each separated from the others by hostility, territorial claims, and tariff barriers, the economy of the region stagnated.

But, since the spread of nationalism after the French Revolution and Napoleonic wars, multinational empires are simply not viable. Their component nationalities demand independence. It was the enormous ethnic diversity of Austria-Hungary that finally doomed it. Only a quarter of the population was German. Another fifth was Hungarian, but close to half was of half-a-dozen Slavic nationalities who owed little loyalty to the emperor.

One solution might have been to grant all the nationalities of the Austro-Hungarian empire equal status within a democratic, federal structure, thus transforming the empire into a Danubian federation. Some far-sighted thinkers of the time suggested it, but the Austrian and Hungarian nobles were basically reactionaries who couldn't compromise with the new forces that were rippling through their empire. They wanted to keep things in a mythical golden age. Only in late 1918, two weeks before the empire collapsed in World War I, did Vienna in desperation suggest turning the empire into a federation. Perhaps if they had done it 10 years earlier, there would have been no World War I, and a "United States of Danubia" would now be a major and wealthy nation.

Even trying to appease a major nationality led to more difficulties for the Habsburgs. Hungarians bitterly resented being treated like second-class citizens and in 1848 rose against Habsburg rule. The tsar sent Russian troops to help put down the uprising. After Austria's disastrous performance in a war with Prussia, in 1867 Vienna granted Budapest equal status within the empire. The emperor of Austria also took on the title of king of Hungary, and the Hungarian parliament, dominated by conservative nobles, ran the Hungarian half of the empire more strictly than the Austrians ran their half. This was called the Dual Monarchy of Austria-Hungary; its symbol was a double-headed eagle.

"Divide and Rule"

How did the Turks and Austrians run sprawling empires in which they were greatly outnumbered? They practiced the ancient art of imperialism first devised by the Romans, who gave it the Latin name *divide et impera*, divide and rule. Keep your subject peoples divided and hostile to each other; play off one against the other. Then you can easily dominate. For example, since Croats did not like being governed by Hungarians, in the last century Vienna used Croatian troops to suppress unrest in Budapest. The trouble with this clever policy is that it left a legacy of great animosities that now prevent the independent nations from cooperating with each other. Most former Ottoman and Habsburg countries cordially hate each other to this day.

Now it was the Hungarians' turn to treat subject peoples like second-class citizens, and Slovaks, Croats, and Romanians were forced to obey Budapest and even to learn Hungarian, a policy called "magyarization." Budapest had no intention of granting its subject nationalities equal status. What Hungarians demanded for themselves they denied to others. In East Europe, "freedom" for one nationality meant its dominance over other nationalities.

Another factor doomed the empire: its desire to expand. In a sense, it couldn't help itself. As the Turks were pushed back in the Balkans, Austria-Hungary almost naturally moved into the vacuum. Specifically, in 1878 Austria occupied Bosnia, the mountainous area between Serbia and the Dalmatian coast, which was partly populated by Serbs. Neighboring Serbia, which that same year had won its full independence from Istanbul, didn't like Austria taking what it felt was Serbian territory. Anger grew in Belgrade when Austria annexed Bosnia into the empire in 1908.

In 1914, Bosnian students, equipped with guns and grenades from sympathetic Serbian army officers, assassinated Austrian Archduke Franz Ferdinand in Bosnia's capital of Sarajevo. Austria felt it had to severely punish Serbia to show the Slavic nationalities of its empire that it would not stand for any breakaway movements. Belgrade rejected Vienna's demands to take over Serbia, and Austria attacked. Serbia turned to Russia for help, Austria turned to an expansion-minded Germany for help, and World War I was on.

World War I, sparked by terrorism, was the seminal tragedy of the twentieth century, the catastrophe that led straight to communism, nazism, and World War II. Could it have been otherwise? Suppose the Serbian government had given in to Austria's demands. Austria would have occupied Serbia, raised its economic, health, and cultural levels, and given Serbs access to a great empire. Austrian rule, after all, was not so bad; it was vastly better than Turkish rule. Serbs could have worked within the empire with other nationalities to turn the empire into a democratic federation. Such is the nature of nationalism, however, that this suggestion is utterly unacceptable and implausible. Once nationalism gets going, rule by foreigners seems horrible, intolerable, a crime against one's people. In this way, nationalism led to East Europe's fragmentation and vulnerability.

The Tsarist Russian Empire

Throwing off the Mongols in the fifteenth century, the Russian state expanded until, under Peter the Great in the early eighteenth century, it broke through the Turks to the Black Sea in the south and overcame the Swedes in the north to reach the Baltic. Much Russian attention was focused southward, against the Turks. In a long series of wars, Russia pushed the Ottomans back until at one point a Russian army was camped at the gates of Istanbul.

Russian motivation was partly religious but mostly geopolitical. Most of the Christians under the Turks in the Balkans were Eastern Orthodox, and the tsar, as head of the Russian church, felt himself to be their natural protector. In varying degrees, Russian military pressure on the Ottomans allowed Orthodox Christian Serbia, Wallachia, and Moldavia to win their autonomy and then their independence from the Turks. The Russians also dreamed of liberating the historic capital of their faith, Constantinople, from Islamic rule.

The geopolitical motives were probably more important. A Black Sea that belonged securely to Russia offered military protection and a commercial outlet to the Mediterranean. Otherwise, the whole southern part of the tsar's empire was landlocked. To obtain full use of the Black Sea, however, required dominating the Turkish Straits. Otherwise, whoever stood astride the Dardanelles and Bosporus could stop or let pass merchantmen and warships as they wished. Turkey, with a history of centuries of rivalry with Russia, could let in foreign fleets and not let out the Russian fleet. During the Crimean War of the 1850s, Turkey did precisely this, letting the British and French through to fight on Russia's soft underbelly. Control

Are Lithuania, Latvia, and Estonia Part of East Europe?

Well, perhaps, but they tend to see themselves as Scandinavian. Between the two world wars, the independent Baltic republics might be included in East or Central Europe, especially Lithuania, which from 1386 to 1795 had been part of the Polish-Lithuanian kingdom. With the partition of Poland in the late eighteenth century, Lithuania came under tsarist Russian rule. Latvia and Estonia had long been part of the tsarist empire but were left largely alone.

Stalin took all three of the Baltic republics in 1940 and had their inhabitants treated brutally. Hundreds of thousands were deported to Siberia. A big majority of Lithuanians, Latvians, and Estonians fervently wanted independence and gained it in 1991. They did not identify with East or Central Europe, however, but with their Scandinavian neighbors on the Baltic.

The Partitioning of Poland

In three stages, from 1772 to 1795, Austria, Russia, and Prussia, in mutual agreement with each other, took larger slices of Poland until it disappeared from the map of Europe. The weakness and helplessness of Poland in the face of the three empires encapsulates the tragedy of East Europe in general.

Poland was governed by an ancient and unworkable constitution that continued the feudal pattern whereby nobles were more powerful than the king. Recall how in West Europe monarchal absolutism reversed this situation. Poland's nobles, independent and arrogant, met in a council in which each had right of veto over any new law. That is, even one vote against could block any measure. This *liberum veto* (free veto) led to immoderate, insoluble quarrels among factions of nobles. To gain advantage, they turned to outside help, some to the Russians, some to the Prussians, and some to the Austrians. The outsiders simply helped themselves to parts of Poland. Too late, in 1791, Poles produced a modern, reformed constitution inspired in part by the new U.S. Constitution. This effort, however, simply provoked Russia and Prussia into making a second partition in 1793 and abolishing the reform attempt.

Polish patriots hated the partition and rose heroically in 1794, 1830, 1863, and 1905 in unsuccessful attempts to restore an independent Poland. Thousands were killed, jailed, or forced into exile. Some of Poland's greatest artists, such as pianist-composer Fryderyk Chopin and novelist Joseph Conrad, went abroad. Still, the Poles' struggles kept alive the hope that they would one day regain Poland's independence.

of Istanbul, therefore, became one of the great wishes of Russian and later Soviet foreign policy.

With the partition of the once-large Polish-Lithuanian state between 1772 and 1795, Russia took the eastern territories of the country and after 1815 came to control central Poland, including the capital of Warsaw. These areas Russia ruled as its "Vistula provinces" until the end of World War I. In Poland, as elsewhere in the tsarist empire, the Russians tried to "russify" the population by requiring Russian as the official language and discouraging the use of local tongues. This policy created nothing but resentment. Austrian policy in Galicia, its part of Poland, was far more enlightened and permitted a certain autonomy, including the use of the Polish language and an elected assembly.

Russia, too, was a vast multinational empire, but it didn't have quite the same problem as Austria-Hungary, for Russians formed a majority of the population. Nonetheless, World War I wrecked it, too. By mobilizing the gigantic Russian army in July 1914, the tsar panicked the German kaiser into doing the same. As the tsarist empire collapsed in the war, its restless nationalities saw their chance for freedom. Lithuania, Latvia, Estonia, and Finland took their independence. The

Ukraine nearly did. And Polish independence fighters in the Russian sector of Poland united with colleagues in the German and Austrian zones of the partitioned land to put Poland back on the map of Europe after a century and a half.

The Prussian (German) Empire

During the Middle Ages, Germans pushed eastward along the Baltic, exterminating or enslaving the local populations. These Germans became known as Prussians and their ruling class as *Junkers*, from the German for young gentlemen (*junge Herren*). Frederick the Great of Prussia in the eighteenth century continued the process by seizing Silesia and eagerly participating in the partition of Poland. German colonizers were brought in, Polish landowners were dispossessed, and the Polish language was suppressed.

In 1871, under Prussian leadership, Germany unified. The Second Reich stretched from Alsace (now French) to East Prussia (now Polish and Russian). Half of present-day Poland was part of Germany. The Germans, to be sure, brought industry to these territories, but Poles resented them and longed for independence and unification with Russian and Austrian Poland. Deprived of a nation-state, Poles rallied to the Catholic Church, to literature, and to music as a statement of their national identity.

THE EASTERN QUESTION

Where these empires collided, there was war. Notice particularly how the Ottoman Empire at its high point included portions of both Russian tsarist and Austro-Hungarian lands. These areas of overlap were the scenes of fierce battles in which the Turks were slowly pushed back, giving the Russians and Austrians enlarged holdings. What to do with the declining Ottoman Empire was for over a century known as the "Eastern Question."

One may quarrel at length over the net impact of empires. Some bring with them signs of progress. The Austrians in the Balkans, for example, did some good in modernizing backward Ottoman provinces and in bringing them into Europe. In the main, however, empires stifle the freedom, creativity, and economic progress of their subject peoples. The worst thing about empires, though, is that they invariably end, and when they do they leave behind the instability, ambition, and rivalry that lead to new wars.

Is East Germany Part of East Europe?

No, at least not any more. Now unified with the Federal Republic of Germany, the former German Democratic Republic has joined West Europe. Still, because it was very much part of the Soviet bloc for forty years, we will refer to it from time to time as part of East Europe.

Key Treaties of Ottoman Decline

Step by step, Turkish power was pushed back. Each major step was marked by one or more treaties. These are some of the more important ones:

Karlowitz, 1699. Beaten by the Habsburgs, the Ottomans turned over to Austria a vast area that included most of Hungary, Transylvania, and the northern part of what later became Yugoslavia.

Kuchuk Kainarji, 1774. The Ottomans conceded to Russia the right to protect Christians in Wallachia and Moldavia (which later formed Romania). The tsar later grandly claimed the treaty gave him the right to protect all Christians in the Ottoman Empire.

Adrianople, 1829. Confirmed the autonomy of the Serbs, Wallachians, Moldavians, and Greeks, who had revolted against Istanbul. The treaty also awarded Russia the mouth of the Danube.

Unkiar Skelessi, 1833. The weak Ottoman Empire turned to Russia for help in putting down breakaway Egypt. The Treaty of Unkiar Skelessi marked the first time Istanbul had to turn to outside powers to try to hold its empire together.

Straits Convention, 1841. The first of many treaties governing the strategic Turkish Straits, the 1841 agreement put the straits under nominal international control.

San Stefano, 1878. This treaty ended another Russo-Turkish war by giving Russia major gains in the Balkans and by setting up a pro-Russian state of Bulgaria.

Congress of Berlin, 1878. Alarmed that the Russians had gained too much influence in the Balkans in the Treaty of San Stefano, the major European powers scaled back its provisions, set up a smaller Bulgaria, and confirmed Serbian and Romanian independence.

London, 1913. The Ottomans, after five centuries of rule and influence in the Balkans, are pushed out of all Europe except for the present small corner of European Turkey.

The retreat of the Ottoman Empire is a case in point. As the Turks were pushed back, by a series of wars and revolts, they left behind small, dissatisfied states with undefined borders and exaggerated ambitions. Serbia, for example, attempted to grab a piece of Bulgaria in 1885. (The Bulgarians still claim Macedonia as part of Bulgaria's ancient kingdom, and linguistically Macedonian is a branch of Bulgarian. Most Macedonians, however, wish to be independent.)

Furthermore, as the Ottoman Empire declined, the other great powers quarreled over who would pick up the spoils. In the nineteenth century, Austria and Britain feared Russia pushing into and taking over Ottoman holdings in the Balkans. The British specifically feared Russian control of the Black Sea and the Turkish Straits, seeing this as a threat to Britain's "imperial lifeline" to India. These concerns led

The Good Soldier Schweik

Czech writer Jaroslav Hasek penned great truth in his satirical novel *The Good Soldier Schweik*. Schweik, a Czech subject of the Austro-Hungarian Empire, is drafted to fight for the empire in World War I. This is the last thing he wants to do. But instead of resisting openly, which would only lead to the firing squad, Schweik uses the tricks of subject peoples. Always appearing to be a "good soldier," Schweik pretends to go along, carrying out orders literally and stupidly, until he bollixes up the Austrian war effort. Schweik became a literary symbol of Czech passive resistance to overlords, first the Austrians, then the Germans, and finally the Russians. Poles and Hungarians historically have resisted more heroically, but the Schweik strategy has served the Czechs well. In Prague today you can drink rich Czech beer in the very tavern frequented by Hasek and described in the novel as Schweik's hangout.

to the curious situation of some of the major Christian powers of Europe propping up the major Muslim power, Ottoman Turkey, against whom in earlier centuries they had conducted crusades. From 1851 to 1856, Britain, France, and Austria fought Russia in the nasty Crimean War (where Florence Nightingale founded modern nursing) in order to stem Russia's southward advances. These same fears of Russia taking too much territory were apparent in the two treaties of 1878 (see box). With San Stefano, Russia got what the others thought was too much; the Berlin Conference was called to trim back Russian gains in the Balkans.

As the Ottoman grip on the Balkans weakened, these provinces seemed ripe for the picking by other imperial powers. Austria took over Bosnia from the Turks in 1878 and tried to take over Serbia in 1914 (provoked, to be sure, by the Sarajevo assassination of Franz Ferdinand). Russia took territory down to the Danube and set up protectorates with an eye to extending its power to Istanbul and to controlling of the Turkish Straits. The Russian and Austrian empires began to bump into each other as they moved in on the Turkish empire. In the early twentieth century, the rival ambitions of Austria and Russia in the Balkans turned what might have stayed a small Austro-Serbian war in 1914 into World War I.

WORLD WAR I IN EAST EUROPE

Both world wars intimately concerned East Europe. Some thinkers note that both wars started in East Europe, and that is true—the Austrian invasion of Serbia in 1914 and German invasion of Poland in 1939—but the stakes were much bigger than mere control over East Europe. The weak states that succeeded the four empires were tempting targets for conquest, and this struck the sparks that lit the conflagrations of both world wars.

East Europe in 1914

As we have considered, the peoples of East Europe grew increasingly restless under the yokes of their respective empires in the nineteenth century. As Ottoman power receded in the Balkans, Austria and Russia moved in to fill the vacuum, and this rivalry was one important cause of World War I. All four of the empires we have discussed fought and destroyed themselves in the war, including Turkey (which fought on the side of Germany), although by World War I Turkey was effectively out of the European picture.

All East European nationalities contributed to the war effort, mostly as soldiers in the armies of their respective imperial masters. At first little Serbia held off Austria, but the arrival of German troops put the Serbs to rout. The Serbian army escaped to Corfu and was thence mobilized into the Allied cause to fight under a French general on the Salonika front in northern Greece. Croats, on the other hand, were drafted into the Austro-Hungarian army. Sergeant Josip Broz, for example, joined a German-speaking unit and was captured on the Russian front.

Woodrow Wilson on East Europe

President Wilson, one of the founders of political science in the United States, brought with him to the Versailles peace conference of 1919 the legalistic and idealistic bent of the subject at that time. Wilson gave his famous "Fourteen Points" address to Congress in early 1918; three of the fourteen points directly concerned East Europe:

"X. The peoples of Austria-Hungary, whose place among the nations we wish to see safeguarded and assured, should be accorded the freest opportunity of autonomous development.

"XI. Rumania, Serbia, and Montenegro should be evacuated [of German and Austrian forces]; occupied territories restored; Serbia accorded free and secure access to the sea; and the relations of the several Balkan states to one another determined by friendly counsel along historically established lines of allegiance and nationality; and international guarantees of the political and economic independence and territorial integrity of the several Balkan states should be entered into...

"XIII. An independent Polish state should be erected which should include the territories inhabited by indisputably Polish populations, which should be assured a free and secure access to the sea, and whose political and economic independence and territorial integrity should be guaranteed by international covenant."

One immediately senses that there would be some difficulty carrying out these grand aims.

When the Bolsheviks took over, he converted to their revolution and later became Tito, the Yugoslav Communist chief. Hungarians, Czechs, Slovaks, Poles, and Romanians were likewise part of the Austrian armed forces. In 1914, Austrian mobilization orders had to be issued in a dozen different languages.

It was here that Austria-Hungary paid the price for failing to integrate its many nationalities. Why should Czechs and Croats fight for a German dynasty? The subject peoples did not fight enthusiastically; some even wished the empire to split apart. For this, the reactionary Habsburgs had only themselves to blame. They had never defined themselves as anything but a Germanic dynasty with non-German subjects. If over the decades they had converted those subjects to citizens, the empire might have held together.

What was to become of East Europe was not the chief concern of the major powers for most of the war. Then the United States entered the war in 1917, when it was two-thirds over, and President Wilson introduced a new, idealistic set of war aims. These included the liberation of East Europe from its imperial shackles. The aims were wonderful, but were they realistic? The test here is not their lofty intentions, but how they worked out in practice. For that, we turn to Chapter 2.

SUGGESTED READINGS

CHIROT, DANIEL, ed. *The Origins of Backwardness in Eastern Europe: Economics and Politics from the Middle Ages Until the Early Twentieth Century.* Berkeley, CA: University of California Press, 1989.

GARTON ASH, TIMOTHY. "Mitteleuropa?" *Daedalus* 119 (Winter 1990), 1.

HUPCHICK, DENNIS P. *Conflict and Chaos in Eastern Europe*. New York: St. Martin's, 1995.

HUPCHICK, DENNIS P., AND HAROLD E. COX. *A Concise Historical Atlas of Eastern Europe*. New York: St. Martin's, 1996.

KANN, ROBERT A., AND ZDENEK V. DAVID. *The Peoples of the Eastern Habsburg Lands, 1526-1918.* Seattle: University of Washington Press, 1984.

KAPLAN, ROBERT D. *Balkan Ghosts: A Journey Through History.* New York: St. Martin's, 1993.

JUDT, TONY. "The Rediscovery of Central Europe," *Daedalus* 119 (Winter 1990), 1.

SETON-WATSON, HUGH. *The Decline of Imperial Russia, 1855-1914.* New York: Praeger, 1952.

SETON-WATSON, ROBERT W. *The Rise of Nationality in the Balkans.* New York: Howard Fertig, 1966 (originally published in 1917).

TURNOCK, DAVID. *Eastern Europe: An Historical Geography, 1815-1945.* New York: Routledge, 1988.

WOLFF, ROBERT LEE. *The Balkans in Our Time.* Cambridge, MA: Harvard University Press, 1956.

CHAPTER TWO

Flunking Democracy: The Interwar Years

The nationalities of East Europe were quite old when they at last won their freedom at the end of World War I, but as independent states they were very young. Indeed, as states most of them were artificial creations with unclear boundaries and uncertain popular support. The question of borders looms large in the interwar years. Unsupportable borders both caused and symbolized the turmoil and brevity of East Europe's states between the two world wars. In West Europe, most borders had long been clearly established. The only remaining dispute was over Alsace-Lorraine; it took World War II to settle that quarrel between France and Germany. East Europe was beset by a dozen boundary disputes that were at least as nasty and bitter as the Alsace-Lorraine question. The situation of East Europe between the wars was inherently unstable and had to collapse. This it did, first into the hands of the Nazis, and then into the hands of the Communists.

BORDERING ON MADNESS

Each East European nationality had a grand view of its territory. Some romantic nationalists harkened back to the boundaries of ancient kingdoms, as if temporary possession of a piece of real estate conferred permanent title. History gives no such title deeds. Typically, the new states of East Europe that emerged from the peace conferences of 1918-1920 out of the wreckage of the German, Russian, and Austrian empires staked out maximal rather than realistic boundary claims; such claims had to bring them into conflict with neighboring states.

The problem, one found worldwide, is that few nationalities have clearly defined natural borders. If every country could be like Iceland, the world would be spared many wars. Instead, almost everywhere, peoples are dispersed and interdigitized, making clear and fair borders impossible to draw. Drawing borders always includes people of one ethnic group in the territory of another. Between the world wars, an estimated 31 percent of East Europeans were classified as minorities. The solution, if there is one, is to make a state so strong that it can define nationality and inculcate that nationality into all its citizens, so that ethnic backgrounds become irrelevant. Most Alsatians, for example, after centuries of belonging to France, feel, speak, and act French, even though they have Germanic names and also speak German. Rather than change boundaries, you change psychologies.

This solution in East Europe proved difficult if not impossible. The countries were too new, the ethnic identities too strong, and the memories of past hurt or past glory too vivid. Hungarians living in Romania or Slovakia do not willingly turn themselves into Romanians or Slovaks. With this in mind, let us review some of East Europe's interwar border problems.

East Europe in 1930

Poland

The new Poland, reappearing on the map of Europe after more than a century, tried to obtain the borders of the old Poland, the Poland of the seventeenth century. This was done largely by military force, not by negotiation. Poland's new borders were problematic, for the old Poland had included a great deal of Lithuania, Belarus, Ukraine, and areas that had become German. The new Poland was beset by boundary disputes on every side.

Germany kept most of its territory—the big butterfly shape of Lower Silesia and Pomerania—but Poland took the most heavily industrialized part of Upper Silesia and Poznan (German: Posen), areas that in earlier centuries had been Polish and still had a Polish majority. Many of the "Germans" of the region, in fact, were of Polish descent; Prussian and German policy had been to Germanize the Polish population. Germany also lost part of Pomerania for a "Polish corridor" to the sea, as Wilson had urged and a friendly Versailles conference had accepted. Poland, after all, was an ally that had suffered greatly during the war, and Germany was a defeated enemy that deserved to be punished. The Polish corridor, however, left East Prussia cut off from the rest of Germany, a loss that many Germans found intolerable. Hitler later played into this longing to recover lost German territory. The largely German city of Danzig (Polish: Gdańsk) was declared a "free city" in which Poland had many rights.

To the south, a disputed area on the Czech border, Teschen, was divided between the two new countries, but this left some 140,000 Poles under Czech rule. To the north, Poland also took pieces of present-day Lithuania, including the capital, Vilnius (Polish: Wilno, Russian: Vilna). From 1386 to 1795, Poland and Lithuania had formed one kingdom, and Vilnius had a Polish majority even in the interwar period.

The real problem, though, was to the east, Poland's border with the new Soviet Union. Because ancient Poland had included Lithuania and Ukraine, the new Poland felt entitled to get at least part of them back. As we noted, history provides no guide to these questions. In two years of fighting between the new Polish army and the new Red Army, the front seesawed back and forth. In May 1920, the Poles were in Kiev, deep within Ukraine. By June, the Bolsheviks had pushed them out and by August were at the gates of Warsaw. It was the Bolshevik dream, especially the dream of Trotsky (who founded and organized the Red Army), that, once the Bolsheviks took Poland, spontaneous revolution would spread westward over all Europe. But the Poles threw the Bolsheviks back deep into Russian territory, and the two sides settled with the 1921 Treaty of Riga (capital of the newly independent Latvia).

This border, though, was not the "right" one, if such a thing is discoverable. It was a hundred or more miles too far east and included lands inhabited chiefly by Lithuanians, Belorussians, and Ukrainians along with a considerable Polish minority. Lwow (Russian: Lvov, Ukrainian: Lviv) had a Polish majority. Some 32

The Curzon Line

In late 1919, an international commission under British Foreign Secretary Lord Curzon came up with an "ethnographic" eastern boundary for Poland, one that took into account which ethnic groups lived where. The Curzon Line, as it was called, placed most Poles to its west and most Lithuanians, Belorussians, and Ukrainians to its east. It was a reasonably fair boundary but never went into effect; both the Bolsheviks and the Poles ignored it. The Polish Legions ended up well east of it and were not about to give territory to the Bolsheviks, who had tried to conquer them. The current Polish-Soviet border, seized militarily by Stalin in 1939, approximates the Curzon Line.

percent of Poland's population in the interwar period did not speak Polish as a first language. Was a fair border possible? The Allies at Versailles tried to draw one and did a pretty good job with the Curzon Line (see box), but Warsaw dismissed the notion of surrendering what it had just conquered. The Polish-Soviet border was fraught with problems and contributed to subsequent events that were disastrous for Poland.

Czechoslovakia

Like Poland, interwar Czechoslovakia was born with some difficult boundary and ethnic problems. Bohemia and Moravia (the Czech lands) were the most advanced and industrialized region of East Europe. The Austro-Hungarian Empire had selected them for industrial development, and the Skoda iron and steel works provided much of the empire's heavy equipment. Educationally and culturally, too, Czechs were at least as advanced as Austrians. Slovakia, on the other hand, was a backward region and in 1867 was consigned to the not-so-tender mercies of Hungarian administration. Czechs and Slovaks are two distinct peoples and do not especially like each other. Their languages are close but different. Slovaks, like Poles, are strongly Catholic. Czechs had largely turned to Hussite Protestant ideas after 1410 and were forcibly recatholicized after their crushing defeat by the Habsburgs at White Mountain in 1620. This left many of them secular in outlook. Bohemia had a large German settlement, and many Czechs spoke German. Slovakia had a considerable Magyar population, and Budapest required Slovaks to learn Hungarian. Czechs love beer (and make some of the world's best); Slovaks prefer wine. There was never such person as a "Czechoslovak"; you were either one or the other.

To the east of Slovakia stood an even more backward land, Ruthenia, now known as the Carpatho-Ukraine, inhabited largely by Ukrainians. It too had been under the Hungarian crown, and Hungary wanted it back. Ruthenians, like Slovaks, did not like being ruled from Prague.

During World War I, Czech and Slovak representatives agreed in talks in Pittsburgh, Pennsylvania, to form a new country that granted considerable self-government to Slovakia. (Czechs had a long and benevolent American connection. Many had immigrated to the United States. Woodrow Wilson especially liked their American-educated leader, Tomás Masaryk.) The 1920 Czechoslovak constitution, however, created a unitary state, governed by Prague, with Czechs in all the key administrative positions, even within Slovakia. This angered not only Slovaks but the 3 million Germans who lived in a large horseshoe-shaped area around three sides of Bohemia. This area, the Sudetenland, was passed on to the new state of Czechoslovakia with the breakup of the Austro-Hungarian Empire. A Hungarian minority, as it does today, lived in southern Slovakia. Thus the brave little Czechoslovak democracy was born with a large percentage of its people resenting the Czechs as the new imperial folk who, many felt, had no business bossing around Germans and Slovaks. These resentments paved the way for Hitler's takeover of Czechoslovakia in 1938 and 1939.

Hungary

Poland and Czechoslovakia were among the East European territorial winners from World War I. Hungary was among the losers, and a major one. The 1920 Treaty of Trianon (so named because it was signed in the Trianon Palace at Versailles) gave 72 percent of the prewar kingdom of Hungary, with 64 percent of its population, to Czechoslovakia, Yugoslavia, and Romania. Although most of the people living in these areas were not Hungarian, a sizable minority was, especially in Transylvania. Altogether, a third of Hungarians now lived outside Hungary's borders, a recipe for extreme Magyar nationalism and revenge. Virtually all Hungarians hated the dismemberment of their kingdom, and "Trianon" became for Hungarians what "Versailles" became for the Germans, an unfair treaty that had to be revised. This climate of bitterness contributed to the rise of reactionary and even fascistic political movements in Hungary. In the 1990s, concern for Hungarians in Slovakia, Romania, and Serbia is still prominent in Hungarian politics. After three-quarters of a century, "Trianon" still echoes.

Yugoslavia

Yugoslavia, like Czechoslovakia, was a new and artificial country, born only in 1918. Serbia had won autonomy from the Turks in 1804 and gradually expanded as a small kingdom. Serbs also developed the idea of expelling all foreign occupiers from the region and of founding a "South Slav" state. Using the example of the Piedmont region leading Italian unification, Serbs thought of themselves as freedom fighters for a new monarchy that would gather in and protect the neighboring South Slavic peoples. The flaw in this concept is that it did not accord equality to the other peoples. As we considered in Chapter 1, Serbian nationalism set off the spark that ignited World War I.

Hungary after World War I

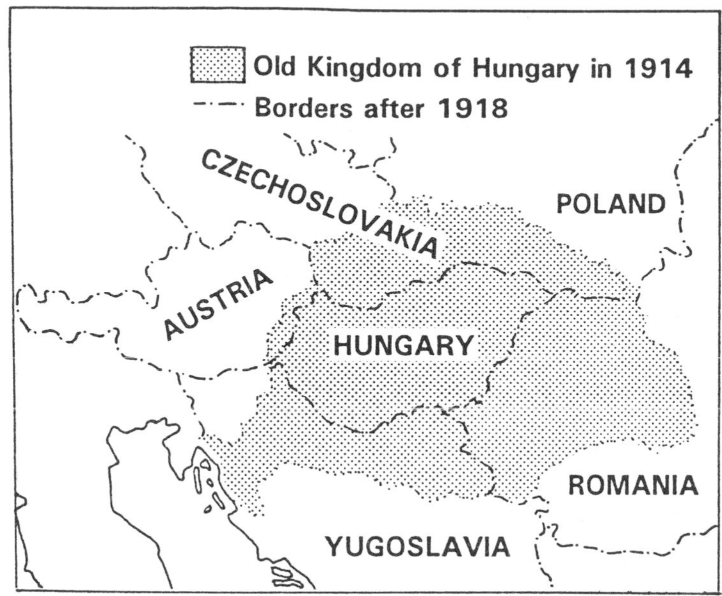

During World War I, King Alexander of Serbia obtained the sometimes half-hearted agreement of the various nationalities to form a new state. The effort had the support of the Versailles victors, for Serbia had fought on the Allied side. The Croats, the second largest nationality after Serbs and speaking essentially the same language, went along with the deal, for they did not like being ruled by Hungary and feared Italy would take Croatia's Dalmatian coast. In December 1918, King Alexander proclaimed the Kingdom of Serbs, Croats, and Slovenes. The name Yugoslavia only became official in 1929.

Yugoslavia was immediately a problem country, one stitched together from former Austrian, Hungarian, and Turkish provinces, with all the cultural and economic differences that implies. In the northwest, the Slovenes were virtually Slavic Austrians, prosperous and Catholic. On the coast, the Dalmatians were sort of Slavic Venetians, fishermen and seafarers. The Croats were heavily influenced by centuries of Hungarian rule (which they disliked). As one moved south, the country got poorer and more backward. Macedonia was nearly a Slavic Turkey, and it was claimed by Bulgaria. Montenegro (meaning "Black Mountain"), nestled in the mountains north of Albania, had never been conquered; it had preserved a backward independence under a prince-bishop and was still dominated by clans. Bosnia had a mixed population of Serbs, Croats, and Muslim Bosniaks (local Slavs who had been converted to Islam by the Turks). Furthermore, there was an important Hungarian community in the north and an Albanian community in the south.

Yugoslavia after World War II

This description of Yugoslavia at its birth requires little change to describe the Yugoslavia that collapsed in 1991 and 1992. Between the two world wars, as in the 1980s, Yugoslavia increasingly fell apart due to ethnic strife. Perhaps Yugoslavia was simply not meant to be.

Romania

Romania also gained from World War I, but was unable to keep its territorial gains through World War II. Romania was neutral at the start of World War I but joined the Allies in 1916. This paid off after the war when Romania was awarded the large area of Transylvania and the Banat region (just south of Transylvania, bordering Yugoslavia) from Hungary and Bessarabia and Bukovina from the collapsed Russian tsarist empire. Hungary always wanted Transylvania back, and the Soviet Union always wanted Bessarabia and Bukovina back. There are still strong feelings over these areas.

Suddenly after World War I, Romania more than doubled in size and population. This meant new political problems as the newly acquired minorities, especially Hungarians and Jews, triggered contrary Romanian chauvinist feelings,

Transylvania: Hungarian or Romanian?

In the twentieth century, Transylvania (meaning the "land beyond the forest") changed hands three times. Long part of the Kingdom of Hungary, the 1920 Treaty of Trianon gave Transylvania to Romania, because Hungary had been on the losing side and Romania, nominally at least, on the Allied side.

Hungary joined Hitler's Axis in 1939. Romania came under unbearable pressure from both Germany and Russia, which had agreed to divide East Europe in the 1939 Nonaggression Pact, and in 1940 Hitler stripped off the northern half of Transylvania and gave it to Hungary in the so-called Vienna Award.

Romania later joined the Axis but dropped out in time to technically be on the winning side in World War II. Because Hungary was again on the losing side, Romania was awarded all of Transylvania in 1945. Romanians and Hungarians are interspersed in Transylvania, making a fair partition impossible. The only two counties with a Hungarian majority, for example, are deep inside Romania, at the elbow formed where the Carpathians meet the Transylvanian Alps. Romanians now form some 80 percent of Transylvania's population, and, as far as Romania is concerned, that settles the issue. Hungary does not consider the issue completely settled and seeks, at a minimum, minority rights for ethnic Hungarians.

heightened existing Romanian anti-Semitism, and led to the founding of the fascist Iron Guard party of the extreme Romanian nationalists. This ultimately pushed Romania to the Nazi side in World War II.

Bulgaria

Bulgaria has been one of the losers in East Europe. Harkening back to the large medieval Bulgarian kingdom, Bulgarians in this century have dreamed of a "Greater Bulgaria." In combination with Greece, Serbia, and Romania, Bulgaria succeeded in pushing Turkey back to its present European frontiers in the First Balkan War of 1912-1913. This splendid victory even gave Bulgaria Western Thrace (now part of Greece) and thus access to the Aegean. But Bulgaria still claimed Macedonia (to which it indeed had historical and linguistic ties), and Serbia and Greece divided Macedonia between them after the First Balkan War. Unable to live with this, Bulgaria attacked them in the Second Balkan War of 1913. Romania and Turkey opportunistically joined in; Bulgaria was at war on all fronts and lost. Macedonia stayed divided between Serbia and Greece; Turkey got back Western Thrace; and Romania took Southern Dobrudja. (Dobrudja is the coastal region south of the mouth of the Danube; most of it went to Romania in 1878.)

The 1913 loss left Bulgaria longing to recover these territories. In 1915, the German side made Bulgaria a better offer than the Allied side, so Bulgaria entered

Bulgarian Expansion During World War II

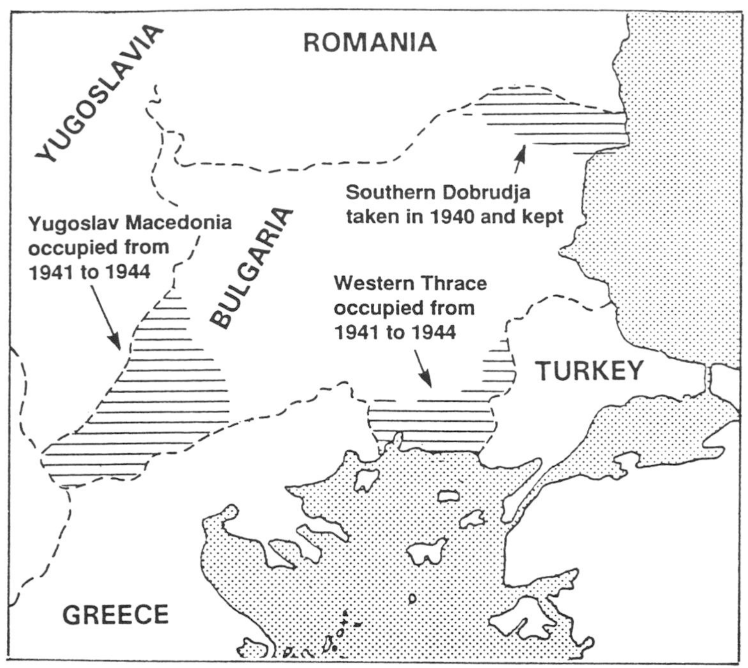

World War I and fought well against Serbia, Romania, and Russia, but unfortunately on the losing side. With the 1919 Treaty of Neuilly, Bulgaria again lost its disputed territories. "Neuilly" became for Bulgaria what "Trianon" was for Hungary, a symbol of the fatherland's dismemberment. Poor, agricultural, and now awash with refugees, some Bulgarians still dreamed of a Greater Bulgaria. Bulgarian nationalists sponsored the Internal Macedonian Revolutionary Organization (IMRO), which practiced guerrilla warfare and terrorism in the Macedonian areas of Greece and Yugoslavia. The purpose of IMRO was to recover Macedonia for Bulgaria. Between the world wars, Bulgaria was the wild man of the Balkans, rather like Iraq in the Persian Gulf today.

Bulgaria's irredentist aims moved it closer to Germany in the late 1930s, especially in trade. Hitler arranged the return of Southern Dobrudja to Bulgaria from Romania in 1940, and in 1941 Bulgaria joined the Axis. Hitler's victories in the Balkans allowed Bulgaria to take Yugoslav Macedonia and Greece's Western Thrace in 1941, only to lose them in 1944.

Albania

Tiny Albania, the poorest and most backward country of Europe, has been both occupied and occupier. Achieving independence in the First Balkan War,

Albania was overrun by five different armies during World War I. Some thought Albania would be divided between Greece and Serbia, but President Wilson wouldn't stand for it, and Albania emerged intact. During the interwar years, Albania fell under Italian control. Since ethnic Albanians also live in Kosovo (part of Serbia), Macedonia, and Greece, Albanian forces on the Axis side during World War II occupied these areas.

East Europe's territorial disputes resemble West Europe's during the Middle Ages and Renaissance. West Europe, after centuries of fighting and the establishment of strong states, worked out most of its boundaries. East Europe, held in a sort of suspended animation by the empires that occupied it for centuries, resumed its boundary quarrels as the empires withdrew or collapsed. We should not poke too much fun at the sometimes crazy way East Europe's borders heaved to and fro. The East European states were making up for lost time, advancing claims to create Greater Serbia, Greater Hungary, Greater Bulgaria, and so on that could not be sustained. By trial and error, they were finding out who had the wealth, power, geography, and allies to get and keep what they claimed was theirs. These boundary and ethnic issues are not settled; some of them burst out with pent-up fury in the early 1990s.

POLITICAL INSTABILITY

East Europe's conflicting territorial claims set the stage for political instability. They added one more brick to the already intolerable loads placed on the new democracies of East Europe after World War I. Economies were in shambles; with the collapse of empires came the disappearance of markets as each new little country tended to protectionism. The new regimes had little legitimacy to begin with; that is, many citizens doubted the right of the new governments to rule. Further weakening their legitimacy was the massive corruption, at Latin American levels, that pervaded most of East Europe. Irredentism fired nationalist politicians to demand the return of lost territories. Refugees, unfair treaties, and discontented minorities tended to push East European politics between the wars in an extremist and nationalistic direction. Every East European state started out after World War I with a democratic constitution. By the mid-1920s, only Czechoslovakia continued to function as a democracy. All the others were taken over by conservative parties with rigged elections, nationalist generals, royal dictators, or fascistic movements. They quickly flunked their first test as democracies.

In fairness to the East European states, we should note that numerous other democracies failed during the interwar period. Spain, Italy, Portugal, Germany, Brazil, Japan, Greece, and others went from weak, unstable democracies to dictatorships, some of them bloodthirsty and expansionist. We now see that democracy is not something that can simply be transplanted into a country. However democratic the constitution may be, democracy depends on widespread attitudes of moderation, tolerance, compromise, and restraint. You cannot thrust a democracy on a poor, badly educated population with no experience in self-rule and expect it to work. Democracy takes practice. Without experience and moderate attitudes, democracy becomes chaotic and tumultuous; politicians and parties don't play by the rules; and the democracy soon ends.

We should also note that all East European countries, except Poland and Czechoslovakia, were constituted as monarchies. This, theoretically, could have been a stabilizing factor; a monarch can sometimes give people a unifying and legitimizing figure to focus on. But East European kingdoms were small and weak. In greatly expanding their kingdoms, Yugoslavia and Romania brought their monarchs new subjects who did not feel that the monarchs were legitimate, as did the subjects in the original core area of their kingdoms, respectively, Serbia and the Regat.

It was no accident that democracy worked (and not without problems) in the only East European state with a partly industrialized economy and a rather well educated population, Czechoslovakia. East Europe on the whole was poor, much poorer than West Europe. The majority of East Europeans were peasants, some landless, others only smallholders. Yields per acre were much lower than in West Europe. Population increases and subdivision of holdings reduced some peasants to the subsistence level on tiny plots; these peasants were called "dwarfholders." Industrial growth was not nearly rapid enough to absorb the population surplus being generated in the countryside. For much of East Europe, poverty in the interwar years grew worse. And one important escape hatch closed in 1924: That year the U.S. Congress passed the Johnson Act that imposed national-origin quotas on immigration, which effectively snipped off immigration from East Europe.

The East European middle class was small and often connected to government bureaucracy. A modern business mentality was alien to East Europe. A disproportionate share of East Europe's business was in the hands of Jews, who, because they had been barred for centuries from farming, had long been merchants and moneylenders. The concept of "going into business" was rare in East Europe and is still something of a novelty today. Instead, a bright young person might aspire for a university degree and a position in the civil service. Unlike Americans, East Europeans (and Europeans generally) assumed that the state should take a leading role and that the private sector should be subordinate to the government. A tiny noble class, some with large land holdings, continued to exercise a disproportionate and overwhelmingly conservative influence in politics.

Anti-Semitism has a long history in East Europe, but between the wars it generally grew worse. Although Jews were rarely more than a small fraction of the population, they were regionally concentrated, especially in the towns. Anti-Jewish feeling ranged from maniacal in Romania to strong in Poland and Hungary. It was often quite regional within one country: moderate anti-Semitism in Croatia and Slovakia, but little in Serbia and Bohemia. Only Bulgaria and Albania developed no anti-Semitic movements.

Anti-Semitism is worth noting for at least two reasons. Its rise indicates that the society is under great stress and that this stress is pushing people to lash out at handy scapegoats. East Europeans, with new countries and illegitimate regimes, under economic hardship (which got much worse in the 1930s), tended to blame the people who had long been stigmatized on religious grounds. Jews tended to be small shopkeepers; they were visible and somewhat better off than average and became perfect scapegoats. A rise in anti-Semitism indicates a country is cracking up. (A current example of this can be seen in Russia.) Second, anti-Semitism feeds the growth of fascistic movements, which both utilize existing hatred of Jews and whip up more. In East Europe between the wars, the rise of anti-Semitism contributed to fascist takeovers and thence to alignment with Nazi Germany.

The Great Depression that started in 1929 hurt East Europe terribly. Farm prices virtually collapsed, and poor peasants got poorer. Industrial growth stopped and sometimes declined. Only Czechoslovak industry weathered the downturn; Austrians used to apply to get into Czechoslovakia for the good factory jobs. But elsewhere, many East Europeans were either indifferent to democracy or welcomed a strong-handed government that would restore order and put some bread on the table. Whatever chance democracy had in East Europe, it went down the drain with the Great Depression.

Poland

Józef Piłsudski fled from the repression of Russian Poland to the relative freedom of Austrian Galicia, the southern part of Poland. A military officer, Piłsudski trained Galician infantry that took part in the Austro-Hungarian war against Russia. His aim, however, was Polish freedom, not Habsburg hegemony. With Russia effectively out of the war by 1917, Poles began to think of fighting Austria. The German army didn't trust Piłsudski and jailed him. Wanting to stir Polish patriotism against the Germans and Austrians, the Allies declared Poland a member of the Allies so that technically Poland was on the winning side in World War I. In 1918, when the German, Austrian, and Russian empires split their defeat in the war three ways, Piłsudski's rapidly growing Polish Legions (they numbered 600,000 by 1920) moved in to fill the vacuum. Piłsudski became the powerful and revered president of a new Poland.

Originally defining himself as a socialist, Piłsudski shifted from democracy to authoritarianism. Admittedly, it would have been awfully hard to have stayed a pure democrat amid the turmoil of interwar Poland. About a third of the population was non-Polish, and minority nationalities—Germans, Ukrainians, Jews, Lithuanians—formed their own political parties. Furthermore, within the Polish majority, political infighting was immoderate and tumultuous. There were too many political parties, few of them willing to compromise.

Piłsudski, who often governed from the shadows as defense minister, pushed for stronger and stronger presidential rule and obtained it in 1935, shortly before his death. Political parties and the *Sejm* (parliament) were rendered powerless.

Piłsudski can be seen as a kind of de Gaulle, who also stood on the sidelines until he got a strong presidential constitution (in 1958). Both generals disdained parties and parliaments as weakening the country and saw a strong presidency—virtually an elected dictatorship—as the only way to save the nation. The mediocre Polish colonels who took over after Piłsudski lacked his vision and charisma. The political parties resented and opposed the presidential dictatorship, which grew repressive, nationalistic, and anti-Semitic. Polish politics resembled those of Perón's Argentina.

Czechoslovakia

Symbolically, just as modern Poland was founded by a soldier, Piłsudski, Czechoslovakia was founded and governed by intellectuals, Tomás Masaryk and Dr. Eduard Beneš. Politically, Czechoslovakia was, relative to the rest of East Europe, a success story between the two wars. While all the other lands moved to authoritarianism, Czechoslovakia continued as a democracy, with fair elections, a free press, and civil liberties. A major land reform turned millions of peasants into smallholder farmers, and they in turn supported the democratic government. Land reform was easier in Czechoslovakia than elsewhere because many of the large estates had belonged to Austrian and Hungarian nobility, and they were now foreigners without political influence in Prague.

Prague, to be sure, made mistakes. The Czechs, much better educated and economically more advanced than the Slovaks, defined themselves as the founders and leaders of the new state. They were slow in according home rule and local administration to the other nationalities. Most of the civil service was Czech. This provided fertile ground for German and Slovak nationalists. With the rise of Hitler in the 1930s, the Sudeten Germans, who lived on the borders of Bohemia, fell under the sway of Nazism and demanded autonomy and then union with Germany. The Slovaks demanded at least genuine federalism and then opted for independence. Czechoslovakia, then and now, was pulled apart by its nationalities.

Hungary

Interwar Hungary was born angry and stayed that way. Democracy had only the slimmest chance. A brilliant liberal nobleman, Count Mihály Károlyi, tried to set up a democratic system as soon as the Habsburg empire collapsed. Free elections and a free press, civil rights, land reform, and other sweeping reforms were quickly introduced. But a majority of Hungarians, still smarting from defeat and the loss of their gigantic kingdom, failed to rally to Károlyi. The nobles who owned the large estates hated any thought of land reform. Furthermore, Károlyi tried to retain the subject peoples of old in a federation that included Transylvania, something the Allies had no sympathy with. The Allies blockaded Hungary and forced Károlyi to withdraw Hungarian troops from Transylvania in March 1919. Károlyi resigned, and Hungarian democracy died in its cradle.

Conservatism and Fascism

These two terms, used to describe the "right" of the political spectrum, need to be clearly differentiated, especially as applied to East Europe. Conservatives want to preserve what is. Sometimes they want to go back to what was; this may earn them the title "reactionary." In East Europe, and indeed in much of West Europe as well, conservatism meant political systems in which democracy was curtailed by means of limited voting rights, the suppression of radical parties, and resistance to economic or social reforms. Political power stayed in the hands of aristocratic or wealthy persons.

Fascism was actually a radical philosophy that called for the revolutionary overthrow of old systems. Some thinkers suggest that fascism doesn't really fit on the right of the political spectrum. Fascists are lunatic nationalists. Nation is everything for them, and they define nationhood in racial terms. Jews are seen as not part of the nation; anti-Semitism is usually one of the building blocks of fascism. Additionally, fascist movements generally include some fake socialism; they talk about jobs and welfare for all. One tip-off of fascist movements: They love to wear uniforms. For them, politics should be structured along military lines: obedience and order!

It is here we may become confused in understanding the difference between fascism and conservatism. A conservative such as Poland's Marshal Piłsudski or Hungary's Admiral Horthy may come from a military background, but he has no interest in militarizing society. Such a leader also wishes to reestablish order, but it is the order of the old days, not of a radical new system. Both conservatives and fascists are firmly opposed to leftists, but the conservatives merely wish to suppress them, the fascists to kill them. Conservatives may also be nationalistic, but they generally practice live and let live with neighboring states. Fascists want to conquer; for them, war proves superiority. Under certain circumstances, as in interwar East Europe, conservatives and fascists may temporarily cooperate, but ultimately they are at odds with each other.

Into the vacuum moved the short-lived Communist takeover of Béla Kun. An officer of the Austro-Hungarian army, the socialist-minded Kun had been captured by the Russians in 1915 and as a prisoner had been converted to the aims of the 1917 Bolshevik Revolution. (Yugoslavia's Tito, also a prisoner in Russia, was likewise converted to communism at that time.) Under Moscow's orders and with Soviet money, Kun returned to Budapest and with local Communist and Socialist supporters seized power and instituted a small version of the Russian Bolshevik Revolution. The Hungarian Socialist Republic was opposed by just about everyone. In August 1919, Romania defeated Kun's Hungarian Red Army and looted Budapest. Kun fled to Russia. (In 1937, amid Stalin's purges, Kun was arrested and tortured and then executed in 1939 for alleged espionage.)

Hungary's interwar politics was an uneven struggle between what have been called "populist" and "urbanist" forces. The populists, by far the stronger, were nationalistic, conservative, peasant oriented, and anti-Semitic. They aimed at getting Transylvania back into Hungary. The urbanists, heavily concentrated in Budapest, were liberal, westward looking, intellectual, and partly Jewish. Most interesting, exactly the same division reappeared with free Hungarian elections in the 1990s, again won by the conservatives.

After Kun, conservative forces took over led by Admiral Miklós Horthy. (How could landlocked Hungary have an admiral? Prewar Austria-Hungary did have outlets to the Mediterranean, at Trieste and Fiume.) Horthy was a conservative, maybe even a reactionary, but it is not clear that he was a fascist, as the Communists later claimed. Horthy occupied a strange office in interwar Hungary: regent, the person who stands in until a new king is ready to take the throne. As conservatives, Horthy and his followers did not want a republic, so they restored the monarchy, but the surviving Habsburg, Karl, was unacceptable as king. Thus interwar Hungary was a monarchy without a monarch, presided over by an admiral without a sea, who served as regent with no expectation of a king.

Conservatives consolidated their hold. Kun's radical forces were brutally suppressed. The leading party became the populistic and conservative Smallholders party (which reappeared in 1990), but the elections were rigged. Horthy was moderately successful at curbing inflation and boosting industry and education. Still, the gap between rich and poor (mainly peasants) remained huge, and anti-Semitism bubbled closer to the surface. Jews, a sizable and better-off minority, were blamed for everything. The Great Depression hit Hungary hard, tensions mounted, and increasingly right wing governments permitted the rise of the fascistic Arrow Cross movement, paving the way for Hungary's alignment with Germany.

Yugoslavia

Yugoslavia, like Czechoslovakia, was pulled apart by its nationalities. The Serbs, like the Czechs, saw themselves as the founders and leaders of the new South Slav state; the other nationalities were seen as junior partners. The Croats intensely disliked the unitary and centralized Serbian monarchy; they found being governed by Belgrade no improvement over being governed by Budapest.

Matters came to a head in 1928, when a fanatic Montenegrin deputy gunned down the top leaders of the Croatian delegation on the floor of the national parliament. Croats, Bosnian Muslims, Macedonians, and even Serbs turned extremist and even fascistic. King Alexander was so exasperated with the turmoil that in 1929 he proclaimed a royal dictatorship. Renaming the country Yugoslavia, Alexander tried to erase the mentality of national areas by setting up artificial districts named after their principal rivers, the old trick of the French revolutionists that set up France's current departments. Alexander was assassinated in Marseille in 1934 by an IMRO gunman with ties to a Croatian fascist movement that in turn was backed by Hungary and Italy. Many forces wanted Yugoslavia dismembered.

Yugoslavia then limped along with a regency until Prince Paul came of age, but every year the country became a little more unstuck. Paul, seeing support from Germany as the only way to hold his kingdom together, drifted in a pro-Axis direction. He was overthrown by pro-British Serbian officers in 1941. Interwar Yugoslavia simply did not jell.

Romania

Romania's interwar politics paralleled those of its neighbors: a monarchy that for a time was a regency, unrest among its minorities, a large agrarian party, a royal dictatorship, and the growth of anti-Semitic and fascist parties. One of the most backward countries in Europe, Romania, by transforming itself into Greater Romania with the addition of Transylvania from Hungary and Bessarabia from Russia, took on problems it couldn't handle.

Under King Ferdinand, a major land reform was politically successful—it calmed millions of landless peasants—but economically counterproductive, as their holdings were too small to be worked efficiently. A soaring birthrate compounded the problem of rural poverty. Romania had one economic trump card: the only major oilfield then known in Europe. Foreign, especially German, capital rapidly began to develop Romanian industry.

The two leading parties were the National Liberal party and the Peasant party, who were elected and governed as a National-Peasant coalition. (Their descendants reemerged in the 1990 election to unsuccessfully challenge the ruling National Salvation Front.) Both these parties were fairly conservative and easily manipulated by large landowners. In 1927, Ferdinand died, but his son Carol abdicated, choosing to live openly with his mistress rather than stay with his queen. Carol's son, Michael (still the pretender to the Romanian throne) was only six at the time, so a regency was set up.

But Carol still had some legitimacy, especially as the Romanian economy suffered under the Great Depression and the National-Peasant regime splintered. Carol returned, ended the regency, and took the throne as Carol II. Building on traditional rabid anti-Semitism, the fascist Iron Guard party grew, and Carol, a conservative of the Horthy mold, could not contain it. In 1938, as chaos grew, Carol declared himself royal dictator. With everything collapsing about him in 1940, he fled with his mistress, and Romania fell into Hitler's clutches.

Bulgaria

Reflecting the peasant economies of East Europe, Bulgaria's leading party between the wars was the Agrarian party. Unique to East Europe at the time, the second largest party (but nevertheless much smaller) was the Communist party, the result of the early spread of Marxism to Bulgaria in the 1880s. The Bulgarian Communist party was founded in 1891, one of the first in the world and well ahead of its Russian counterpart. Bulgaria's Communists staged an uprising in 1923 but were suppressed, decimated, and outlawed. The key conflict in Bulgaria, however, was between the government and IMRO, the revolutionary organization that aimed at the recovery of Macedonia from Yugoslavia and Greece. Agrarian leader Aleksander Stambuliski, with overwhelming electoral support, became prime minister. King Boris had only a weak role. Stambuliski, a farsighted man, recognized that Bulgaria had to make peace with its neighbors, especially Yugoslavia, so he tried to turn off IMRO demands. The IMRO, which regarded any abandonment of their cause as treason, along with nationalist officers, staged a bloody coup in 1923 and gunned down Stambuliski along with thousands of helpless peasant supporters. Bulgaria thus gained a bloodthirsty reputation in the western press.

IMRO raids into Yugoslavia increased, and Sofia moved closer to Mussolini's Italy, which also wished to dismember Yugoslavia. Another coup in 1934 brought to power officers who had had enough of the IMRO and crushed it. The following year, King Boris, with army support, took over and set up a royal dictatorship. Boris moved Bulgaria closer to Nazi Germany, which established great economic influence in Bulgaria. In 1941, Bulgaria joined the Axis.

LEEDS METROPOLITAN UNIVERSITY LEARNING CENTRE

Albania

Interwar Albanian politics was a struggle between democratic and authoritarian forces that the latter won. On the liberal side was Fan Noli, a Harvard-educated Orthodox bishop. On the authoritarian side was the son of a Muslim tribal chief, Ahmed Zogu. Zogu gained control in 1921, lost it to Noli in 1924, and regained it in 1925. In 1928, Zogu turned the Albanian republic into a monarchy with himself as King Zog I. Zog did modernize Albania, crushing banditry and building roads and schools. But he drifted closer to Italy, which dominated Albania in the 1930s.

In sum, East European democracy between the wars scarcely had a chance. Struggling from the destruction caused by World War I, the new governments soon faced the disaster of the Great Depression. Untried institutions thrust upon unprepared citizens quickly collapsed into various types of authoritarianism. In every case, boundary and ethnic disputes played a major role in the domestic politics of these lands and helped determine their international alignments. Not one statesman of the region could see beyond his limited and nationalistic concerns to notice that all of East Europe was about to be swallowed by monsters. As today, there was no cohesion among nations in facing common threats.

INTERNATIONAL ALIGNMENTS

Simply by knowing which countries lost territories in World War I we can predict (with one major exception) how they would line up for World War II. The territorial losers, Hungary and Bulgaria, inclined toward the German-Italian Axis. The territorial winners—Poland, Czechoslovakia, and Yugoslavia—fearing revenge and dismemberment at the hands of Germany or Hungary, looked westward for help and thought they had found it in France, which also had a stake in keeping Germany down and retaining newly regained Alsace-Lorraine. The exception is Romania, which won big after World War I but nonetheless inclined toward the Axis as these territories were stripped away in 1940.

France sponsored the Little Entente in 1920-1921. This was a treaty among Czechoslovakia, Yugoslavia, and Romania to keep what they had won against chiefly Hungarian claims. Unfortunately, for several reasons the Little Entente could not serve as an overall defensive alliance for the region. Obviously, Hungary was opposed to it. Poland, which had no worries from Hungary but focused on Russia and Germany instead, saw little reason to join the alliance. Furthermore, Warsaw exaggerated the importance of the small Teschen region that Czechoslovakia took, but which had a Polish majority. Anger toward Czechoslovakia prevented Warsaw from entering into a defensive alliance with Prague. So the Little Entente started with two major holes in it, Poland and Hungary. Poland did conclude separate treaties with France and Romania. Overall, however, there was no East European alliance.

Overreliance on France was another problem. France was simply not well situated, geographically, militarily, or psychologically, to come to East Europe's rescue. Terribly weakened and embittered by World War I, Paris governments had no stomach for any policy that might seriously lead to war. As early as 1933, Piłsudski suggested joint Polish-French action against Hitler's new government; Paris demurred. Again, in 1936, as Hitler remilitarized the Rhineland, a direct threat to France, Warsaw promised Paris and Brussels support in a showdown with Germany. No response. After a while, the governments of East Europe could see that France was not a pillar of support, and French-sponsored alliances became a dead letter.

The only other power capable of backing up East Europe was the Soviet Union, and it was a nonplayer, with major territorial designs of its own on the region. As far as Stalin was concerned, squabbles between capitalist neighbors were all to the Soviet good; the capitalists would destroy themselves and leave the Soviets alone. Then the Soviets would pick up the pieces. Stalin thus pursued a rather isolationist policy toward East Europe, with no interest in joining in a common cause against a German threat.

Economically, Germany penetrated virtually all of East Europe by means of trade. This was in part natural—Germany was and still is the economic giant of Europe and the natural trading partner of the small, poor countries of EastEurope—and in part deliberate policy. Especially under the Nazis, Germany arranged major barter deals of East European food and raw materials in exchange

The Dismemberment of Czechoslovakia

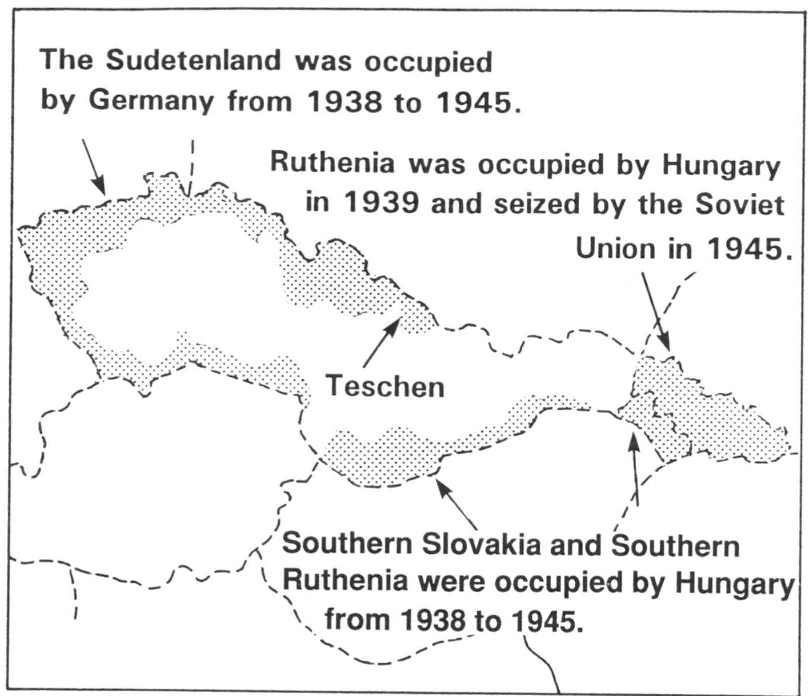

for German manufactured goods, effectively tying the economies of East Europe to Germany. (Any resemblance to the current situation is purely intentional.) If East Europe had had other big trading partners, things might have been different, and they might not have ended up in a dependency relationship with Germany. But during the Great Depression, trade shrank, and Germany was the only country willing to work by barter instead of with scarce hard currency.

The main thing Hitler had going for him in East Europe was his understanding of how much the East European states hated each other. He could ply them with trade and territorial promises, working one against the other, and take over all of them when the time came. With no sense of solidarity among themselves, the East Europeans let themselves be picked off one at a time.

"Munich" illustrates Hitler's strategy. Munich, in Bavaria, is widely known as the place where the British and French gave away Czechoslovakia to Germany in 1938 in an attempt to appease Hitler. Munich was that, but it was also more complicated, a multiparty backstabbing arrangement. First, Hitler had a plausible argument that the Sudeten Germans did not wish to be ruled by Prague and did wish to be part of the Reich. It was, of course, more than an ethnographic boundary question, for Czech defenses were well bunkered into the mountains of

Hungarian Expansion during World War II

the Sudetenland. Once Britain and France had pressured Czechoslovakia, which was not even present at the Munich meeting, into giving up the Sudetenland, then with its surrender went Czechoslovakia's main line of defense.

Second, Hitler knew that Slovaks also disliked rule by Czechs. When he moved into the now defenseless Czechoslovakia in the spring of 1939, he handed Slovaks their independence, and they eagerly took it, becoming a German dependency with a pro-Nazi government too weak to resist Hungarian territorial demands.

Third, other territorially interested states participated in Munich. Poland was awarded the tiny Teschen area that it had long demanded from Czechoslovakia. This enabled Hitler to point out that Czechoslovakia's borders needed correcting for more than just Germans. It also undermined Poland's moral position in standing up to German territorial demands the next year. In a small way, Poland stabbed a fellow Slavic country in the back.

Hungary got in on the deal, too. With the so-called Vienna Award of 1938, Hitler let Hungary take southern Slovakia and southern Ruthenia with their Hungarian minorities. With the breaking away of Slovakia in 1939, Hungary then took the rest of Ruthenia, snipping off the easternmost 125 miles of Czechoslovak

The Dismemberment of Romania in 1940

territory. This tied Hungary to German foreign policy, and Hungary joined the Axis. Simply by using East European territorial claims as a diplomatic tool, Hitler thrust German power far to the east in 1939 without firing a shot. Among East European lands there was no sense of solidarity, and this doomed them.

Next, Hitler used Soviet claims against Poland to neutralize Stalin. Knowing that Stalin had always wanted the Curzon Line as Russia's border, Hitler gave it to him in the secret protocol of the 1939 Molotov-Ribbentrop pact. (As a sweetener, Stalin turned over to the Gestapo some 500 German Communists who had fled to Moscow.) Seriously misnamed as the Nonaggression Pact, Hitler was promised Soviet noninterference as he invaded Poland on September 1, 1939. On September 17, Stalin invaded Poland from the east, firmly knifing a fellow Slavic state in the back.

As part of the Molotov-Ribbentrop pact, in 1940 Stalin occupied Lithuania, Latvia, and Estonia. In 1940 Stalin took Bessarabia, now the ex-Soviet republic of Moldova, and Northern Bukovina from Romania. With the Second Vienna Award of 1940, Hitler gave Romania's Northern Transylvania to Hungary and shortly thereafter Southern Dobrudja to Bulgaria. To whom could Romania turn? Russia was the hated Communist land that had taken Bessarabia. With massive fascistic agitation by the Iron Guard, Germany appeared as Romania's only protector against further dismemberment. Strangely, Germany had precipitated Romanian territorial losses and yet Romania had to turn to Germany for help.

With the German conquest of Yugoslavia and Greece in 1941, their neighbors moved in for the pickings. Hungary took portions of Northern Yugoslavia that had a Hungarian population. Bulgaria took Western Thrace from Greece (territory that Bulgaria had briefly held in 1913) and Macedonia from Yugoslavia.

Hitler barely had to fight to take over all of East Europe. Only Poland and Yugoslavia resisted, and they were overrun in a matter of days. The rest of East Europe fell into Hitler's hands because he knew their borders were terribly disputed and that they hated each other. Hungary, Bulgaria, and Romania were enrolled as allies. As if in response to Benjamin Franklin's quip to the Continental Congress, "Either we all hang together or we all hang separately," the East Europeans eagerly put nooses around their own necks.

SUGGESTED READINGS

HELD, JOSEPH, ed. *The Columbia History of Eastern Europe in the Twentieth Century.* New York: Columbia University Press, 1992.

LIVEZEANU, IRINA. *Cultural Politics in Greater Romania: Regionalism, Nation Building, and Ethnic Struggle, 1918-1930.* Ithaca, NY: Cornell University Press, 1995.

SETON-WATSON, HUGH. *Eastern Europe Between the Wars, 1918-1941.* New York: Harper & Row, 1967.

WALTERS, E. GARRISON. *The Other Europe: Eastern Europe to 1945.* Syracuse, NY: Syracuse University Press, 1988.

CHAPTER THREE

East Europe and World War II

Between the two world wars, the Communist parties of East Europe were generally small. In elections during the 1920s, Communist parties won an average of 10 percent or so for the region as a whole. A temporary high of 20 percent came in Bulgaria in 1920. A Communist vote does not necessarily indicate members or even believers. Much Communist electoral support is a protest vote, cast by people who don't much know or care what the Communists stand for but who dislike the existing system. A great deal of the French and Italian Communist vote is of this nature. French President Mitterrand understood this and, by offering a more attractive way to protest in his Socialist party, drained off a third of the Communist electoral support.

As R. V. Burks pointed out in his important study, *The Dynamics of Communism in Eastern Europe*, the groups that tended to vote more strongly Communist tell us a good deal about communism and its appeal. The Communists, following Marx's theory of a coming proletarian revolution, always liked to portray themselves as the party of workers. There is little to substantiate this picture in East Europe between the wars. The Communist vote was quite mixed: some workers, many peasants, and surprising numbers of middle-class people. Many Communist leaders were intellectuals of middle-class origin.

Burks finds that Communist voting, membership, and leadership were concentrated among groups with grudges, people who felt they had been treated unfairly and discriminated against. For example, Communist voting was high among the Magyar population that was left outside Hungary's borders by the Treaty of Trianon. Hungarians in Slovakia or Romania could show their resentment against their unhappy national status by voting Communist. Again, a protest vote. Jews in Poland, about 10 percent of the interwar population, were discriminated

Ulbricht: A Stalin Puppet

Typical of the pre-World War II Communist leaders whom Stalin held on ice was the German Communist Walter Ulbricht. His story could be the story of many of East Europe's first generation of Communist leaders, those who were installed by Soviet bayonets after World War II. Ulbricht was born in 1893, the eldest son of a poor Leipzig tailor, who raised Walter as a devout Marxist. Bright but without funds, Ulbricht completed only eight years of schooling before apprenticing himself to a cabinetmaker—a typical German working-class pattern. In 1912, at age 19, Ulbricht joined the Social Democratic party (SPD), then the largest and strongest socialist party in the world. In the Leipzig Workers Educational Institute he picked up a sort of Marxist college education.

As World War I began in 1914, the SPD split. The largest part stayed with the mainstream leaders and supported Germany's war effort. A minority left-wing faction under Karl Liebknecht denounced the war, and Ulbricht aligned himself with this wing. Drafted against his will in 1915, Ulbricht deserted twice and was caught both times. As Germany lurched to collapse in 1918, Ulbricht escaped from military prison to organize soldiers and workers for a short-lived revolutionary takeover attempt. As the new German Communist party (KPD) split off from the SPD in 1919, Ulbricht sided immediately with the KPD and was among its founders. Working his way quickly up through party ranks, Ulbricht was sent as a KPD delegate to the Comintern world congress in 1922, and the following year he was made a member of the KPD central committee. Already he was the party expert on organization. In the mid-1920s he attended a Comintern school in Moscow.

Elected to the Reichstag as a Communist in 1928, in time for the Great Depression, Ulbricht soon was echoing the new Stalinist line of immediate revolution to overthrow the tottering capitalist Weimar Republic. The Social Democrats he reviled as "Social Fascists," no better than the capitalists. The policy was a catastrophe, paving the way for Hitler's rise to power. In 1933, along with many KPD cadres, Ulbricht fled to Paris, where he continued to organize German Communists.

In the late 1930s, Stalin carried out his infamous "purges" of suspected disloyal Communists. These included foreign as well as Soviet party members. Many on the KPD's central committee were summoned to Moscow where they disappeared. Ulbricht, too, was called to Moscow, but he convinced Stalin's police that he was utterly reliable. As the purges executed superiors and rivals within the KPD leadership, they also eased Ulbricht's way to the top.

In 1938, Ulbricht was again ordered to Moscow, this time as the KPD's delegate to the Comintern. With the German invasion of Russia in 1941, Ulbricht organized emigré German Communists and, later, German prisoners of war into a Communist nucleus to take over Germany after the war. In April 1945, as the Red Army pushed into the eastern part of Germany, *Gruppe Ulbricht*, as the Communist group was called, was returned to German soil where it immediately reestablished the KPD and a civilian power structure under Russian military supervision. All over East Europe, trained groups like Ulbricht's were reinserted on their native soil to set up Communist governments as the Germans were pushed out.

In 1949, just after Konrad Adenauer proclaimed a new Federal Republic of Germany in the Western powers' occupation zones, Ulbricht proclaimed a German Democratic Republic in the Soviet zone, and it soon became known as East Germany. Ulbricht was the undisputed boss and president of East Germany through the fiercest years of the Cold War. After watching the GDR's population drain away through West Berlin, Ulbricht built the Berlin Wall in 1961. But Ulbricht was still beholden to Soviet power for his tenure. He was forcibly retired in 1971 for reasons probably having to do with his inflexibility over Bonn's rapprochement with Moscow. Ulbricht didn't like having the Soviet Union deal over his head with West Germany. Although for decades a loyal Stalinist agent, Ulbricht eventually displeased the Kremlin's post-Stalin leadership. His ouster showed how dependent he—and most other East European Communist party chiefs—were on Moscow's support.

Still, it was a remarkable record. By hewing to the right line at the right time, by utterly supporting whatever strategy Stalin proposed, by tireless attention to detail, Ulbricht plodded his way to the top. In contrast to Tito, whom we will consider subsequently, Ulbricht had absolutely no personal charisma. He fought in no battles and led no troops. He came to and retained power on a bureaucratic basis, by loyalty to Moscow and by careful party organizational work. He died in 1973.

against by an anti-Semitic regime, so a higher proportion of them voted Communist. Ukrainians and Belorussians under Polish rule felt the same way, so much of the support for the Polish Communist party was non-Polish. (Ironically, much of Israel's Communist vote now is from Arabs who resent their second-class citizenship but who have few alternatives, for the Palestine Liberation Organization is illegal in Israel. Still, this confirms Burks's thesis that groups with grudges vote Communist in protest, not necessarily out of ideology.)

The point is that there were Communists in East Europe before World War II, but there weren't many. (The good-sized Bulgarian Communist party was an exception here.) On their own, no East European Communist party would have come to power; they would have stayed minor parties. These small parties did contribute one element to the Soviet takeovers in East Europe after World War II: the initial Communist leadership. Most of the first Communist leaders of East Europe had been active in the small, sometimes underground, Communist parties of the 1930s. With the Nazi takeovers, many fled to the Soviet Union, where Stalin groomed them to set up Communist parties and regimes after the war. The fact that Stalin trained them in Moscow through the war indicates he had rather firm plans for using them after the war, namely to take over East Europe.

THE STRUCTURE OF COMMUNISM

In 1919, Lenin laid down strict requirements for any party that wished to join the new Communist International he had founded. There was then and still is a Socialist International (called the Second International), a loose grouping of democratic socialist parties. Lenin wished to have nothing to do with that. As far as Communists were concerned, socialists were cowards and fakes. They had long talked about the international solidarity of workers, but in practice they had mellowed into trade unionists and welfarists. Worse, they had cooperated with the capitalist governments' march to war in 1914. German Social Democrats had supported Germany's war effort, French Socialists had supported France's war effort, and British Labourites had supported Britain's war effort. In Bolshevik eyes, the socialists during World War I were as bad as capitalists.

The Third, or Communist, International—known as the "Comintern" for short—was to be not a debating society but a highly disciplined, centrally controlled network of parties that voluntarily and enthusiastically followed Moscow's every lead. Lenin's purpose was to split off the serious revolutionaries from existing, moderate socialist parties. From 1919 to 1921, virtually every socialist party did split, its left wing becoming the new Communist party and in short order a member of the Comintern. Promising Communist talent was sent to Moscow for training and indoctrination.

The various Communist parties were supposed to have little or no autonomy, but they were to adapt themselves to local conditions. Strategies to achieve this were set by Stalin (Lenin died in 1924). Where communism was suppressed, as in Hungary after Béla Kun's abortive takeover, Communists were to function underground, organized into small cells. If the police cracked one cell, its members would not be able to reveal more than a few names. In more open circumstances, Communists were to compete in elections, organize unions, and criticize bourgeois governments.

But what if Stalin made a mistake in selecting the strategy? He made many, and it cost Communists a great deal, in some cases their lives. At times, Stalin advised cooperation with bourgeois governments when he should have urged secrecy and a low profile. Once out in the open, Communists could be arrested by conservative regimes. At other times, Stalin ordered Communists not to cooperate with other parties, even against the rise of fascism. This contributed to Hitler's takeover of Germany in 1933 (see box).

However mistaken, Communists were not supposed to question Stalin's strategy. Those who did—or who Stalin suspected did—got taken care of. The Polish Communist party was thoroughly purged in 1938 (and ostensibly dissolved) by simply turning over lists of unwanted members to the Polish police, who in effect did Stalin's dirty work for him. During the Great Purge of the mid-1930s to the late 1930s, East European Communist leaders deemed insufficiently obedient were summoned to Moscow to work at Comintern headquarters and were then arrested,

Stalin and Hitler's Rise

One of the last things Communists liked to talk about was how the German Communist party in the early 1930s helped Hitler rise to power. At that time, Stalin had issued worldwide orders that Communist parties not cooperate with other parties. (Earlier, in the 1920s, the KPD had been instructed to cooperate with other parties.) The theory in the early 1930s was that cooperation with other parties might indicate that they had some merit; this would confuse the masses, who might then vote for a non-Communist party. Communists must avoid compromises and come to power on their own, without partners.

As applied to Germany, Stalin ordered the small but growing German Communist party (KPD) to end its parliamentary alliance with the larger Social Democratic party (SPD), an alliance that might have blocked the takeover by Hitler's National Socialists (Nazis). Stalin evaluated Hitler as essentially a clown (he did resemble Charlie Chaplin), the plaything of sinister but decaying capitalist circles, who was not capable of governing Germany. Even if Hitler did take office, his ridiculous regime would soon collapse. The German Communist phrase of the time was, "Nach Hitler kommen wir" (After Hitler comes us). In other words, the Nazis were the last gasp of a dying capitalism; they would finish off the doomed system and then the Communists would take over.

Hitler did come to power in early 1933, and was soon arresting both Communists and Social Democrats. Some of them paid with their lives for Stalin's monumental misevaluation. In 1935, without ever admitting his error, Stalin cranked out a new line: now any and all nonfascistic parties—Communists, Socialists, and moderate democrats—were to form a "Popular Front" to block fascism. The operative phrase became that of the French Communists, "Pas d'ennemis à la gauche" (No enemies on the left). In other words, we must all get together to fight this menace. But it was five years too late. In 1941, with the German invasion of the Soviet Union, Russians had to pay with millions of lives for Stalin's blunder. The episode shows both Stalin's limitations in dealing with situations in other countries and the slavish obedience of Communists in following foolish advice.

tried, and executed as spies and foreign agents. Several of the founders and first leaders of East European Communist parties went to the Soviet Union in the 1930s never to return. (See the box on Ulbricht.)

What was Stalin up to? Why would he harm the Communist movements of East Europe? The clue is Soviet national interest, or what Stalin perceived to be Soviet national interest. Stalin didn't give a fig for communism in other countries except insofar as it helped or hurt the Soviet Union. This generally meant a conservative line, especially after Hitler consolidated power in Germany. In the mid-1930s, East Europe started taking on some importance to the Soviet Union.

Stalin did not want East European countries to ally with or be used by Germany as a possible invasion corridor. Under these circumstances, it was unwise to urge local Communist parties to try to overthrow conservative governments, not that any would have been able to. But revolutionary activity would only weaken the none-too-strong governments of East Europe and make it easier for pro-German elements to take over. Accordingly, Communists should generally lay low and not make trouble. Some parties were even formally dissolved, although the leading cadres continued to operate quietly underground. Watch and wait was Stalin's game.

WORLD WAR II IN EAST EUROPE

Stalin did not have long to wait. As we discussed in Chapter 2, Czechoslovakia was the first to go. The 1938 Munich conference, in which Britain and France handed Hitler Czechoslovakia's strategic Sudetenland, convinced Stalin that London and Paris were trying to point Hitler eastward, toward the Soviet Union. There is no evidence that they had any such thing in mind, but Stalin was a classic paranoid, quick to believe that others were out to get him. At the same time, Poland and Hungary moved in to pick over the carcass of Czechoslovakia.

World War II, like World War I, started in and over East Europe. In the first war, the problem had been Bosnia and Serbia. In the second war, the problem was Poland, that is, German demands to get back territories that Versailles had given to the new Polish republic. In both cases, strong states saw no reason to accommodate weak states. We are strong, said Austria and Germany, respectively, so we will take what we wish. Only one thing made Hitler pause before attacking Poland in 1939: How would the Soviet Union react? Hitler wished no war with the Soviet Union at that time. As we considered in Chapter 2, Stalin made an incredibly cynical pact with Hitler, the 1939 Nonaggression Pact, which gave Hitler the green light to invade Poland and Stalin permission to annex the eastern part of the Polish state.

What were East European Communists to do as Hitler either lined up the East European states as allies or took them by military conquest? They were to do absolutely nothing, Stalin ordered. Just lay low and wait. Incredibly, Communists were not to resist or plot against German occupiers or fascist puppet governments. That might alarm Hitler, Stalin figured. All that changed on June 22, 1941, for on that date Germany invaded the Soviet Union, and Communists were told that it was suddenly their sacred duty to do everything they could to defeat fascism. Again, the subordination of communism to Soviet foreign policy was evident.

East Europe's Communists liked to boast how they had "fought" the Nazis and local fascists during World War II. This image is accurate only in spots. Here and there, as in Albania, Bulgaria, and Slovakia, Communists organized some guerrilla bands to physically combat the Germans. But most Communist leaders had fled to Moscow, where they sat out the war. In Moscow they trained and organized to set

Tito: Not a Stalin Puppet

In many ways Walter Ulbricht and Josip Broz—better known as Tito—were similar. They were almost exactly the same age; Tito was born in 1892, a year earlier than Ulbricht. Both came from modest backgrounds, both worked their way up through their respective Communist parties, served the Comintern in Moscow and elsewhere, and became the post-World War II leaders of their lands. But they gained power very differently and this strongly influenced the courses they took once in power. Ulbricht, a party bureaucrat, was placed in power by Stalin as an obedient puppet. Tito fought his way to power on his own and owed Stalin little. This was the basis for the Tito-Stalin split.

Born in a village in Croatia—then part of the Austro-Hungarian empire—Josip Broz was the seventh of fifteen children, eight of whom died in childhood. Life was harsh under the Hungarian nobles who ruled the area. Broz's father was a Croat farmer, his mother Slovenian. This mixed background later served him well, for he represented two of Yugoslavia's several nationalities. The family lacked money to send the lad to America, so Josip was apprenticed to a blacksmith and mechanic. At night school, he trained himself to become a voracious reader. At age 18, in 1910, Broz began to wander, picking up various jobs, in Austria, in Bohemia, and in Germany, and learning German and Czech. In Zagreb, he joined the Metalworkers Union and the Social Democratic party of Croatia, his first political involvement, a leftist one.

In 1913 Broz was drafted for the standard two-year stint in the Austrian army and was promoted to sergeant. At the Carpathian front in 1915, Sergeant Broz was lanced in a Russian cavalry charge and captured. (Note that at the same time Ulbricht was busy dodging the German draft.) Broz worked as a mechanic while a prisoner. Hearing of the tsar's overthrow in March 1917, Broz escaped to join the Bolsheviks, who themselves seized power under Lenin in November 1917. By now he was a committed Communist. Marrying a Russian girl (the first of his four wives), Broz returned to the new nation of Yugoslavia in 1920. He had been five years in Russia.

Back in Zagreb, he engaged in union and party activity, working quickly up the ranks of the new Communist party, which was soon declared illegal. In 1928, Broz was sent to prison for more than five years. (Ulbricht was never sent to prison.) Tito later reflected that prison was his university, for there he could read and converse with other Communists. Upon release in 1934, Broz went underground as a professional party leader. In 1935, as a Comintern delegate in Moscow, Broz was among the first to receive Stalin's new line of "Popular Fronts"—all left parties against fascism. Part of this was aimed at aiding the Republican government in the Spanish Civil War. Traveling around Europe with forged passports, Broz helped organize Comintern volunteers to fight in Spain. In early 1939 Broz was named general secretary of the Yugoslav Communist party. Several earlier leaders had perished in Stalin's purges.

Taking the *nom de guerre* of Tito, Broz organized and led the Communist-dominated Partisans who battled and outlasted the Germans in the mountains of Bosnia. By 1945, the Partisans had liberated roughly the southern half of Yugoslavia; the Soviet army swept through the northern half. This fact gave Tito an independent power base that no other East European Communist chief had. Tito had his own army, and it had fought heroically and supported him devotedly. The new Communist leaders elsewhere in East Europe had sat out the war in Moscow and had been put in power by Soviet bayonets. This made the difference when Stalin tried to oust Tito in 1948. Stalin could purge other East European Communists with a raised eyebrow, but he could not topple Tito, who stayed president of Yugoslavia until his death in 1980.

Both the situations and the personalities of Ulbricht and Tito were quite different. Guerrilla warfare inside Germany was impossible, and Ulbricht was essentially a bureaucrat with zero charisma. Yugoslavia is largely mountain and forest, perfect for guerrilla warfare. Many Yugoslavs hated the Germans. And Tito was a strong, tough, and charismatic leader. Ulbricht and Tito illustrate that different circumstances call for entirely different types of leaders.

up the first postwar Communist systems in East Europe. Much of East Europe's anti-German resistance, as in Poland, was led by non-Communist nationalists, often at odds with Communist resistance groups. Only one Communist-led outfit really fought the Germans, the Yugoslav Partisans of Tito. For the most part, other Communists organized underground in preparation for the arrival of the Red Army.

In the spring of 1941, Hitler conquered Yugoslavia, severely weakened by Serb-Croat enmity, in eleven days. The Yugoslav Communist response? Nothing. That was still the strange period of the Hitler-Stalin pact, and Moscow ordered Communists throughout Europe not to resist. Hitler, knowing that Croats wanted their freedom from Serbia, set up a Croatian puppet state much like Slovakia. Slovenia was incorporated into the Reich. Most of Macedonia was taken over by Bulgaria. Italy occupied the Adriatic coast. Albania seized Kosovo and part of Macedonia.

Only with the German invasion of Russia in June 1941 did the Yugoslav Communists swing into action, organizing Partisan forces that practiced guerrilla warfare, mostly in the mountains of Bosnia. The Partisans never beat the German occupiers. In classic guerrilla fashion, they outlasted the Germans, slipping away when outgunned. Much fighting was with other Yugoslavs, the fascist Croatian Ustasha and monarchist Serbian Chetniks. German reprisals against Yugoslav civilians were murderous, but this didn't bother Tito's Partisans. The more civilians the Germans killed, the more recruits for the Partisans. The occupier does the guerrillas' recruiting for them. By the war's end, over 10 percent of Yugoslavia's population had been killed and 3.5 million were homeless.

guerrillas' recruiting for them. By the war's end, over 10 percent of Yugoslavia's population had been killed and 3.5 million were homeless.

The Communist-led Partisans were neither the only nor the largest armed group of Yugoslavs. Remnants of the army formed a Serbian guerrilla force called the Chetniks (named after the old anti-Turkish bandits), whose goal was a restoration of the old Serbian-dominated monarchy. As such, the Chetniks were not a viable rallying point for other Yugoslav nationalities. In the 1930s, a native fascist movement grew up in Croatia, the Ustasha, which set up a Nazi puppet state, doubling the size of Croatia and exterminating the sizable Serbian communities that had existed inside Croatia for three centuries. Obviously, the Ustasha could not unite all of Yugoslavia. Only the Communist Partisans were above the old national quarrels; they alone held out the hope of a new system with justice for all national groups. The Chetniks fought for Serbia, the Ustasha for Croatia, only the Communists for all Yugoslavia. It was a potent recruiting device for the Communists, giving them a certain moral authority.

Augmenting this moral authority was the fact that only the Partisans actually fought the Germans. The Partisans suffered some 350,000 dead and 400,000 wounded. Did guerrilla warfare against the Germans do any good? A little. It disrupted communications and tied down several German divisions that were desperately needed elsewhere. By itself, however, it did not defeat the enemy or liberate the country. What it did was secure the Communist guerrilla leaders as their country's next rulers. Partisan chiefs knew they couldn't beat the Germans; they focused on seizing power after the Germans had been beaten by the Allies.

To see how this strategy was attempted elsewhere and how it failed, let us compare Yugoslavia with Poland. First, under Stalin's orders, the Polish Communist party was purged and ostensibly dissolved in 1938 as Stalin was trying to improve relations with Warsaw. Underground, however, a trimmed-down Polish Workers party continued to exist. Poland was conquered by the Nazis in 1939; most of the Communists who did not flee to Russia were killed by the Germans. Accordingly, the Polish Communists were much fewer in number by June 1941—when guerrilla warfare suddenly became desirable—than the Yugoslav Communists.

Second, there were no nationality quarrels among Poles as there were among Yugoslavs. Offering a solution to the nationalities question was one of the Yugoslav Partisans most important recruiting devices. Poles have a strong sense of national identity, something the Yugoslavs never attained.

Third, especially among Serbs and Montenegrins, Russia still had a favorable image, that of the big Slavic brother who would save them from the Turks. The Russophile Montenegrins, the tiny nationality just north of Albania, used to boast, "Us and the Russians make 200 million." Poles, on the other hand, for centuries had feared and despised Russia, and they had recent memories of the tsarist Russian administration of the central portion of their country. Poles had just gotten rid of the Russians in 1918, and they didn't view the Soviet Union as their savior.

These factors added up to a main Polish underground movement that was thoroughly non-Communist. Forming the Home Army, it answered to the Polish government in exile in London, the so-called London Poles. Thousands of Poles who escaped in 1939 (most via Romania) served under British command. Polish Communists formed a much smaller resistance movement that was commanded from the Soviet Union. Tens of thousands of Poles who had fallen under Soviet control as the Soviets overran eastern Poland in 1939 also served in the Red Army. (Such was the military background of General Wojciech Jaruzełski, later president of Poland.) Thousands of Polish reservists, though, were murdered under Stalin's orders in the Katyn Forest in the spring of 1940 (see box).

There was some Polish partisan activity in the forests, but in the main the Home Army laid low, knowing that moving too soon against the Germans could be fatal. The Polish underground, for example, offered little help to Jews, who were shipped to Nazi death camps, most of which were on Polish soil. Many Poles were anti-Semitic, and some didn't mind what the Nazis were doing to Jews. In fairness, it should be noted that other Poles risked their lives to aid Jews. Few Europeans of any nationality stepped forward to save Jews; only Danes and Bulgarians massively resisted the Nazi deportations of Jews to death camps. When the Warsaw Ghetto at last revolted in 1943, the Polish underground did little, figuring the revolt was a useless gesture. Many Polish guerrilla units did not welcome Jewish partisans; some even shot them. It was the classic East European story of backstabbing and disunity in the face of adversity.

Perhaps the high point of wartime backstabbing came as the Soviet army pushed the Germans back to Warsaw in the fall of 1944. The Home Army saw this as their chance to liberate Warsaw from the Germans and proclaim a free (that is, non-Communist) Polish government before the Soviets could set up a Communist government. On August 1, some 35,000 Poles of the "Warsaw Army Corps" rose up with captured and smuggled weapons. Immediately, the Polish fighters called for the nearby Soviet army to help them drive out the Germans. Instead, the Red Army sat on the other side of the Vistula River from Warsaw and let the Nazis get rid of troublesome Polish patriots for them. In 63 days of heroic fighting against five German divisions, the Poles were either killed or fled into the sewers. The Germans turned much of Warsaw into rubble; it was the most damaged city of World War II. After it was over, the Soviets crossed the Vistula and took Warsaw. The Warsaw horror can be seen as a continuation of the Katyn massacre.

Notice how all players in these games, whether Yugoslavs, Poles, or Soviets, whether Communists or non-Communists, have chiefly in mind the seizure of power after the war. Americans are a bit naive on this point; they think wars are fought to beat an enemy. Americans think all should join in selflessly to attain victory and not worry about the postwar situation. The East Europeans were much more cynical; they understood that the big payoff was in who gained power after the war. Fighting the Germans (or simply waiting) were but tactics to this end.

The Katyn Massacre

As Hitler's Wehrmacht overran the western two-thirds of Poland in September 1939, Stalin's Red Army took the eastern part of Poland as per the dictators' agreement of the previous month. The Soviets captured more than 230,000 Polish soldiers, mostly reservists, without a fight and interned them in Russia. The following spring, all word from about 15,000 of these prisoners—8,000 to 9,000 of them officers, most of the others sergeants—ceased. What had happened to them?

In 1943 the world found out, but some didn't want to believe it. The German invaders unearthed, in the Katyn Forest deep inside Russia, mass graves of thousands of Polish officers and non-coms, each of them shot in the back of the head with a revolver. Gleefully, the Germans showed the graves to the Red Cross and to captured British officers so they might get the word out about what the Russians had done. The London Poles, who had long wondered where the missing officers were, believed the story. The Soviets hotly denied it, blamed the Germans, and huffily broke relations with the London Poles. The following year, Stalin set up his own puppets, the Lublin Polish group, in newly liberated Lublin, Poland.

The facts clearly blame Stalin and his secret police for the Katyn massacre. First, all word of these captured Poles ceased in the spring of 1940. The Germans didn't invade Russia until the summer of 1941. Second, Katyn Forest is deep inside Russia; the Germans did not arrive there until the fall of 1941. Third, the uniforms and boots of the murdered Polish officers showed only moderate wear, as if they had been imprisoned only a few months. Fourth, why would the Germans publicize the horror if they were guilty?

But why would Stalin do such a thing? The Polish officers would have been a welcome addition to the Red Army. They would have fought well against Germans. (Of course, in 1940 Stalin couldn't have known that Germany would invade the next year.) Some 100,000 Poles were, in fact, later recruited into Polish units under overall Soviet command. But the captured Polish officers were not Communists; they would answer only to the London Polish government. After the war, these officers could provide leadership to a non-Communist Poland. In short, if Stalin didn't own them, he didn't trust them. His solution: decapitate a portion of the Polish leadership stratum so they wouldn't give him any trouble after the war. Stalin was perfectly capable of thinking this way.

News of Katyn was officially prohibited in both the Soviet Union and Poland, but by word of mouth not a single Pole was unaware of the massacres. It deepened Polish hatred of Communism and Russians. Finally, in 1990, the Soviet Union handed over to Poland cartons of documents that Soviet President Gorbachev said "indirectly but convincingly" pointed to Stalin's secret police as the culprits. "It is not easy to speak of this tragedy, but it is necessary," he said, trying to establish new and friendly relations with Poland. After half a century of lies, a Soviet leader admitted what Poles had known all along.

"People's Democracy"

It sounds incredible now, but during the Cold War the Communists claimed that the "people's democracies" and "people's republics" of East Europe were actually more democratic than the ordinary liberal or "bourgeois" democracies in the West. In Communist theory, bourgeois (middle-class) democracy really wasn't very democratic at all, for it left overriding power in the hands of rich capitalists, who structured parties, the press, and politics to protect their own wealth and power. Free speech and opposition parties didn't count for much because they didn't have a chance in competition with the capitalists' money, went Marxist theory.

Real democracy, argued the Communists, came when you got rid of the capitalists. This was "people's" or "popular" democracy, for now the will of the masses, undistorted by the bourgeois parties and media, would stream into political power. Naturally, someone would have to organize and lead the people, and this would be the Communists, who are best equipped to understand what the people really need. Competing parties and opposition viewpoints and media would not be needed since there would now be only one class. Indeed, any attempt to resurrect other parties and news media would indicate the capitalists were trying to sneak back into power and must be squelched. Applying this weird Marxist logic, Stalin justified his "people's republics" in East Europe.

STALIN'S APPROACH TO EAST EUROPE

Stalin was ultracynical about East Europe. Whoever conquered a piece of territory, he said, imposed his political system on it. To him, it was a sort of natural law. The Western Allies did not consult with him in setting up "bourgeois democracies" in Belgium and Italy, and he did not mind. But neither should Britain or America object to his setting up "people's democracies" in East Europe, he reasoned.

Behind Stalin's Marxist rhetoric stood some plausible geopolitical arguments. East Europe had repeatedly been used as an invasion corridor against Russia. From the Teutonic knights, to the Swedes, to Napoleon, to the Germans in the two world wars, whoever held East Europe was a threat to Russia. That had just been proved by the Hitlerian onslaught, which cost some 20 million Soviet lives. Stalin therefore wished to keep East Europe not on ideological grounds—to spread the Communist revolution—but as a defensive shield for the Soviet motherland. The only way to make sure it stayed a reliable shield was to implant Communist regimes; bourgeois regimes in East Europe would soon incline westward and link up with Russia's enemies. Communism in East Europe was secondary to Soviet security considerations.

By the fall of 1944, the Red Army had liberated the Soviet Union and was pushing the Germans back through East Europe. The Red Army, except for

The Balkan "Percentages" Deal

One of the war's most cynical geopolitical deals was reached by Stalin and Churchill in Moscow in 1944 as the Soviet army pushed into Romania and Bulgaria. Churchill, a classic British imperialist, wished to outline spheres of influence in the Balkans so that Britain and Russia would "not get at cross-purposes in small ways." Stalin, a classic Russian imperialist, understood exactly what he meant: who was going to own what. Churchill wrote what percentages of predominance the two powers should get in the Balkans:

Rumania	
Russia	90%
The others	10%
Greece	
Great Britain (in accord with USA)	90%
Russia	10%
Yugoslavia	50-50%
Hungary	50-50%
Bulgaria	
Russia	75%
The others	25%

Wrote Churchill: "I pushed this across to Stalin, who had by then heard the translation. There was a slight pause. Then he took his blue pencil and made a large tick upon it, and passed it back to us. It was all settled in no more time than it takes to set down."

Did Stalin intend to abide by this partition plan? Probably not, but strangely that is how things approximately worked out. Except for Hungary, which was within a few years a firm Soviet satellite, the note describes the postwar lineup. Stalin did not attempt to take over Greece; he even ordered Greek Communists to give up their guerrilla war (which they nearly won). Yugoslavia from 1945 to 1948 was a strong Soviet satellite, but after Stalin kicked it out of the Soviet camp, it really turned neutral, and Stalin did not invade it. Perhaps Stalin meant what he told Churchill in 1944.

liberating the most and biggest Nazi death camps (which were on Polish soil), did not generally make a good impression. Looting and rape were frequent, and many East Europeans feared and disliked the backward, primitive Russian soldiers, who were inclined to "liberate" anything that struck their fancy. After the Red Army had swept through an area, for example, there were few wristwatches left.

Yalta, 1945

As the Allies neared the borders of Germany, the Big Three leaders met at Yalta to set up a postwar world. The series of agreements, some coming before Yalta and some coming after, are sometimes referred to simply as "Yalta." They included the following points, some in writing and some in verbal understandings.

1. **A United Nations was to be set up.** Some of the elements of the UN Charter were mentioned, including the bizarre provision for counting Ukraine and Belorussia as separate UN members, thus giving the Soviet Union three votes in the General Assembly. Roosevelt thought that gaining Stalin's acceptance of the UN was the main thing that had happened at Yalta.

2. **Russia got the Curzon Line** as its western border. As we discussed in Chapter 2, Poland had taken parts of Ukraine and Belorussia in 1920, well to the east of the Curzon Line recommended by the Western victors at Versailles. Stalin had always wanted this territory back and had indeed gotten much of it back in his 1939 pact with Hitler. Poland's eastern border was therefore moved about 100 to 200 miles westward, a point that the Allies had agreed to at their 1943 meeting in Tehran, Iran.

3. **Poland got a large chunk of Germany** in compensation for its losses to the Soviet Union. This was confirmed at the Potsdam meeting near Berlin in July. The gigantic butterfly of German territory—Silesia, Prussia, and Pomerania—was snipped off at the Oder and Neisse rivers and handed to postwar Poland. The area had been German for three centuries; millions of Germans fled westward to be replaced by Poles who had been displaced from the eastern part of Poland now taken over by the Soviet Union. Poland was in effect picked up and moved about 100 miles westward. Germany's East Prussia was split in two, the northern half taken by the Soviets, the southern by the Poles. The Russian portion, Kaliningrad Oblast, still exists as the coastal wedge of land between Poland and Lithuania.

4. **Germany was divided into occupation zones**, at first three—British, American, and Soviet—and later four, when France was added. The military occupation was to be temporary. The splitting of Germany into two states, East and West, was not envisioned. Berlin was to be likewise divided, but under joint military administration.

5. **Germany was to be disarmed** and was to pay heavy reparations for the terrible war damage it had inflicted.

6. **The nations of East Europe were to be democratic and friendly to the Soviet Union.** This agreement, admittedly vague, became the snarling point between Washington and Moscow, and it caused much controversy within U.S. domestic politics. The Soviets read "democratic" to mean "people's democracy," which, as we considered earlier, meant Communist control. And "friendly" to the Soviet Union meant occupation by and under the control of the Soviets.

7. **The Soviet Union would attack Japan** within three months of Germany's defeat. The Soviet Union and Japan had signed a nonaggression pact shortly before the German invasion in 1941 and had scrupulously adhered to it. The Soviets stayed out of the Pacific war until we persuaded them to enter, which they did just as we were dropping the first atomic bombs. Yalta provided for the return of Russian territory taken by Japan in the Russo-Japanese War of 1905.

YALTA

Stalin wanted East Europe. Did Yalta give it to him? Critics of President Franklin D. Roosevelt for years lambasted the Democrats as the architects of the giveaway of East Europe. Yalta is a resort town in the Soviet Crimea where in early 1945 the wartime Big Three leaders met—Roosevelt, Stalin, and Churchill. Their attention focused heavily on Poland (Stalin and Churchill having taken care of the Balkans the previous year).

The situation on the ground when Yalta took place in February 1945 did not favor Roosevelt and Churchill. The Western Allies had liberated only France while the Soviets had taken most of Poland, Hungary, and Yugoslavia, half of Czechoslovakia, and all of Romania by that time. A major German counteroffensive had recently taken the Americans by surprise in the Ardennes (the Battle of the Bulge). Soviet forces were about 100 miles from Berlin, the Western Allies about 300 miles from Berlin. No one knew at that time that the Americans would be able to cross the Rhine over the unexploded bridge at Remagen on March 7 and move rapidly across Germany.

There was little Roosevelt or Churchill could do to change Stalin's mind about the territories he had conquered and paid for in Soviet blood. It is possible that the two Western leaders viewed Yalta as a mechanism to keep Stalin from taking any *more* of Europe. Basically, Roosevelt and Churchill conceded to Stalin what Stalin already had in his possession, in return for some nice phrases about the United Nations and democracy in East Europe after the war. Notice how much of Yalta concerns boundaries.

At the time, Roosevelt and his assistant Harry Hopkins thought they were getting a pretty good deal at Yalta. Stalin would enter the war against Japan, which at the time was thought to be necessary for victory. Roosevelt didn't know that the atomic bombs, then being frantically developed in the Manhattan Project, would work and that Japan was near surrender anyway. Roosevelt also got Stalin's acceptance of the UN idea, one of Roosevelt's pet projects. Did Roosevelt comprehend the utter cynicism of Stalin and his geopolitical designs on East Europe? Probably not. Roosevelt, who had been an official of the Wilson administration, carried over some of Wilson's internationalist vision. Roosevelt was

Poland Is Moved Westward

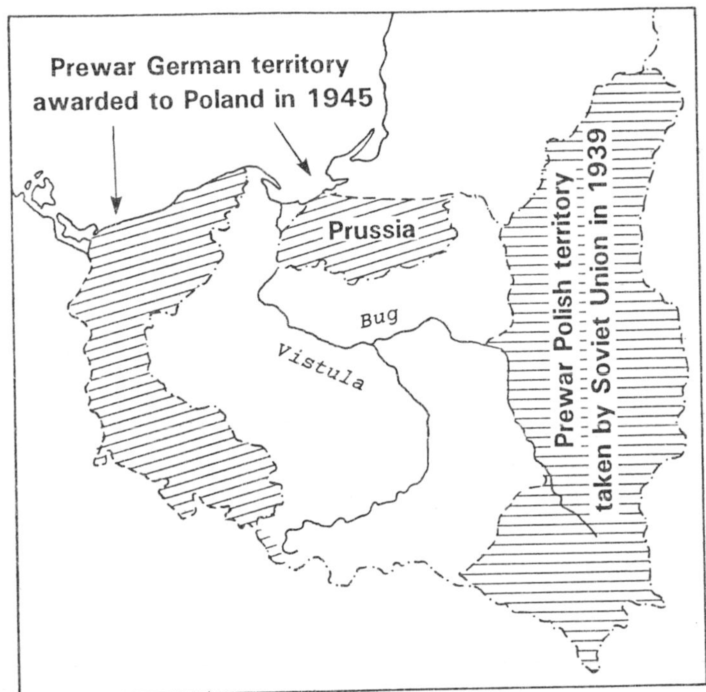

personally charming and thought he could persuade Stalin to join in the idealistic open world that Roosevelt envisioned. We know now that Stalin regarded Roosevelt not as an idealist but as a crafty imperialist trying to expand U.S. power. Stalin projected his own cynicism onto Roosevelt.

Roosevelt really was a bit naive. Clues to Stalin's behavior were available; some had come from the warning cables of George F. Kennan in the U.S. embassy in Moscow, who noted that our Soviet ally was not a great deal better than our German enemy. Few listened to Kennan at the time. There was a war on, and the Soviet Union was seen as a heroic, embattled ally. American opinion of the Soviet Union during the war was favorable, and Roosevelt shared it. To have said no or to have engaged in tough bargaining at Yalta would have confused and bothered the American people. Stalin's promises on a democratic East Europe seemed fair enough.

Could things have gone differently at Yalta? Only if the United States and Britain had invaded Europe earlier than 1944. If they had taken the chance and invaded France in 1943, they likely would have been able to take large areas of East Europe. (The British and Americans did invade Italy in 1943, but made only slow progress working their way up that mountainous peninsula. Some historians regard the whole Italian campaign as a mistake; others say it was an important gesture to show the Soviets, who had been demanding a second front in the west since 1941, that we were still in the war. Otherwise, some feared, Stalin might have sought a separate peace with Hitler.) Actually, the western area of Czechoslovakia, including Pilsen, was liberated by General George S. Patton's army, but it was turned over to the Soviets as per the Yalta agreement. If the British and Americans had taken an extremely high risk strategy and invaded the Balkans, they might have been able to liberate most of East Europe. Of course, they might also have gotten bogged down in the Balkans, as they did in Italy.

Another possibility, suggested by famed diplomat-historian George F. Kennan among others, was to have cut off U.S. war supplies to Russia as soon as the Soviet army had liberated its own territory. This would have occurred around August 1944, and such an action could have enabled U.S. and British forces to reach East Europe first. U.S. help to the Soviets was a major factor during the war; many of the trucks hauling fuel for Soviet tanks were American made. Continuing U.S. aid helped the Soviets take over East Europe. But in August 1944, the German army still had plenty of fight left. To have encouraged the Soviets to drop out of the war at that point would have permitted the redeployment westward of the bulk of the German army. Remember, most of World War II in Europe was fought on the eastern front; some 90 percent of the German forces were deployed there. In World War I, we called the Bolsheviks traitors and agents of the Germans when they withdrew Russia from the war. Would we have wanted them to withdraw at a similar stage in World War II?

General Dwight D. Eisenhower, supreme commander of the Western Allied forces, did not relish the thought of fighting all the way through Germany to Berlin. He shuddered to think of the American casualties. If Eisenhower had been willing to expend more American lives, Western forces would have liberated most of Germany and the western part of Czechoslovakia ahead of the Soviets. Stalin and his generals shared no such compunctions over sacrificing their young men in order to seize territory and put themselves in a strong postwar position. Remember, the Soviets lost some 20 million citizens during the war. The U.S. lost half a million in both Europe and the Pacific. In short, in 1945 the Soviets were in East Europe, with guns. We weren't, and that made all the difference.

How did Yalta work out in the long sweep of history? Ironically, in 1989 and 1990, Yalta began to be implemented the way Roosevelt envisioned it. The unpopular Communist governments were chucked out, the Soviet troops began to depart, and the Warsaw Pact became a dead letter. East Europe opened to the West. The borders agreed to at Yalta remained. Germany, which was never to have been divided, was reunited. After a 45-year delay, the correct interpretation of Yalta was finally put into practice.

SUGGESTED READINGS

BORSODY, STEPHEN. *The Tragedy of Central Europe: The Nazi and Soviet Conquest of Central Europe.* New York: Collier Books, 1960.

BURKS, R. V. *The Dynamics of Communism in Eastern Europe.* Princeton, NJ: Princeton University Press, 1961.

MACLEAN, FITZROY. *Josip Broz Tito: A Pictorial Biography*. New York: McGraw-Hill, 1980.

ROTHSCHILD, JOSEPH. *Return to Diversity: A Political History of East Central Europe Since World War II*, 2d ed. New York: Oxford University Press, 1993.

CHAPTER FOUR

The Communist Takeovers

World War II in East Europe closed with the major shift westward of the Soviet frontiers, in some areas by as much as 200 miles. As well as adding territory to the Soviet Union, the shift changed the geopolitics of East Europe, giving the Soviets direct land access to more countries. Before the war, the Soviet Union on its west bordered only Poland and Romania. Poland and Romania bordered each other at that time, sealing off Czechoslovakia and Hungary from Soviet territory. The Soviet Union even had no border with Lithuania, as Polish territory actually abutted Latvia, effectively insulating Lithuania from Russia.

With the pushing back of Polish and Romanian borders at the close of the war, the Soviet Union gained direct access to Czechoslovakia and Hungary, as well

Stalin Expands the Western Ukraine

as Poland and Romania. The Soviet takeover in 1945 of Ruthenia or the Carpatho-Ukraine gave Stalin a Ukrainian salient that extended toward the middle of Europe. Ostensibly, the new government in Prague voluntarily gave Ruthenia to the Soviet Union in 1945. Ruthenia, although it had a Ukrainian-speaking majority, had never belonged to the Russian empire. It had belonged to old Hungary and later to interwar Czechoslovakia. The official Soviet explanation was that the Ukrainians demanded to be united into one country. More likely, Stalin had geopolitical reasons for the annexation. First, it gave him direct access to Hungary. Second, to have left sizable numbers of Ukrainians outside Soviet control but now directly adjoining Soviet territory could have been a source of infectious ideas about freedom and independence for the long-discontented Ukrainians within the Soviet Union. The border change in this region meant that, during the long Cold War period, unrest in any four of these East European lands could be crushed by Soviet troops, who did not have to transit any third countries to reach their destinations. A change in borders greatly facilitated Stalin's hold over East Europe.

A series of bilateral treaties between the Soviet Union and each East European state further cemented the region into the Soviet orbit. Under the standard but misleading title of a "treaty of friendship and mutual assistance," these treaties were actually defensive alliances that prohibited the East European country from allying with a Western power. The treaties mentioned Germany by name as a dangerous revanchist (out for revenge) power that they must unite against. This is the one area where the genuine national interests of Poland and Czechoslovakia coincided with those of the Soviet Union: rejection of and defense against any German claims to the Oder-Neisse territories, East Prussia, or the Sudetenland. Even today, Warsaw and Prague still worry a little about eventual German designs on these territories. The treaties also mentioned economic cooperation, thus forming the basis for the Council on Mutual Economic Assistance (Comecon).

SALAMI TACTICS

In general, the Communists did not immediately take over the governments of the newly liberated East European countries. Where they did, in Yugoslavia and Albania, it was because local Communist partisans had fought their way to power against both the German occupiers and local non-Communist forces. Tito saw no reason to wait in communizing Yugoslavia, a point that irritated Stalin and contributed to the later Tito-Stalin split.

In the other countries, Stalin ordered his Communist puppets, most of whom had sat out the war in Moscow, to take over their countries gradually, one slice at a time. Hungarian Communist boss Matyas Rákosi referred to this as "salami tactics." The idea was, first, not to alarm the West, especially the United States. Roosevelt made the tactical mistake of telling Stalin at Yalta (see Chapter 3) that he expected all U.S. forces to be withdrawn from Europe within two years of the war's end. With this bit of information, Stalin knew all he had to do to avoid difficulty with the Americans was to wait two years, until they were gone, before clamping down with full-fledged Communist dictatorships.

Second, a full-fledged and immediate takeover could provoke violent opposition by non-Communist resistance fighters, many of whom distrusted the Communists and had kept their arms. Best to lull them into accepting the mixed regimes, then disarm and isolate them, and finally institute the Stalinist system. Uprisings in East Europe could attract American attention and support, so best to take over slowly and cleverly to head off uprisings. The idea was to make things look confused and chaotic, to blame non-Communist leaders as obstreperous personalities who were standing in the way of national unity and progress for the sake of personal power. The Communists could then claim to be "saving" the country from disunity and reactionary forces. It might be difficult to blame any given incident on the Communists, but when one stood back and looked at the whole process, one saw the unmistakable Communist strategy for seizing power. Unfortunately, for some this recognition came too late.

Could anti-Communists really have done anything about it? Alas, no. Protest, especially armed protest, would simply have been crushed by the local Communist police and army. If supplementary force was needed, the Soviet forces were now never far away. Bloody struggle, with no hope of winning, might have alerted the world a little sooner as to what was happening in East Europe after the war. But by taking over with salami tactics, the Communists were able to lull some people, in both East and West Europe, into accepting the Communist regimes as legitimate and permanent.

We might compare the Communist takeovers with the earlier Nazi takeovers. Both erected essentially fake regimes, but the Germans were much more blunt and direct; they arrested and murdered thousands, in some countries millions of people. They immediately installed either Nazi officials or pliant local quislings into power. The Communists were willing, for appearance's sake, to take a year or two to do the job. They were a bit more clever and subtle than the Nazis; in most countries they arrested only thousands and executed only hundreds. (The bloody exception to this rule was in Bulgaria.) Their victims were mostly leaders who opposed them; they counted on intimidation to cow others into silence. In the long run, it did the Communists little good. The regimes they erected with little popular support could not stand once the Soviet prop was pulled out.

Typically, the first governments immediately after liberation were mixed cabinets containing representatives of all or most prewar parties who had not been tainted with fascism or collaboration with the German occupiers. In almost every East European country, the biggest party was the peasants' party (peasants were called "smallholders" in Hungary). The first stage of the Communist takeovers resembled the old prewar Communist policy of establishing coalitions or "popular fronts" out of all the antifascist parties. The presidents and prime ministers were not Communists, but generally leaders of revived peasant, liberal, or socialist parties. The press was reasonably free, and most parties were permitted to organize and recruit. It looked like a pretty decent setup, one not too different from many West European countries.

But it was intended as a temporary stage. The Communists always arranged to get themselves or stand-ins named to lead the interior and defense ministries. In the United States, "interior" suggests redwoods and buffalos, but in Europe the interior minister runs the national police. With Communists appointing all the leading personnel of the police and army, soon all means of coercion were in Communist hands. This "mixed stage" lasted from several months to a year or so, depending on the country.

Another important advantage the Communists took in these mixed governments was control of land reform. In some countries this consisted of merely confiscating the great estates of nobles and prewar millionaires and distributing these estates to peasants, thus gaining peasant gratitude and their dependency on the Communists. This gave the Communists votes and support they would not have otherwise had.

In Poland and Czechoslovakia, though, there was an additional and major element: the lands and dwellings of millions of Germans who fled or who were expelled as World War II ended. Some 7 million Germans were pushed out of the Oder-Neisse territories taken over by Poland, and some 2 million Germans fled the Sudetenland, the area Hitler had gained at Munich in 1938, now returned to Czechoslovakia. This was a rich bounty for Communist officials to distribute, and they used it to ensure reliability, like a big-city politician uses patronage jobs. Poles from the eastern territories taken over by the Soviet Union and landless peasants from the crowded central area of Poland were awarded productive farms, houses, and apartments recently vacated by Germans. The people who received these bounties were naturally grateful and a bit worried that their original owners might some day demand them back. Accordingly, the recipients tended to support the Communists, who had bestowed these gifts upon them and who were the best protection for keeping them.

The next stage consisted of the gradual tightening of Communist control, slowly enough so that many people were not completely aware of what was going on. Non-Communist parties had trouble organizing and holding meetings, which were sometimes broken up by Communist toughs. The police took no interest in these disturbances. Non-Communist newspapers had difficulty getting published and distributed; shortages of newsprint and

Stalinism

The word "Stalinist" connotes an especially rigid, centralized, cynical, and brutal type of Communist ruling style. Stalin ruled the Soviet Union with a heavy hand from 1927 to 1953, creating the Soviet system that endured until Gorbachev began to significantly alter it in the late 1980s. Stalin also demanded and got strict compliance with his policies from Communists all around the world. They rationalized as follows: Stalin is the leader of the Soviet Union, the world's first socialist country and the path to the future, so by supporting Stalin we are supporting the homeland of socialism and assisting the liberation of humanity from capitalism, imperialism, and fascism. Even if Stalin were a little on the gruff side, he was working for socialism, and that's what ultimately counted, Communists figured. Among the party faithful of the 1930s through 1950s, such attitudes became an almost religious fixation that members refused to question. A word against Stalin was aid to the enemies of socialism. Even after Stalin's crimes and bloodthirsty nature had been abundantly documented, some refused to believe it. Stalinism included the following elements:

1. **Worship of Stalin.** In all Stalinist systems a personality cult was built around the Soviet dictator. Statues of Stalin were built throughout East Europe, as they had been in the Soviet Union. (Now rapidly vanishing, destroyed or melted down, they have become valuable for their rarity.) Boulevards, parks, and factories were named after Stalin. His every public word was elaborately quoted in the media. Policies were justified with Stalin's rhetoric. The heads of satellite states identified themselves with Stalin and copied his political style.

2. **Obedience.** In carrying out policies—economic, political, and foreign—individuals were expected to obey. Discussion was held to a minimum and focused only on how to implement the policy, not on overall strategy or goals. Those who opposed or even openly doubted Stalin's wisdom were defined as enemies and dealt with accordingly. Said Stalin of one such doubter: "We will shorten him by a head."

3. **Manipulation.** In Stalinist thinking, politics existed to be manipulated. Public opinion had no life of its own but was to be massaged into shape by lies, provocations, and primitive fright campaigns. Said Stalin on the subject of lies: "The paper will support whatever is written on it." By clever propaganda, Stalinists thought they could manipulate the masses to follow the Communist line. Unpopular, illegitimate regimes could be set up against the will of their citizens, who would soon be brainwashed into supporting them. This type of thinking is shortsighted. The regimes thus created come tumbling down when their coercive props are removed. Lies achieve only temporary results; eventually the truth comes out.

4. **Centralization of the economy.** Only the smallest of economic activities (for example, shoe repair) were left out of state control.

Everything else was controlled by a central planning agency, which emphasized heavy industry at the expense of consumer goods. In most countries, farming was collectivized (not in Poland). Production and trade were tied heavily to Soviet needs.

5. **Strict control of the arts and media.** Movies, music, painting, literature, the theater, and so on, were supervised by party hacks to make sure they cranked out the correct messages. Classical materials were left generally untouched, and many educated people sought refuge in them. The themes of new material had to be wholesome, upbeat, heroic, pro-Communist, and easily understandable. Western art was denounced as "bourgeois formalism" and was depicted as a cesspool that reflected the decline of capitalism.

6. **Scrutiny of individuals.** The security forces, usually under the interior ministry, kept tabs on anyone who dissented, had contacts with foreigners, or traveled abroad. Part-time informers could be in any organization, so people learned to watch what they said. Jail terms were frequent.

"Stalinist" in nonruling Communist parties, as that of France, indicated faithful support for whatever Moscow was doing at that moment. Everything the Soviet Union did was good, from the purges to farm collectivization. When Stalin said unite against fascism, they cheered the Popular Front. When Stalin said stop denouncing fascism, they came up with rationalizations for the Hitler-Stalin Nonaggression Pact.

Stalinist systems outlived Stalin, who died in 1953. How and when Communist countries de-Stalinized forms an important part of the story of East Europe. Romania under Ceauşescu was essentially a Stalinist system, as was Albania under Hoxha. North Korea, where children worship giant statues of Kim Il Sung, may be the last surviving Stalinist system. "Stalinist" at one point was considered synonymous with Communist. Was it? Or were the two logically separable? Can you have a non-Stalinist Communist system? Or is Stalinism the natural culmination of the system and tendencies that Lenin initiated?

trucks hit non-Communist newspapers. Non-Communist leaders, including ministers and prime ministers, who saw the jaws closing and tried to raise alarms, were depicted as reactionaries or imperialist spies and forced to resign. Some died under suspicious circumstances.

Non-Communist parties that grew wary of the Communists found themselves split. One or two leaders, possibly planted earlier by the Communists, would break away and set up a "new" peasant or socialist party, which would then repudiate the parent party as inflexible and mistaken. The new party, essentially a fake, attempted to attract adherents away from the original party. The fake party would enter into the governing coalition and thus enable the Communists to say, "What do you mean, the Peasant party has withdrawn from the coalition? One branch, led by Western capitalist agents, has withdrawn. But the other branch, led by farsighted progressives, has joined us." This tactic fooled some people for a while.

Virtually all the Communist parties of East Europe had been small. To boost their apparent numerical strength, socialist or social-democratic parties, which had historically usually been larger, were pressured (or even forced) to merge with the Communist parties. The resulting parties—the United Workers party in Poland, the Socialist Unity party in East Germany—could then claim to speak for the majority of the toiling masses, the true voice of the people, and so on. It didn't fool many.

In the third and final stage, the mask slipped away to reveal Stalinist rule. Non-Communists were dismissed from the cabinets, and only fake non-Communist parties were permitted to exist, usually as members of a united front totally dominated by Communists. Opposition views, both spoken and printed, vanished. All leading positions in industry, agriculture, education, and so on, were staffed with Communists. Travel and contact with the West were severely circumscribed. The countries of East Europe introduced new constitutions, each modeled on the Soviet Union's 1936 constitution, dubbed the "Stalin constitution." Along with the new constitution, the East European country usually changed its name to "People's Republic of..." or a variation thereof. (See the box in Chapter 3 on "People's Democracy.") The Stalin economic model was then put into place.

THE POSTWAR TAKEOVERS

Poland

Stalin used the London Poles' 1943 outcry over the massacre at Katyn as an excuse to break relations with them. Their leader, Gen. Wladysław Sikorski, was killed in a plane crash in 1943. His successor, Stanisław Mikołajczyk (pronounced "me-kol-why-chick"), head of the important Peasant party, found himself under British pressure to cooperate with the Soviets. After Stalin set up the Polish Committee of National Liberation in newly liberated Lublin (the so-called "Lublin Poles") in 1944, Mikołajczyk joined it. The Warsaw government of 1945 consisted of the Lublin Poles, who were Communist puppets, plus some non-Communists who had been invited in. Seizure of the former German Oder-Neisse territories took place under this government and was quite popular among all Poles, who felt they were entitled to compensation for the German devastation of their country. Resettlement was generally in Communist hands, though, and enabled them to build some Communist sympathies among the recipients of land and houses.

The shift of Polish territory from east to west turned postwar Poland into one of the most ethnically homogeneous countries of Europe. Before the war, the eastern part of Poland contained many Belorussians and Ukrainians; now these lands were Soviet. Poland's 3 million strong Jewish community had been largely wiped out by the Nazis; most of the surviving Jews emigrated. The result was a Poland where over 95 percent of the citizens spoke Polish and were Catholic.

Slowly, the Communist noose tightened around Mikołajczyk. His Peasant party was increasingly harassed, even terrorized, and he was accused of being a British agent (he had spent the war in London). The Lublin committee organized a fake Peasant party in competition with Mikołajczyk's. The Communists and their helpers arranged for rigged elections in early 1947, with each party assigned a fixed number of seats beforehand. Had the elections been free, Mikołajczyk and his Peasant party would likely have won, for by then there were no other non-Communist alternatives. In the January 1947 elections, the Communists and their puppets "won" 382 out of the 444 seats of the *Sejm* (pronounced "same"), Poland's parliament. The Peasant party took only 28 seats. The packed Sejm then elected veteran Communist Bolesław Bierut (who even had Soviet citizenship) president. At that point, it may be fairly said that Poland was officially Communist; it had entered the third stage discussed previously. Seeing no hope for democracy, Mikołajczyk fled to the West in October 1947.

East Germany

At this point, East Germany becomes relevant to our study, for during the long Cold War it served as the keystone or plug that locked in much of the rest of the East bloc. When East Germany collapsed in 1989, it was impossible to hold the East bloc together; Gorbachev didn't even try. Starting with Soviet occupation in 1945, East Germany began to take shape as a different country, one very similar in structure to its eastern neighbors. The Soviets did hesitate, however, before setting up a separate East German state.

The Soviet Occupation Zone assigned by Yalta was initially treated like the conquered country it was. The Soviets, who had lost more than 20 million in the German invasion, were vindictive toward Germany. Uppermost in their minds were economic reparations, not setting up an East German Communist state. The Russians immediately began dismantling whole factories in their zone and shipping them home to the Soviet Union. But, as in other East European lands, the Soviets also set up a Communist structure. In April 1945, in the wake of Red Army advances into Germany, the "Ulbricht Group" (see Chapter 3) was flown into Soviet-occupied Germany and began setting up a civil administration and reviving remnants of the old German Communist party. At one point (1932), the German Communists had won 13 percent of the German vote, but it had always lagged behind the Social Democrats. In April 1946, Ulbricht persuaded or forced the Social Democrats to merge with the Communists to produce the Socialist Unity party, a Communist party in all but name. By this point or shortly after, we may speak of a Communist regime in East Germany.

But the area was still the Soviet Zone, not a separate country. That came formally only in the fall of 1949. As discussed more fully later in this chapter (see "The Cold War"), conflict between the Soviets and the Western Allies over the fate of East Europe and the treatment of occupied Germany led to the Berlin Blockade and Airlift in 1948-1949. By this time, there were political figures in both Eastern and Western zones working for statehood under, respectively, Soviet and American sponsorship. In the West, Konrad Adenauer urged the founding of the Federal Republic of Germany and achieved it in September 1949. This pushed Stalin to give Walter Ulbricht, just a month later, what he had been wanting, the German Democratic Republic. East Germany was very much a child of the Cold War and did not long outlast the Cold War.

Czechoslovakia

With the only democratic tradition in East Europe that had been carried over from the interwar period, Czechoslovakia held out the longest against a complete Communist takeover. Perhaps the Communists waited in Czechoslovakia because they thought they had a good chance to take over legally and electorally. Many Czechs, including President-in-exile Beneš in London, distrusted the Western powers for selling them out at Munich in 1938; they looked with hope to the Soviet Union, the Slavic big brother who liberated them from the Nazis. Czechoslovak Communists built on this feeling. They also gained votes from Czechs who received appropriated German property. In combination with fellow-traveling Social Democrats, the Communists received 38 percent of the vote in reasonably free elections in 1946. That was by far the highest Communist vote obtained fairly anywhere in East Europe, and that was under the unusual circumstances of postwar uncertainty.

As in Poland, the Communists organized a new government in the eastern part of the country that had been liberated first by the Soviet army, in this case in Košice. It was a National Front of several parties and was joined by Czechoslovakia's prewar leaders, including Beneš. It soon moved to Prague.

Beneš was chosen president and, in recognition of Communist strength, he named Communist chief Klement Gottwald prime minister. In turn, Gottwald picked a cabinet with ministers from several parties, with the really important posts going to Communists. Local committees, dominated by

Masaryk: Murder or Suicide?

Jan Masaryk was the son of Tomás Masaryk, the famed founding president of Czechoslovakia after World War I. Jan Masaryk served as foreign minister of Czechoslovakia after World War II. Like his father, Jan was a devoted democrat and patriot. He saw the Communists taking over power and opposed it. By 1947, all the other East European countries had become openly Communist. Only Czechoslovakia held out, but with a mixed government that the Communists increasingly dominated.

On March 10, 1948, the body of Jan Masaryk was found in the courtyard of the foreign ministry atop Prague's Charles Hill. He had apparently died of a fall from a high window. Or was he thrown out? The official story was suicide, but many believe Masaryk, a hindrance to complete Communist takeover, was taken care of by the Communist-controlled security forces.

"Defenestration" (from the Latin *fenestra*, meaning "window"), the pitching of someone from a window, plays a prominent role in Czech history. The spark that started the Thirty Years War was the Protestant defenestration of Habsburg representatives in Prague in 1618. Masaryk's suspicious death shocked the world and marked the final clanging shut of the Iron Curtain around East Europe.

Communists, accused opponents of collaboration with the Germans, a charge that was often unfair. The interior ministry, increasingly packed with Communists, announced an alleged conspiracy in Slovakia and arrested many members of the Slovak Democratic party. Most non-Communists in the cabinet, sensing the rigged nature of the police, resigned in February 1948, hoping to topple the government. Instead, the Communists mobilized their police and unions to stage mass demonstrations to make it look like "the people" were supporting Gottwald. The new cabinet was almost completely Communist except for Foreign Minister Jan Masaryk. And he did not last long (see box). What was called the "Prague Coup" of 1948 marked the formal and complete Communist takeover of Czechoslovakia, democracy's last holdout in East Europe.

Hungary

Unlike Poland and Czechoslovakia, Hungary had a fascistic government and was an ally of Germany. There was no government in exile in London. This fact actually made things easier for the Soviets, because the provisional government set up at the end of 1944 under Soviet sponsorship in liberated Debrecen in the eastern part of the country faced no competition. The Soviet army fought its way across Hungary; Budapest was beseiged for seven weeks at the beginning of 1945.

In late 1945, the Soviet occupiers permitted a free election. The results were so disappointing to the Communists—who, with some fellow travelers, won only 17 percent of the vote—that they never permitted another free election. The prewar Smallholders party was revived to win 57 percent of the votes and a majority of parliamentary seats. Their leader, Ferenc Nagy (pronounced "nadj"), became prime minister. The Soviet occupiers, though, would not let the Smallholders fully staff the ministries; key offices, as usual, went to Communists. When the Smallholders complained of the growing Communist takeover, the Communists arrested them as "conspirators" and accused them of being former fascist collaborators. The Peasant party's charismatic second in command, Bela Kovacs, was accused, arrested by the Soviet army, and never seen again.

Under Communist control, new elections were held in 1947. The Peasant party had been broken by arrests, and the electoral franchise had eliminated all persons judged suspicious by the Communists. The Communists still won only 22 percent of the vote, and that was with multiple balloting by Communist toughs. By now Communist domination, in fact if not in name, was nearly complete. Nagy, still prime minister, called for Western help, but there was nothing the West could do. Like another peasant-based party leader, Mikołajczyk in Poland, Nagy fled abroad in 1947. Power was in the hands of Vice-Prime Minister Rákosi, an obedient Stalin puppet who had spent the war in Moscow. In 1948 the Communists, having purged the Social Democratic party of anti-Communists, merged the rump of the Social Democrats with the Communists to produce the Hungarian Workers party, really just another name for the Communist party.

Yugoslavia

By the end of the war, the Communist-led Partisans of Marshal Tito had liberated roughly half of Yugoslavia. The Soviet army swept the Germans out of the northern portion of the country. The only national political force left was the Partisans, and they saw no need for a gradual takeover. They had fought heroically, taken many casualties, and were impatient to install a Communist system. Prewar politicians, returning from exile or from internal anonymity, were given a few offices but quickly dismissed and sometimes tried as "British agents." The Chetnik leader Mihailović was hunted down, tried, and shot for allegedly cooperating with the Germans. Democratic newspapers were suppressed after one or two editions.

A People's Front, totally Communist controlled, "won" elections in late 1945 with an alleged 96 percent of the vote. There were no opposition candidates. Industries were quickly expropriated and farms collectivized on the best Soviet model. The 1946 Yugoslav constitution was nearly an exact copy of the 1936 Soviet constitution. The official name of the country was now the Federal People's Republic of Yugoslavia. Tito was president and all ministries were staffed with Communist Partisan veterans.

This was a problem, for the Partisan forces had been composed almost entirely of peasants, people who hated the Germans for the simple reason that the Germans had killed their relatives and razed their villages. The *Partizani* were sturdy and brave mountain fighters, but few were educated and none had experience in governing a country. They mistrusted city people and intellectuals, most of whom had simply stayed in Belgrade or Zagreb and waited out the war. Close to Tito, only Milovan Djilas had attended university. This gave a clumsy, rough-hewn quality to the Communist takeover, which was more brusque and brutal than elsewhere in East Europe.

Stalin did not like the way or the speed of the Yugoslav Communist takeover, even though the Yugoslav leaders aped him with almost embarrassing exactness. Stalin did not want a showdown with the Americans or British, for the Soviet Union was exhausted from the war. Especially difficult for Stalin was Yugoslavia's claim to Trieste, formerly an Austro-Hungarian seaport on the Adriatic, taken after World War I by Italy. Most of Trieste's inhabitants spoke Italian, but most of the surrounding villagers were Slovenians. At the end of World War II, Yugoslav Partisans battled the Germans for Trieste just before the British arrived to claim it. Tension was high. The Yugoslavs swore *"Trst je naš!"* ("Trieste is ours") and demanded Soviet support for their position. An armed conflict with the Western powers over Trieste was the last thing Stalin wanted at that time, and he demurred, urging Tito to take it easy (Trieste later went to Italy, the surrounding countryside to Yugoslavia). The Yugoslavs were quickly becoming a pain to Stalin, who preferred obedience and control.

Romania

Romania, like Hungary, was an ally of Hitler during the war but contributed far more troops to the Russian front than did the Hungarians. The military government of General Ion Antonescu, in league with the fascist Iron Guard, had a major grudge against the Soviets, Stalin's seizure of Bessarabia in 1940. In August 1944, as Soviet troops started moving into Romania, the hitherto silent King Michael (who had taken over when his father, Carol, abdicated in 1940) announced that Romania was changing sides and supporting the Allies.

This gesture did little to appease the Soviets, as they followed the general pattern described previously. After a brief period with pro-Soviet Romanian generals as prime ministers, Moscow ordered King Michael to appoint Communist Petru Groza to the office in March 1945 as head of a National Democratic Front composed of several parties but dominated by the Communists.

Elections in late 1946 were rigged. Anti-Communists and other "unreliable" persons were not registered, and the balloting was carried out in a climate of intimidation that gave the bulk of the vote to the National Democratic Front. As elsewhere in East Europe, the large National Peasant party, led by the popular Iuliu Maniu, was harassed and its leaders arrested, including Maniu, on trumped-up charges. A Communist-dominated "Ploughmen's Front" was offered as an alternative to the Peasant party. In late 1947, the mask came off. The Social Democratic party was forced to merge with the Communists. King Michael was ordered to abdicate (he went into exile in Switzerland), and the monarchy was replaced by a Romanian People's Republic.

Bulgaria

Bulgaria, too, was a member of the Axis, but unlike Romania sent no troops to fight in Russia. That would have provoked mass unrest among the russophile Bulgarians, who harkened back to the Russia that liberated them from the Turks. Unlike Romania, Bulgaria developed an armed resistance movement, Communist-led like Yugoslavia's Partisans, but much smaller, totaling perhaps 30,000 fighters. Earlier than Romania, the wartime Bulgarian government of King Boris decided it did not wish to be on the losing side. Boris visited Hitler in 1943 to explain this and mysteriously died. By mid-1944, however, Sofia announced its neutrality. Moscow nonetheless declared war on Bulgaria in September 1944 and Soviet troops swept in. At this same moment, a Fatherland Front, composed of Communists and democratic elements, took over in a coup.

As usual, the key positions in the Fatherland Front government were held by Communists. The guerrilla forces of Todor Zhivkov set up people's tribunals that quickly tried and executed some 2,800 wartime political figures, marking Bulgaria's as one of the bloodiest takeovers in East Europe. Within the Fatherland Front, the Communists arrested the other elements. A 1946 referendum abolished Bulgaria's monarchy, and the boy king, Simeon, left for Spain. Rigged elections later that year gave the Communists a big majority, and they took over totally.

The leader of the Bulgarian Communists—one of the few Communist parties of East Europe to have an early and substantial following—was Georgi Dimitrov, who had fled to Moscow following the abortive Communist uprising of 1923. There, Dimitrov helped direct the Bulgarian Communist party from afar. In 1933 Dimitrov was arrested and tried in Leipzig, Germany, for the infamous Reichstag fire that Hitler tried to blame on the Communists. Defending himself brilliantly and aided by an international outcry, Dimitrov went free. In 1935, Dimitrov was named head of the Comintern, the Moscow-run worldwide Communist organization.

From Moscow, Dimitrov supervised the Communist takeover of Bulgaria until 1945, then he returned to Bulgaria and became prime minister in 1946. He had the leader of the important Agrarian Union, Nikola Petkov, executed on fake charges despite strong U.S. and British protests. Dimitrov paid no notice to reminders that similar protests had saved him from a Nazi noose in 1933. Dimitrov, a perfect Stalinist, then told another opponent: "In this assembly I many times warned Nikola Petkov's group, but they would not listen. They lost their heads, and their leader lies buried. Reflect on your own actions lest you suffer the same fate." Dimitrov's warning captures some of the cold evil of Stalinism.

Albania

Like Yugoslav Communists, the Albanian Communists fought their way to power, partly against Italian and, later, German occupiers, but mostly they fought against non-Communist Albanians. As the Germans withdrew in November 1944, the Communist-led National Liberation Movement entered Tirana, took over under their chief Enver Hoxha, and shot their rivals in the pro-Western National Front. Again like the Yugoslavs, the Albanian Communists moved quickly with rigged elections and the proclamation of a people's republic in early 1946.

In this way, by early 1948, all of East Europe had been turned into what were called Soviet "satellites," each closely adapted to the Stalin model. An "iron curtain," in the words of Winston Churchill, had fallen across the middle of Europe. It has lifted only in our day.

THE START OF THE COLD WAR

The brutal Communist takeover of East Europe alarmed the West, and that was the crux of the Cold War. If Stalin had observed the letter and spirit of Yalta, there would have been no Cold War. Stalin's behavior in East Europe immediately raised the question: Is this what he intends to do in West Europe as well?

It is likely that Stalin and his successors never intended expanding westward into West Europe by military force, but in the atmosphere of heightened fear that characterized the Cold War, a Soviet attack was seen as a real possibility. Starting with Truman, American presidents found it convenient to simplify the problem by portraying it in military terms: Get ready for a Russian attack. There were, to be sure, some indications that a Soviet attack might be possible. Communist guerrillas nearly took over Greece. (The West didn't learn until later that Stalin had actually told the Greek Communists to desist and that they operated largely on their own.)

The Cold War

The Cold War was a long period of armed tension between the United States and the Soviet Union that followed World War II. It never erupted into a direct conflict between the two superpowers, but they fought each other indirectly, by means of arms races, alliances, and proxy wars, as in Korea, Vietnam, and Afghanistan. The probable reason why the Cold War was conducted at arm's length was the possession by both superpowers of nuclear weapons. They feared, with good reason, that if they ever started fighting each other directly, the conflict would soon escalate into a nuclear exchange that would devastate both nations.

The precise start of the Cold War is hard to pinpoint. A few writers claim it started with the 1917 Bolshevik Revolution, which the Western Allies strongly opposed. U.S. troops intervened in Russia and fought Bolshevik forces in 1918-1919, confirming the bad will between Russia and the West. More writers say it began as soon as Stalin's designs on East Europe emerged in 1946. By the spring of 1947, Washington was alarmed over Stalin's takeovers in East Europe and announced policies to counter them in the Truman Doctrine, in the Marshall Plan, and in George Kennan's influential "X" article in *Foreign Affairs.* These three moves, coming within weeks of each other, laid down respectively the U.S. political, economic, and theoretical responses to the Soviet threat. Kennan coined the term "containment," the long-term application of U.S. political and military counterforce wherever and whenever the Soviet Union tried to expand until the Soviet empire either mellowed or broke up. Containment was U.S. policy for 40 years. By 1947 the term "Cold War" was in use. The events of 1948—the Prague coup and the Berlin Blockade—confirmed the Cold War.

It is also difficult to pinpoint when the Cold War ended. Some see the Cuban Missile Crisis of 1962 as its dangerous peak; thereafter it slowly subsided. Others think it ended when Nixon turned to a policy of détente (a relaxation of tensions) with Moscow in the early 1970s. Still others claim it didn't end until Gorbachev threw in the towel in the late 1980s.

The United States quickly sent most of its troops home from Europe after the war and cut its armed forces and defense budget to low levels in the late 1940s. But Stalin kept large numbers of troops in East Europe. Why? He could not have feared Western attack. (Actually, General Patton had urged precisely that.) Therefore, went the reasoning, Stalin must be contemplating an attack of his own. (We now see that Stalin wanted to make sure that East Europe stayed completely under his control, and massive troop strength guaranteed that.)

Compounding the problem was the American tendency after World War II to make a too-exact analogy between Stalin and Hitler. See how Hitler had gobbled up one country after another? Well, Stalin is doing exactly the same thing, went the highly simplified reasoning. The comparison was poor. Hitler was reckless, hot-tempered, and in a hurry. Stalin was cautious, cold-blooded, and felt he had all the time in the world. According to Marxist-Leninist analysis, capitalism would soon crumble. Why start another war when you will be history's winner without one?

What Stalin had in mind for West Europe seems to have been more subtle than military conquest and satellitization, as he had done in East Europe. After World War II, Stalin ordered the West European Communist parties—the most important by far were the large Communist parties of France and Italy—to practice a double strategy of both open political opposition and underground preparation for armed overthrow. Aboveground, the French and Italian Communists attempted to attract adherents with a militant prolabor line of "power for the workers." They organized France and Italy's largest unions and frequently called them out on strike. In parliament, they opposed tenaciously the moderate governments set up after the war. Underground, though, they collected arms from the anti-German resistance (in which both parties had been prominent) and organized for a possible coup.

It seems likely that Stalin sought a weak, fragmented, and neutral West Europe. Some years later, Stalin likely calculated, after the Soviet Union had recovered its strength, a weakened West Europe would fall into his hands. The local Communist parties should prepare and work for that day but not attempt an armed uprising, which would only provoke the U.S. and British imperialists, a point that always obsessed Stalin.

The West did stem Soviet designs on West Europe, but by a combination of economic, political, and military policies, not by armed strength alone. The determination shown by the Berlin Airlift and by the economic aid from the Marshall Plan was more important in the late 1940s than the few thousand American troops still stationed in West Europe. And one of the key factors in stiffening West European resolve was the Iron Curtain itself and what was happening behind it. Except for some committed Communists, few West Europeans wanted to be under Soviet domination.

It was in this political and economic context that the line between the two systems stiffened and solidified in the center of Europe. In Germany, Stalin didn't quite know what to do with his zone, except to loot it for an estimated $20 billion worth of equipment. The Cold War context forced matters to a head in Germany. As Stalin took over the rest of East Europe, the Western occupiers of Germany—the United States, Britain, and France—grew more alarmed. They decided to build up rather than tear down their zones of Germany and to turn them into a bulwark against the further spread of Communism. Economic revival was the first step. In 1948, millions of Marshall Plan dollars began to arrive in Germany and the currency was reformed, replacing the worthless reichsmarks (German currency from 1924 to 1948), military script, and American cigarettes (a popular currency) with the new deutsche mark. Every citizen got 60 of the new D-marks, and the West German economic miracle began.

The Soviets objected to the currency reform in the Western zones, as they had been flooding the Western zones with reichsmarks as part of their looting campaign. In retaliation, they blocked ground traffic to West Berlin, which was 110 miles inside their occupation zone, figuring the Western Allies, who were assigned zones of Berlin as part of Yalta, would clear out of Berlin. Instead, the Americans and British answered the Berlin Blockade with the Berlin Airlift. For nearly a year, 1948-1949, West Berlin was supplied with everything—food, coal, even animal fodder—by round-the-clock cargo flights. By now the Cold War was clearly in full swing. Stalin solidified his grip over East Europe, and lines that were envisioned as temporary became permanent—or, as things turned out in 1989-1990, semipermanent.

Could things have gone differently? Could the Cold War have been avoided? There were, theoretically, three possibilities, none of them very probable. First, if Stalin had not seized East Europe there likely would have been no Cold War. World War II ends, Soviet troops return home, and both East and West Europe settle down to economic reconstruction with U.S. aid. But Stalin was determined to retain East Europe. With his East European satraps, trained and organized during the war in Moscow, he had been preparing to take over East Europe for years.

A second unlikely possibility might have been for the United States to take immediate U.S. military measures. World War II ends and Allied forces then lay down the law to Stalin to fulfill Yalta and to leave East Europe alone. In such a case, major U.S. forces stationed in West Europe, plus the U.S. monopoly (until 1949) over the atomic bomb, would have backed up Western resolve to get the Soviets out of East Europe. While intriguing, this scenario was psychologically impossible. The American way of war is a massive but brief outpouring of energy to get the war over with; then the boys come home. American politicians had promised to "bring the boys home by Christmas" of 1945, and few American citizens would have stood for a prolonged occupation of Europe. Although, eventually, that is precisely what happened. In 1945, however, the United States and Soviet Union were allies. When their troops met on the banks of the Elbe River in Germany, they embraced like brothers. How could we suddenly turn on them? And if there had been fighting to dislodge the Soviets, the battleground would have been precisely the East European countries we were trying to liberate. With nuclear weapons, there would have been little worth liberating.

A third possibility would have been to adopt early and publicly a Churchill-like spheres-of-influence policy and divide Europe. Stalin wants East Europe? He gets it, provided he leaves West Europe alone. We leave East

Europe alone. Again, psychologically this would have been difficult. Many Americans are of East European descent and care about their homelands. They could not turn their backs on the Stalinist brutalities, therefore neither could American politicians. As mentioned earlier, Americans tended to read into Stalin's actions those of another Hitler. Ultimately, the United States did quietly accept a kind of spheres-of-influence policy. By the late 1960s, busy in Vietnam, Washington lost interest in East Europe. It didn't seem to matter much any more. The Soviets seemed intent on keeping East Europe forever, and we were not about to go to war over it. The futility of the Cold War led to a de facto recognition of East Europe as a Soviet sphere of influence.

Actually, U.S. policy in East Europe was not bad in the long run. Starting with Kennan in 1947, there was the realization in Washington that eventually the Soviet empire in East Europe would collapse. President Eisenhower especially understood that the Cold War was not to be fought but waited out. The wait was frustrating, but it was better than war, and ultimately we won. Few Americans would have understood or accepted this strategy if you had presented it to them in the early years of the Cold War. Americans like to get their wars over with fast; they lack patience.

So the worst was avoided, but the tragedy in this long wait was that East Europe fell so far behind the West. The original Marshall Plan was offered to all Europe, even to the Soviet Union. But the Marshall Plan required open economies and the sharing of economic data, something Stalin would never permit. Traditionally, the Soviet Union held its economic data as secretly as its military plans. Stalin ordered his puppets in East Europe not to attend the initial Marshall Plan session. Czechoslovakia had been about to attend. Then came the early 1948 Prague coup, and Czechoslovakia too turned its back on the Marshall Plan. To a very considerable extent, we are now picking up four decades later where we left off when Stalin cut East Europe off from the West. The flow of economic aid and trade that would have modernized East Europe is at last underway, and it will eventually make East Europe a part of the global economy.

SUGGESTED READINGS

FOWKES, BEN. *The Rise and Fall of Communism in Eastern Europe*. New York: St. Martin's, 1993.

GRAEBNER, NORMAN. "Cold War Origins and the Continuing Debate: A Review of the Literature," *Journal of Conflict Resolution* 13 (March 1969), 131.

SETON-WATSON, HUGH. *The East European Revolution*, 3rd ed. New York: Praeger, 1956.

TURNOCK, DAVID. *Eastern Europe: An Economic and Political Geography*. New York: Routledge, 1989.

CHAPTER FIVE

The Hated Regimes

Probably the worst time in the life of East Europeans was the age of Stalinism between the complete Communist takeovers of the late 1940s and the death of Stalin in 1953. Thousands were arrested, tried, and sentenced to long prison terms, merely because they were suspected of opposing the Communists. In some East European countries, thousands were quietly killed. Only recently have their unmarked mass graves been discovered. Within a few years after the tyrant died, things began to ease, slowly and sporadically, in most of East Europe. While Stalin lived, though, the features of Stalinism, discussed in the previous chapter, were laid on with a trowel in East Europe. The governments of the region liked to call themselves either "people's democracies" or "socialist" states, but they clearly qualified as Communist regimes (see box). The "socialism" in East Europe should in no way be confused with the socialism found in West Europe, where it has long since mellowed into democratic welfarism.

THE STALINIST MODEL

The Party in Power

Perhaps the defining element in a Communist system is that the Communist party overlaps with and very nearly *is* the government. When the two start to split, with government throwing off Communist-party control and direction, it means the end of the Communist system. In these systems, the most powerful figure is invariably the head of the Communist party, usually bearing the title first secretary or general secretary, but referred to in the West as "party chief." In addition, such figures often take on government jobs, usually the presidency. When they lose one

Communism and Socialism: What's the Difference?

There is much confusion and overlap in meaning between these two terms, some of it fostered by Communist regimes themselves. Many of the countries we used to call "Communist" called themselves "socialist." Most of the Communist parties of East Europe in 1990 renamed themselves socialist, and most probably are socialist now. However, the East European governments that existed from the late 1940s until about 1989 were clearly Communist.

Karl Marx, writing in the second half of the nineteenth century, viewed socialism as merely the beginning stage of communism, and the Communist regimes of East Europe followed Marx's notion. Capitalism, Marx predicted, would suffer a series of economic depressions until the impoverished working class could stand it no longer. The working class would turn revolutionary and eventually overthrow the reckless and abusive capitalist system, replacing it with socialism. Socialism, according to Marx, would abolish both private ownership of the means of production and profit, which he regarded as unjust and historically doomed. Marx was vague about socialism, but he suggested that it would mean state ownership of the means of production, a drastic leveling of social-class differences, and material abundance for all. Eventually, when socialism had reached this happy level, it would turn into communism, a utopian society of material plenty and no government or state coercion. It would be perfection, the end stage of human development. Bear in mind that no Communist government claimed to have achieved communism. They had achieved socialism and were working on communism, according to the theory.

Early in the twentieth century, Lenin made some theoretical changes in Marxism so it might apply to a backward economy like that found in Russia. Marx had envisioned socialism growing where capitalism was most developed, as in Britain and Germany. Lenin's main contribution, however, was his theory of tight organization and of control over the Russian Social Democratic Labor party, which at that time was underground or in exile. Lenin, in fact, was living in Switzerland. The party, which was later renamed the Bolshevik and then Communist party, was not to be a party like others, Lenin wrote. Instead, professional revolutionaries were to be controlled by a disciplined hierarchical structure that reported back to a Central Committee, which Lenin controlled personally. Lenin added the concept of the party as "organizational weapon" to Marx's economic, social, and historical theories about the inevitable collapse of capitalism. The amalgamation "Marxism-Leninism" is another name for communism.

As used in this book, socialism is the broader concept, and communism is a mistaken off-branch of socialism. Socialists have many viewpoints and only one thing in common: All are strongly democratic. Some (a dwindling number) still advocate state ownership of industry, at least certain industries. A few British Labourites still like the nationalization of some industries. Most socialists, however, having noted the failure of state ownership, seek only a certain amount of governmental regulation and control of the economy to correct distortions and abuse. The French Socialists, for example, backed away from state ownership in the 1980s. The mildest socialists, the social democrats, simply urge welfare programs to put a safety net under the poorest and most vulnerable members of society. The German and Swedish Social Democrats could be called "welfarists." And some honest socialists will tell you they no longer know what "socialism" means.

Communists have been the main militant wing of socialism. (There are other militant wings, such as Trotskyists, but they are tiny minorities.) Communists are undemocratic and elitist by nature; they feel that only they know what's best for society. They do not like other viewpoints because, since they already know the answers, they can't stand being challenged. Communists advocate (or advocated) not only state ownership and central control of the economy along with a gigantic welfare state, but also the administration and implementation of this by a disciplined "vanguard" party (that is, the Communist party) that will lead society to a utopia. Under communism's Stalinist highpoint, Communists around the world had to obey Moscow and follow every twist and turn in the Kremlin line. The standard U.S. State Department rule of thumb for distinguishing Communist regimes from socialist regimes was that the former regimes obeyed and were controlled by Moscow; the latter were independent. This might have been a useful distinction in the 1940s and 1950s, but by the 1960s even hard-line Communist regimes increasingly carved out some space for themselves and sometimes repudiated Moscow's leadership.

or the other position, it usually means they are on their way out. This happened repeatedly in East Europe in 1989: an old Stalinist would be bumped out as party first secretary but keep the presidency. Usually in a few months, he was out of that job too.

As is usual in European governments, a separate prime minister serves under the president to carry out most of the day-to-day governance. In 1989, prime ministers often changed while presidents, usually hard-liners, did not. The prime minister in turn picks a cabinet composed of ministers, who run each branch of government and the economy. All ministers are high-ranking Communist-party members. Some East European systems—Poland, East Germany, Czechoslovakia, and Bulgaria—permitted fake little parties under Communist leadership to have a few seats in parliament, but everyone knew they obeyed the Communists. The Communists never won a free election in East Europe. In coming to and staying in power, they depended heavily on the following institutions.

Warsaw Pact

The Soviets totally dominated the armed forces of their satellite countries through a series of bilateral "friendship and mutual assistance" treaties. Promotions at the higher ranks were reviewed by Moscow, and most generals had been trained, in whole or in part, in the Soviet Union. Until 1956, Poland's defense minister was actually a Russian general, and Soviet officers were laced through the Polish army. Arms and equipment were standardized on Soviet models; tanks and aircraft (rarely the latest models) were purchased from the Soviet Union. In short, East European armies were carefully tied to the Soviet army.

In May 1955, to firm up this arrangement, all the Soviet satellites of East Europe met in Warsaw to set up the eastern equivalent of the North Atlantic Treaty Organization (which had been in existence since 1949). The Warsaw Treaty of Friendship, Cooperation, and Mutual Assistance soon became known as the Warsaw Pact. Like NATO, it attempted to better integrate command and control. It also provided legal grounds for keeping Soviet forces stationed throughout the East bloc or for having Soviet troops enter member countries to conduct "joint maneuvers," which might include the crushing of a breakaway regime, as in Hungary in 1956 and Czechoslovakia in 1968.

The armed forces of East European countries were always a problem for Moscow. Arming their satellites too well could mean that someday these weapons could be used against the Soviets. Trying to strike a balance, Moscow encouraged a modest level of preparedness in East Europe, but reserved the most powerful and modern weapons for itself.

Ostensibly, Soviet forces were in East Europe to dissuade the imperialist West, especially revanchist West Germany, from invading. In reality, it was to make sure the East European lands stayed firmly in the Soviet camp. The northern tier of East European countries had Soviet troops garrisoned permanently on their soil. The biggest contingent by far was in East Germany—over twenty Soviet armored divisions totaling more than half a million soldiers. Poland, Czechoslovakia, and Hungary had fewer Soviet troops. Soviet forces were kept out of sight, in inconspicuous barracks in the countryside, which the Soviet troops were seldom allowed to leave. Soviet officers, aware of the problems that could grow from the combination of soldiers, alcohol, women, and defection, kept their troops under tight control, which included giving them no local currency. The Balkan lands of Yugoslavia, Albania, Romania, and Bulgaria, since at least the 1960s, have had no Soviet troops on their soil. Yugoslavia and later Albania had gone their own way. Albania dropped out of the Warsaw Pact in 1961, costing the Soviet navy strategic submarine pens on the Mediterranean, which they could no longer use. Romania exhibited a spiky sense of independence and would not allow Soviet forces on its soil, although it did continue as a Warsaw Pact member. And Bulgaria, a loyal Soviet satellite, didn't need any Soviet forces to ensure its loyalty.

Security Services

The first instrument Stalin's agents in East Europe perfected, even before the final seizure of full power, were internal security services on the Soviet model. Sometimes wrongly called in the West the "secret police" (probably after their Nazi equivalent, the Gestapo), the security services were actually rather public, with uniforms, headquarters, and a presence everywhere. True, they had secret informers and conducted much of their casework behind closed doors. The security forces were neither army nor regular police but a paramilitary force especially trained to do the party's bidding. In 1989, when the security services either couldn't or wouldn't crush anti-Communist protests, the system was doomed.

The leading officers of the various East European security services were trained under careful Soviet supervision, often in Moscow. Most of the top officers thus spoke Russian. In each national organization, many officers reported to Soviet security officials, sometimes secretly, so that the Soviet security organization interpenetrated the local agency. It is safe to say that the Lubyanka, the Moscow headquarters of the KGB, soon knew whatever the East European daughter agencies had learned.

The Communist argument for their security services, starting with the Bolshevik seizure of power in 1917, went like this: We are besieged by hostile capitalist, imperialist, and reactionary forces who want us dead and our revolution demolished. To give them even one inch, to grant them any right to exist inside our country, means they will spread their infection by whipping up discontented elements. They give us no quarter, and we give them none either. Actually, that rationalization is a fairly accurate picture of the Russian Civil War of 1917-1920. It was kill or be killed, defend the revolution or the reactionaries will win. To this end, Lenin had Feliks Dzerzhinsky, of noble Polish origin, set up the dreaded Cheka (Extraordinary Commission) to root out enemies of the revolution. The square in front of the Lubyanka was known as Dzerzhinskaya until the giant statue of Dzerzhinsky was toppled in 1991. The Cheka went through several name changes; under Stalin it was mostly known as the NKVD (People's Commission for Internal Affairs). For its last decades, it was called the KGB (Committee on State Security), the most powerful Soviet ministry.

To be sure, every country has a security service. What was different about those of the Communist countries? In democratic countries, security agencies fight against penetration by foreign spies and gather intelligence abroad. They are concerned about their own citizens only insofar as they may be working as foreign agents. Granted, sometimes security forces in democratic countries exaggerate dangers and harass people on dubious grounds. In the United States an exaggerated Red Scare brought the Palmer raids of 1918-1920. In West Germany in the 1970s, student radicalism plus the Baader-Meinhoff gang (which was supported by East German agents) brought antiradical decrees that demanded numerous loyalty checks. Typically, though, only a minute fraction of the effort of security services

Stalin's Daughters

	Security Service	Party Newspaper
Soviet Union	KGB	Pravda
Poland	UB	Trybuna Ludu
Czechoslovakia	SNB	Rude Pravo
East Germany	Stasi	Neues Deutschland
Hungary	AVH	Népszabadság
Yugoslavia	UDBa	Politika
Romania	Securitate	Scinteia
Bulgaria	DS	Rabotnichesko Delo
Albania	Sigurimi	Zeri i Popullit

in democratic countries is directed at their own citizenry, for the vast majority of citizens are loyal. In Communist countries, the situation is nearly reversed, with most of the security agencies' attention focused on their own citizens. The agencies suspect (with good reason) that many citizens oppose the Communist regimes and that foreign contact may indicate espionage or antiregime propaganda activities. The problem, at root, is one of legitimacy. Where legitimacy is high, that is, where most people accept the government as rightful and where most people are generally loyal, as in most Western countries, security services need concern themselves very little with citizen behavior. Where legitimacy is low and citizens have little respect for the regime, the security services must mount a gigantic effort to oversee vast numbers of citizens. In other words, Communist countries have large, intrusive, and sometimes brutal security services because they need them; their citizens really are disloyal.

Communist security forces, though, make matters worse. Just knowing they are being watched makes people irritable and jumpy. A citizen who has been interviewed for merely exchanging letters with an American relative resents the security forces and the government they represent. A young person who has been denied university admission because of an alleged reactionary family background may turn into a real reactionary. A weekend mountain climber who has trouble getting a passport to climb peaks in another country feels trapped and limited. And anyone who has had a relative killed or imprisoned by security forces will never forget it. Even after the worst excesses of Communist security services subsided after Stalin, they left a bitter taste among people with long memories. One of the questions of post-Communist East Europe is how much of the files, personnel, and informers of the security services should be revealed and prosecuted. The issue, called "lustration," divided societies between those who wanted justice and those who wished bygones to be bygones.

Information Monopoly

As the Communist regimes consolidated their hold over East Europe, they made every effort to choke off alternate sources of information. Communist thinking ran: If we can structure their information world, we can control them. Free media accompanied and hastened the demise of Communist regimes in East Europe in 1989. For party believers, as well as the many opportunists who watched out for the success of their careers, following affairs from the party perspective in the leading party daily could aid in carrying out one's duties and in getting promoted. Each East European country had a party daily newspaper that carried major speeches, policy shifts, and ideological discussions. Distributed nationwide, these party dailies (see earlier box) ensured prompt and uniform fidelity to the party line among those who cared, generally only a small percentage of the population.

At a more popular level, daily newspapers for each city and region restrained the amount of policy discussion in favor of sports and local coverage. Still under party control, stories were slanted to emphasize progress, well-being, and national achievements; the tone was upbeat and positive, like the nationwide party daily, but simpler and more eyecatching. Stories reporting on the West emphasized crime, unemployment, poverty, urban blight, and nuclear weapons. There was nothing neutral or objective about Communist news coverage.

The controlled media never worked very well, as many citizens systematically disdained what they read in the press or heard on the radio. Catholic churches, especially in Poland, cautiously offered alternate views from the pulpit, in church-related organizations, and in church-sponsored publications. Furthermore, after a while many developed access to Western news reports, chiefly through radio broadcasts transmitted by Radio Free Europe, Voice of America, Deutsche Welle, or the BBC. Most European radio sets, in both the East and the West, come with a short-wave band, and this proved to be a weak spot in the Communists' information monopoly.

Radio Free Europe (RFE) was set up in Munich, Germany, at first covertly by the U.S. Central Intelligence Agency, to break the Communist party's monopoly on information in East European countries. By means of close readings of the local press, interviews with travelers, and careful analysis, RFE often came up with solid news stories that the local Communist media had tried to bury. By broadcasting such news back into the East European country, RFE sometimes forced the local media to come clean and the regime to admit that something was wrong. Several RFE newscasters were familiar voices; they had been popular on local radio and then fled to Munich. RFE originally broadcast in every East European language but later dropped Serbo-Croatian (the chief language of Yugoslavia) and Albanian. Yugoslavia had moved into a nonhostile relationship with the United States, and Albania, RFE research discovered, had too few radios to bother with. RFE broadcasts were often "jammed" by the Communist regimes—simply by

How Much Did Ideology Count?

Some writers on Communist systems place—or used to place—major emphasis on ideology. They argue that the Communists of these countries really believed in Marxism-Leninism and used it to build support for the regime, to guide policy, and to ensure discipline among party members. I see no such thing in Communist countries, especially in East Europe. Communist party members, including those at the very top, were terribly cynical about ideology. Almost uniformly they were opportunists who joined the party only to further their careers and improve their standard of living. Most knew little of Marxism-Leninism and cared less. They mumbled a few Marxist phrases like a badly learned catechism. In fact, serious Marxists in East Europe were likely to become doubters and intellectual troublemakers. If you started applying Marxian analysis to East European societies, you soon discovered a pampered party elite and a ruthlessly exploited working class, a situation worse than anything capitalism had brought about. You were quickly told to shut up and apply your Marxist analyses only to Western societies.

In earlier decades, ideology did play a role in recruiting Communist party members. Horrified by the poverty of their countries and the obvious unfair class differences, the original generation of East European Communists, some of whom came to power after World War II, may have initially been driven by ideological motives. The militant evil of nazism convinced others that communism must be the answer. After these people had been in power a while, though, ideology took second place to retaining power and privilege. Ideology was used as window dressing to justify the latest policy twists, including abrupt about-faces. After a while, even believers stopped believing.

To be sure, all Communist regimes taught Marxism-Leninism to young people, but it soon bounced off them, for they saw very little equality and progress. This deepened cynicism and undermined any effort at building a civic culture of legitimacy and honesty. A few talented young people, however, learned that mouthing the right words along with party membership built their careers. By the second generation, 98 percent of the ruling Communist party membership had become opportunists. There could be a few scattered believers, but the regime didn't trust them with anything important. Opportunists are more reliable than believers, because you can closely predict an opportunist's behavior.

The regime shoveled out ideology, but no one believed it, not even the shovelers. The clincher to my antiideological argument, I think, came when the Communist regimes collapsed in 1989. How many citizens were then motivated by Marxism-Leninism? Even former Communists abandoned any pretense at ideology—it no longer served their careers—and announced themselves to be Socialists of a democratic bent. Many Communist managers became enthusiatic capitalist managers. They were, after all, just opportunists.

broadcasting noise on the same frequency—to try to screen them out. Jamming effectiveness is spotty, however; at different locations the broadcast might get through.

Voice of America (VOA) played a lesser role in East Europe. An official branch of the U.S. government (part of the U.S. Information Agency), VOA concentrates on putting out a favorable image of the United States and its foreign policies rather than detailed news about events in East Europe. VOA broadcast fewer hours in East European languages than RFE; some East Europeans tuned to VOA to improve their English. The authoritative English-language station, though, was the BBC. Starting with its wartime broadcasts to anti-German resistance movements, the BBC developed an enviable reputation for fairness, thoroughness, and restraint.

East Germany (the German Democratic Republic, or GDR) had a special problem with its information monopoly: West Berlin, an island of freedom 110 miles inside GDR territory. With several stations broadcasting from West Berlin in German—perhaps the most famous was RIAS, Radio in the American Sector—East Germany was effectively blanketed with Western radio. Even worse, most of the GDR could pick up West German television. The freer, richer life shown on West German television offered a permanent rebuttal to East German Communist propaganda. In sum, the East European efforts at information monopoly did not work; information got through the Iron Curtain as though it were a sieve.

Russian Language and Culture

As the Communists incorporated East Europe into the Soviet bloc, they tried to strengthen and deepen cultural ties. Russian language instruction became required in most East European high schools. As a Slavic language, Russian should be easy for Poles, Czechs, and Slovaks. The amazing thing is how little Russian most East Europeans know. After several years of study and sometimes visits to the Soviet Union, only a few spoke passable Russian. Given a chance to learn English (and sometimes German), however, many gained remarkable fluency in two years. What did this indicate? The students were "voting" by studying the English hard, the Russian not. The motivation to study each language was quite different. The Soviet Union served as an economic, political, and cultural model for very few East Europeans. Traditionally, educated East Europeans looked westward, not to Russia (with the exception of the Bulgarians). English (and German) are useful for foreign trade and tourism, Russian is not. And many young East Europeans love rock-and-roll (partly because their regimes tried to ban it), and rock is almost exclusively sung in English.

Soviet-run bookstores offered bargain prices on the collected works of Lenin, Stalin, and Brezhnev, plus other Communist commentaries by lesser lights, both in Russian and in translation. Sales were less than brisk. Better sellers were translations of Russian classics. The Soviets were also big on folk song and dance groups, and there were many tours and exchanges. The Communist theory here is that folk art expresses the genius of the common people, and this genius is fostered and protected by the Communist system. In folk performances, communism and nationalism were to merge. East European countries also cultivated folk song and dance in an effort to gain legitimacy. None of these cultural efforts worked; in their influence on the people, the efforts rolled like water off a duck's back.

Because it is so important, we will explore more fully the impact of socialist or Communist economics on East Europe in the next chapter. Suffice it to say, Stalin generally imposed on East Europe the nationalization of industry and the collectivization of agriculture that he had earlier imposed on the Soviet Union. In both cases, the long-term results were poor and led to gradual economic decay and ultimately to collapse.

The imposition of the Stalinist model on East Europe resulted in very unhappy East Europeans. It is fair to say that in every country the bulk of the population disliked the regime. An unknown portion hated it outright. A basic tenant of Stalinism is that you can force an unwelcome system on a people and they will learn to adjust to it, even to like it. After all, the reasoning goes, you are in tune with history and know that capitalism is dying and communism is the wave of the future. You're just speeding up history a bit. This nonsense was accepted by few people in East Europe, and their numbers grew fewer over the decades.

THE TITO-STALIN SPLIT

One of the most bizarre episodes of the Cold War was the split between Tito and Stalin that burst out in 1948. It was important, for it both reflected what was happening in East Europe at the time and contributed to subsequent problems in the Soviet bloc. It showed that under the uniform surface of East European politics lurked personal and nationalistic rivalries that not even Stalin could disguise. Few realized it at the time, but the quarrel between the Soviet Union and Yugoslavia was the first and earliest sign that the Soviet bloc would one day break up. The split was one of Stalin's many foreign-policy blunders, all of them related to his very poor understanding of what the people of other countries thought and felt. Stalin thought he knew everything, even what was happening in distant lands.

Tito had been an ultraloyal Stalinist ever since he rose through the ranks of the small Yugoslav Communist party in the 1920s and 1930s. He later remarked that he sensed something was wrong when party comrades were called to Moscow and shot in Stalin's insane purges of the 1930s, but at the time he said nothing. Faint differences emerged during World War II. Stalin was not keen on the Communist-led Partisans; he thought they might alarm the British and Americans. Stalin even urged them to wear the old Serbian monarchist symbol on their caps. Tito insisted they wear the Communist red star, just like Soviet soldiers. In battle, Partisans died with the cry "Stalin! Tito!" on their lips. But the Soviet Union stalled in providing help to the Partisans, and then only a little. The British sent supplies and a team of advisors under the redoubtable Brigadier Fitzroy Maclean.

After the war, the Yugoslav comrades socialized their country faster than Stalin wished. Stalin preferred to go slow to avoid alarming the West. The Yugoslav Communist regime set to work immediately, arresting suspected bourgeois opponents and setting up the above-mentioned artifacts of the Stalinist system, behaving like an overeager younger brother. The 1946 Yugoslav constitution was a word-for-word copy of the 1936 Soviet constitution. It looked as though Yugoslavia were an early and perfect Soviet satellite.

But on June 28, 1948, the Communist Information Bureau, meeting in Sofia, Bulgaria, announced it was expelling Yugoslavia from the Communist camp for alleged deviation and disobedience. The Comintern had been ostensibly dissolved in 1943 as a goodwill gesture to the Western Allies. At the time, it didn't seem right to be fighting a common enemy while one ally was trying to subvert the other. However, in terms of Stalin's control of the world Communist movement, nothing changed, and in 1947 Moscow announced an ostensibly new organization, the Communist Information Bureau—Cominform for short—that was very similar to the old Comintern.

The comrades of the Cominform made a small psychological blunder in picking that particular date for the expulsion of Yugoslavia, for June 28 is the day of St. Vitus (*Vidovdan*), patron saint of Serbia. Eerily, June 28 also marks the historic (albeit losing) battle of Kosovo Polje against the Turks in 1389 and the Sarajevo visit and assassination of Archduke Franz Ferdinand in 1914. If you are going to do something that will arouse Serbs—the largest nationality and the founding element of Yugoslavia—don't do it on June 28.

But why would the Cominform expell Yugoslavia? No other explanation fits but Stalin's personality. He could not stand what he did not control. Tito may have been completely loyal, but he had his own power base not dependent on Stalin, and that was something the paranoid dictator could not tolerate. All the other Communist leaders of East Europe were personally and militarily dependent on Stalin; none had come to power on their own. Stalin wrongly presumed that when he signaled his displeasure with Tito by expelling Yugoslavia from the Cominform, loyal Stalinists in the Yugoslav Communist party would quickly depose Tito. Then, thought Stalin, he could pick a puppet to head the Yugoslav party.

To Stalin's chagrin, the Yugoslav Communists ignored Stalin almost to a man and rallied around Tito. A few "Cominformists," the Yugoslav term for a pro-Stalinite, were jailed. Soviet propaganda blasts depicted Tito as a traitor to communism and an American agent. Soviet troops menacingly maneuvered on Yugoslavia's northern and eastern borders (but at no time did they cross over). At first the Yugoslav comrades could not believe what was happening; they had been trained to worship Stalin. For some months Belgrade expected Moscow to cease its obviously insane charges and patch things up. Gradually the Yugoslavs understood that they were outcasts, on their own, that the Soviet Union was as

Yugoslavia's Maverick Communism

Yugoslav communism is important not because it worked—it was a mess—but because it provided an exciting and enticing suggestion throughout the bloc that there could be a socialism not based on the Stalin model. During the 1950s, Yugoslav thinkers, including Tito's right-hand man, Milovan Djilas, who had served as liaison with Stalin during the war, critiqued and repudiated Soviet-style socialism.

The chief problem, long noted, is that Marx predicted the "withering away" of the state as communism was built. The state and its coercive apparatus of bureaucrats and police were needed only to protect the property and privilege of the ruling class, argued Marx. Nationalize property and make all equal, and the state would grow superfluous. But in the Soviet Union, clearly the opposite was happening. Where was the "withering away" Marx had predicted? Stalin and his hack writers came up with some lame rationales for growing state power: They were surrounded by hostile capitalists; they had to first achieve a considerable material base; history moves in dialectical rather than in straight-line fashion; and so on. Yugoslav thinkers stopped buying these excuses and started calling the Soviet system a mistake, a perversion of Marxism. Actually, Trotsky had developed much the same critique years earlier: "the revolution betrayed."

In place of Soviet-style "state socialism," a system that made the state incredibly large, Yugoslav thinkers proposed a benign "self-managed socialism" in which state power would gradually shrink. This allowed the Yugoslavs to imply that they, rather than the Soviets, were carrying out Marx's designs, a point that made the Soviets very angry, for their way had to be the only way. In a series of reforms during the 1950s, Yugoslavia introduced wide-ranging *decentralization, debureaucratization,* and *worker self-management*. Enterprises were still "socially owned" but run by and for their workers through elected boards. They competed in a partly free market. The Yugoslavs boasted they had taken the best of capitalism and combined it with the best of socialism. (In later years, some wags chortled that it was the worst of both.)

A close-up view of Yugoslavia showed Communist party control, dreaded security forces, and state interference in the economy. State banks determined who got loans. Government funds subsidized money-losing enterprises. Workers voted themselves wage increases out of line with productivity, and inflation became endemic. Tito, almost like Stalin, turned himself into an icon who could do no wrong.

Still, for a while during the 1950s and 1960s, Yugoslavia became a standing rebuke to the Soviet model. Some thinkers in East Europe were intrigued by the idea of each country charting its own path to socialism. Why should the Soviet Union serve as a model for all countries? In this way, Yugoslavia served as an alternative model and, therefore, as an irritant and destabilizing element in East Europe.

great a threat to their national security as the capitalist West and that Stalin had constructed a mistaken system. By 1950, the Yugoslavs had resolved to build their own distinctive system, a non-Soviet socialist system. Stalin's paranoia and misjudgment thus created a competing brand of socialism in East Europe that caused Stalin and his successors no end of trouble.

In a rage at not having been able to oust Tito, Stalin, whose paranoia got worse near the end of his life, started seeing "Titoism" throughout East Europe. Political figures, generally those second in command, who might be interpreted as advocating deviations from the Soviet model for building socialism were given rigged trials; most were executed. In many cases, the accusations of Titoism were covers for getting rid of political rivals, since no one could say exactly what Titoism meant. It was sort of an all-purpose accusation.

The most famous of these purge trials were those of Czech party secretary Rudolf Slansky and several others from 1950 to 1952. In Hungary, Laszlo Rajk, who had been interior minister, was accused of Titoism and executed. In Bulgaria, Traicho Kostov was the comrade most likely to succeed the ailing Dimitrov, but Kostov had voiced some opposition to Soviet economic exploitation of Bulgaria. He was accused of Titoism and executed. In Albania, interior minister and central committee secretary Koci Xoxe represented a pro-Yugoslav faction. He was also a rival for power of Enver Hoxha, who found accusations of Titoism a convenient excuse for executing Xoxe.

Poland was a bit different. In late 1948, Władysław Gomułka, party general secretary and deputy premier, was arrested and accused of "rightist and nationalist deviation," (that is, Titoism) but he was merely imprisoned and reemerged into leadership in 1956. Throughout East Europe under Stalin, lesser figures were fired, many were jailed, and close to one-quarter of the Communist party members were kicked out.

What was Stalin doing? The Communist parties of East Europe had expanded their membership severalfold. Some new members were idealistic fools; most were just opportunists. Stalin, it now seems likely, feared that this rapid expansion of untested members was weakening party control and discipline. For Stalin, any excuse to tighten control was a good excuse. In the 1930s in the Soviet Union it had been "Trotskyism"; now it was "Titoism." And it didn't really matter whether those accused were guilty of any such deviations; most were not. It only mattered that Stalin and his helpers could make an example of someone—anyone—to keep the rest cowed and obedient.

THE RUMBLINGS OF FREEDOM

Inflicting foreign, unpopular regimes on the nations of East Europe engendered smoldering, bitter resentment. Direct, open opposition—even verbal—could be punished, but within the confines provided by friends, family, and the church, many indicated their continuing discontent. At no time did an East European

Communist regime successfully root itself into the hearts and minds of its people. For decades, when there was no hope of change, people got along by going along, although often grudgingly. Hatred of the regime, however, was never far beneath the surface, and from time to time it burst out.

Pilsen, Czechoslovakia, 1953

The western part of Czechoslovakia had been liberated by American forces in 1945. General Patton had gone farther and faster than expected and had arrived earlier than the Soviet army. The U.S. Third Army could have easily taken Prague, but that was left for the Soviets. The Americans meanwhile took Plzeň (spelled in German as Pilsen, birthplace of Pilsner beer) amidst great popular acclaim, for Czechs and Americans had a long and close affinity. The American liberation of Pilsen was officially blotted out by the Communist regime, but citizens remembered "the boys from the U.S.A."

It was against this background that a fair-sized worker revolt broke out in Plzeň in June 1953. (Stalin had died in March.) The regime imposed higher prices and tighter work rules, and workers strongly objected. Demonstrations spread to other cities. The Communist regime handled the situation carefully, backing down a bit on their new policies and boosting production of consumer goods. Collectivization of agriculture was suspended, and some farmers were allowed to resume private production. Although not widely noted, the Pilsen revolt marked the first mass outcry against a Communist system in East Europe.

East Berlin, 1953

What happened a short time later in 1953 in East Berlin attracted far more notice than Pilsen, perhaps because Western reporters (and intelligence agents) could move freely between West and East Berlin. East and West Germans were in close proximity and had easy communication with each other, and East Germans could more easily compare their standard of living and personal freedom with their cousins in West Germany. The East Berlin uprising was bigger, angrier, and bloodier than the Czech one, and it captured the world's attention with a dramatic photograph of unarmed East German workers throwing stones at Soviet tanks.

As in Czechoslovakia, the immediate cause was an economic tightening. In June 1953, the East German regime issued orders raising work norms in order to boost lackluster economic performance. East Berlin construction workers decided they already were working hard enough and struck in protest against the new norms. Soon other trades joined the protest, which quickly spread to other East German cities. The strikes escalated into antiregime riots. Authorities accused Western agents of stirring up the trouble, but it seems to have been spontaneous. Ulbricht had to call for Soviet help, which was close at hand, as more than twenty Soviet divisions surrounded Berlin. The uprising was quickly crushed. Over twenty demonstrators were killed on the street and another seven executed.

The Uses of Anti-Semitism

As we considered earlier, there was a great deal of anti-Semitism in East Europe. Their status as unwanted outsiders drove some Jews to see communism as a liberating force that would make all people equal and erase anti-Semitism. As a result, nearly every Communist party in East Europe had a Jewish contingent. These people served Stalin well in the Communist takeovers of East Europe. In the security services, they could be counted on to mercilessly root out anything that smacked of fascism or collaboration with the Nazis. Often included in this group were old-style conservatives and anti-Communists. As a result, Jews such as Rákosi in Hungary and Ana Pauker in Romania were sometimes prominent among the tougher (and more detested) Communists.

This suited Stalin just fine. A controlled wave of anti-Semitism provided him with another way to manipulate the population and to deflect discontent from its true cause. When difficulties arose in the communization of East Europe, what handier a scapegoat to blame than Jews? By purging them as Titoists, nationalists, wreckers of socialism, or whatever, he tacitly but clearly communicated to the local population that the real problems were caused by the Jews, not by communism. Stalin knew that many East Europeans were anti-Semitic and that Jewish Communists had done a lot of his own dirty work. Besides, Stalin never fully trusted Jewish Communists; they were too "cosmopolitan," meaning they had international contacts. Hanging Jewish Communists in East Europe thus killed two birds with one stone: It pleased local populations, and it got rid of what Stalin suspected was an unreliable element. The two most prominent Jews to get the rope in East Europe were Slansky of Czechoslovakia and Rajk of Hungary. Since then, most of the Jews who had survived the Holocaust left East Europe. They had gotten the message of how communism used and then discarded Jews.

Poznan, Poland, 1956

Since the late 1940s, the old Stalinist, Bolesław Bierut, had, in various offices, been Poland's paramount leader and general secretary of the United Workers' (Communist) party. But, little appreciated by Westerners at the time, not far beneath the surface, the Polish party split, something that happened in most East European Communist parties. The Stalinists of Bierut were in command. These were mostly people who spent the war in the Soviet Union (some in the armed forces and security police) and who enforced a hard-line policy of obedience to Moscow's lead. Other Polish Communists, though, adopted a more "national" approach; that is, they saw things through Polish eyes and envisioned a Polish road to socialism. Some of these people had been in the underground resistance inside Poland during World War II. Others were old-time Polish Socialists who had been forced to amalgamate into the United Workers party, but whose attitudes were more flexible and open than those of the Stalinists.

Khrushchev's moves deepened this split in the Polish party. For one thing, Khrushchev tried to patch things up with Tito; he visited Yugoslavia in 1955 and announced publicly that each Communist party could choose its own path to socialism. This is what the "national" faction of the Polish party had been whispering for years. Its leader, Gomułka, had been dropped as party chief in 1948 for alleged Titoism and had been under house arrest for some years. Then suddenly in 1955, Titoism was not so bad.

Khrushchev's denunciations of Stalin in early 1956 (see box), further weakened the Stalinist leadership of Bierut, who conveniently died in March. Especially devastating was Khrushchev's admission in the speech of how Stalin had brutally and wrongly liquidated the old Polish Communist party in 1938. Although this was probably unintentional, it severely undermined the legitimacy of the hard-line Stalinists in the Warsaw government.

In June, some 50,000 workers rioted angrily against higher prices and work quotas in Poznan, an important industrial city which lies west of Warsaw. They cried for "bread and freedom." Soon the workers were joined by students, and the protests spread, taking on a general anti-Communist tone. The Stalinist leadership, frightened that they could be overthrown, called out units of the Polish army to crush the protests. Fifty-four were killed and hundreds were wounded.

Poland tottered on the edge of a major violent revolution. Thoroughly scared, the Warsaw government, to save itself, turned to the only credible Communist figure, Wladysław Gomułka, the alleged Titoist and nationalist who had been fired in 1948 and isolated ever since. Gomułka was named new party chief in October 1956. Khrushchev flew to Warsaw to try to veto the move; he still didn't trust Gomułka. For a while, it looked like the Soviet army would intervene to block the chain of events in Poland. The Polish defense minister at this time was a Soviet general, Rokossovsky, and there were Soviet officers planted strategically throughout the Polish army. Gomułka reassured Khrushchev that Poland would stay Communist and a member of the Warsaw Pact, and Khrushchev acquiesced to the switch in leadership.

Gomułka, unfortunately, was true to his word. He was not quite the reformer that both Poles and Westerners initially celebrated. He denounced Stalinism in the Polish party, released political prisoners, curbed terroristic police power, admitted there was mismanagement and corruption in the Polish economy, and dismissed Rokossovsky and other Soviets from the Polish armed forces. Things relaxed in Poland a bit; life was freer and people spoke rather openly. Censorship lessened and most collective farms disappeared. The regime improved relations with the Catholic Church and gave it considerable autonomy. But Gomułka did little to change the economy, which stayed centralized, state-run, corrupt, and inefficient. He also made sure that Poland followed the Soviet lead, and he allowed no competition to the Polish Communist party. Under Gomułka, Poland adopted some

Khrushchev's Anti-Stalin Speech

Pilsen and East Berlin were just early rumblings of the discontent that had been smothered under the Stalinist systems of East Europe. What happened in 1956 triggered far greater outpourings. In early 1956, Soviet party leader Nikita Khrushchev gave a stinging, hours-long speech against the "crimes of Stalin" to a party congress of thousands of participants. Khrushchev made the surprise move completely for domestic political reasons. He was at odds, economically and politically, with the Stalinist bureaucrats who still ran the Soviet Union. Trying to prod the system, which was choked with fear and controls, into growth and innovation, Khrushchev went after the chief problem, Stalin's personality cult. He thought he was speaking behind closed doors, but with a little help from the American CIA, copies of the speech soon circulated worldwide.

Around the world, Communists were stunned and shocked. All those terrible things that Western conservatives had been saying about Stalin were now admitted to be true. The purges of the 1930s had murdered loyal party comrades, not British spies or Trotskyist party wreckers. Khrushchev's speech omitted any reference to the millions of ordinary citizens killed in the collectivization of agriculture, for Khrushchev had been one of Stalin's henchmen in that effort. Khrushchev also admitted that Stalin's blunders in World War II cost the Soviet Union millions of soldiers.

In the West, old-time Communists quit the party in disillusionment. In China, Mao Zedong wondered if Khrushchev was rational and reliable; he had rashly smashed the Stalin symbol of Communist unity. And in East Europe, regimes that were still Stalinist and had received no advanced warning of Khrushchev's de-Stalinization, trembled with fear that their symbol of Communist resolve had been suddenly dethroned. They had been basing their policies and style for years on Stalin. His pictures were everywhere. Streets and factories were named after Stalin. Now, all of a sudden, he was a villain. Khrushchev, who seems to have given no thought about the likely impact in other countries of his de-stalinization campaign, thus harmed the stability and legitimacy of the East European regimes. Within months of Khrushchev's anti-Stalin speech, Poland and Hungary erupted in anger. With the god destroyed, the people went mad.

of the symbols of liberalization, but these just whetted Polish appetites for real change.

Budapest, 1956

The real explosion of 1956 came in Hungary just a few days after the "Polish October" installed Gomułka. Emboldened by Khrushchev's de-Stalinization, in 1956 Hungarians, especially writers, began to demand the ouster of their longtime dictator, the Stalinist Rákosi. Budapest intellectuals formed the Petőfi Circle, named after a nineteenth-century nationalist poet who had died in the 1848 insurrection put down by Russian troops. The Petöfi meetings grew to include thousands and featured increasingly antiregime speeches. The admission that Béla Kun and Laszlo Rajk had been wrongfully executed did not calm them; instead, it convinced them that the whole Communist package was rotten. Trying further to calm things, in July the Soviet Politboro member Anastas Mikoyan, a crafty Armenian, flew to Budapest to supervise Rákosi's ouster. His replacement, close associate Ernö Gerö, was no better and calmed no one. Much preferred was Imre Nagy (rhymes with "lodge"), a relatively liberal Communist leader who had been named prime minister in 1953 but who had been ousted by the Stalinist forces of Rákosi in 1955.

On October 23, a major antiregime demonstration gathered in a square facing the Danube to call for the return of Nagy, free elections, and the removal of Soviet troops. Suddenly, security forces fired automatic weapons from buildings, killing several people. That was the signal for the Hungarian Revolution of 1956. Crowds stormed security police headquarters and beat to death security police. A gigantic statue of Stalin in Budapest was pulled down. The revolt spread nationwide. Collective farms were broken up, workers' councils took over their factories, and local committees took over the government. On October 30, Nagy took power and formed a multiparty coalition pledged to fulfilling the demands the demonstrators had made a week earlier. The Nagy government said it sought to build a benign, non-Soviet type of socialism, a middle way between capitalism and communism. The influence of the Yugoslav example was here apparent. It looked like the Hungarian revolution had triumphed and that soon Hungary would no longer be Communist or part of the Soviet bloc.

Khrushchev played a tricky game. He pretended to withdraw Soviet forces from Hungary, but on November 1 they returned in massive strength to crush the uprising. Nagy declared Hungary's withdrawal from the Warsaw Pact, proclaimed its neutrality on the Austrian model, and appealed for Western help. Ashamed, the Western powers delivered no help, nor could they. On November 4, Soviet tanks entered Budapest to cut down the lightly armed Hungarian soldiers and civilians in several days of street fighting. Altogether, some 32,000 died. With the Austrian border still open, over a quarter of a million Hungarians fled to the West, many to the United States. Nagy and his associates took refuge in the Yugoslav embassy. Moscow promised them safe conduct to leave the embassy and the country. Then it arrested, tried, and executed them in 1958. They were buried in unmarked graves in an overgrown corner of a Budapest cemetery.

From obscurity, Moscow plucked Janos Kádár, victim of an earlier purge who had been imprisoned and tortured, to be leader of Hungary. This gave Kádár a kind of *bona fides* as a non-Rákosi, non-Stalinist Communist. The Kádár government restored order, but it did not reimpose the police terror of Rákosi. And Moscow, which took a public-relations beating around the world for its brutality in Hungary, wished no further uprisings, so it treated Hungary with kid gloves, allowing it considerable leeway in developing a Hungarian path to communism and

Did the U.S. Betray the Hungarian Revolution?

For years, Washington had been talking about liberating East Europe from communism. Eisenhower's Secretary of State John Foster Dulles had issued a famous call to "roll back communism" in East Europe. It was a purely electoral ploy to beat the Democrats, who stood accused of not doing enough against communism, but is it possible that Hungarians took Washington's phrase literally? Radio Free Europe (see earlier in this chapter) had been broadcasting anti-Communist messages to the peoples of East Europe, including the Hungarians. These broadcasts gave Hungarians the expectation of speedy U.S. help if they threw off the Communist yoke. The United States seemed to promise something and not deliver. Hungarian freedom fighters were sure the U.S. Army was on the way.

Dulles's rhetoric was revealed as hollow, for there was essentially nothing the United States could do, short of risking World War III with the Soviets. How would Moscow have reacted if U.S. troops had entered Hungary from the west as Soviet forces invaded from the east? Besides, Hungary had no border with a U.S. ally; Austria had been solemnly declared neutral by the Austrian State Treaty of 1955, which the United States had negotiated and signed. We would have had to violate Austrian neutrality to bring U.S. forces to Hungary.

Radio Free Europe claimed its broadcasts had in no way encouraged the freedom fighters to expect U.S. help. To back up this assertion, RFE's Munich headquarters used to eagerly offer visitors a complete replay of their broadcasts of the period. (There is some evidence that a mobile Soviet station broadcast fake RFE promises of help as a way to discredit RFE in particular and U.S. foreign policy in general. The Soviets were no strangers to this sort of "disinformation.") Still, RFE was accused of raising false hopes.

There are a couple of morals to the story. The first is that even speeches intended solely for domestic listeners quickly find their way overseas, where they are heard with a different perspective. Dulles shouldn't have talked about a "rollback" unless he was willing to send U.S. troops. And radio messages of hope cannot be too hopeful, for they may give the impression that the United States is ready to jump in with troops. In late 1956, RFE toned down its militant anti-communism and concentrated on providing accurate news, which in the long run proved more effective. Americans as a whole were a little ashamed for not delivering on their seeming promises.

a comfortable standard of living. In a way, the Hungarian rebels won.

Looked at with several decades' hindsight, we now see how communism has been slowly collapsing since the death of Stalin in 1953. Stalinism was a dreadful system, which not only robbed people of basic human rights but failed utterly at delivering the material bounties it promised. Neither could the system be reformed.

Khrushchev's denunciation of Stalin, for the purpose of domestic reform, destroyed the very cement that held the system together. In a very real sense, Stalin was the system. Much of the history of East Europe since the mid-1950s consists in when and under what circumstances each country could dump the little Stalins the master had left behind.

SUGGESTED READINGS

BEREND, IVAN T. *Central and Eastern Europe, 1944-1993; Detour from the Periphery to the Periphery*. New York: Cambridge University Press, 1996.

BROWN, J. F. *Eastern Europe and Communist Rule.* Durham, NC: Duke University Press, 1988.

BRZEZINSKI, ZBIGNIEW K. *The Soviet Bloc: Unity and Conflict,* rev. ed. New York: Praeger, 1961.

COHEN, LENARD, AND JANE P. SHAPIRO, eds. *Communist Systems in Comparative Perspective.* Garden City, NY: Doubleday, 1974.

FEHÉRVÁRY, ISTVÁN. *The Long Road to Revolution: The Hungarian Gulag, 1945-1956.* Santa Fe, NM: Pro Libertate, 1990.

FELKAY, ANDREW. *Hungary and the USSR, 1956-1988: Kadar's Political Leadership.* Westport, CT: Greenwood, 1989.

HARASZTI, MIKLOS. *The Velvet Prison: Artists Under State Socialism.* New York: Basic Books, 1987.

HIRSZOWICZ, MARIA. *Coercion and Control in Communist Society*. New York: St. Martin's, 1986.

KOSTRZEWA, ROBERT, ed. *Between East and West: Writings from Kultura.* New York: Farrar, Strauss, 1990.

STOKES, GALE, ed. *From Stalinism to Pluralism: A Documentary History of Eastern Europe Since 1945*, 2d ed. New York: Oxford University Press, 1996.

TOMASZEWSKI, JERZY. *The Socialist Regimes of Eastern Europe: Their Establishment and Consolidation, 1944-67.* New York: Routledge, 1989.

WHITE, STEPHEN, JOHN GARDNER, GEORGE SCHÖPFLIN, AND TONY SAICH. *Communist and Postcommunist Political Systems: An Introduction,* 3rd ed. New York: St. Martin's, 1990.

CHAPTER SIX

"We Pretend to Work": The Decay of Communism

MORAL BANKRUPTCY AND MORAL HEROES

By the 1960s, East Europe's Communist regimes were morally bankrupt. Whatever vision they might have been able to offer earlier had vanished amid empty economic promises, police-state repression, and gluttonous opportunism by the party elite. People were resigned and cynical. The Communists controlled the opportunity structure, so if you wanted to go to a university, get a better job, or travel abroad, you got along by going along, usually without enthusiasm. If you publicly opposed the regime, you would have a difficult life. Your writing would not be (legally) published. You would find only menial work. You might go to jail. For most people, there was no point in open defiance. Everyone knew the system was morally bankrupt, but few had the guts to say so openly. It was like the emperor's new clothes: Nobody spoke the obvious. Dictatorship needs not so much enthusiastic believers as a timid and silenced population.

Into this moral vacuum stepped a few cultural and moral heroes, people who, at great personal sacrifice, said no to the regime. They were a diverse lot, ranging from a shipyard electrician to university sociologists to playwrights. Their motivation included religious conviction, humanistic concern over injustice, and the empirical knowledge that communism was a corrupt failure. Their strength was their moral purity; they refused to knuckle under. Through self-published manuscripts (*samizdat*), foreign radio broadcasts, and even being denounced by the regime, these moral heroes gradually became widely known. At the right moment, when the Communist regimes could no longer count on Soviet support, the moral heroes stepped forward to deliver the final puff that collapsed the Communist house of cards.

The context in which these moral heroes became suddenly important and effective is our concern in this chapter. Strength of character by itself did not bring down these police states. It took a series of events that started with the death of Stalin in 1953. After Stalin, things began to loosen up. Could another Stalin have succeeded him, perhaps a dynasty of Stalins? Unlikely. A Soviet Union trapped in the Stalinist mold would have fallen farther and farther behind the West. A society drenched in fear and routine does not produce or innovate enough to keep up with dynamic free societies. This is what Khrushchev was all about: Get the Soviet economic system moving to catch up with the West. To do this, Khrushchev had to de-Stalinize. He permitted the East European countries to do the same.

But with de-Stalinization, the several Communist systems, including those of East Europe, began to lose their way. Under Stalin, things had been brutal but clear: push heavy industry, keep the population silent, follow the Soviet model, permit no factions within the party. After Stalin, things were less clear. Separate paths to socialism might now be permitted. After all, Khrushchev had flown to Belgrade in 1955 to apologize to Tito for Stalin's 1948 ouster of Yugoslavia from the Cominform and to affirm Yugoslavia's right to build the kind of socialism it wished in the way it wanted. If Yugoslavia could develop its own path to socialism, why not Poland? And if party members could discuss this possibility, you had automatically allowed a faction of "third-way" or "middle-way" thinkers to grow up within the party. If you eased up on political controls, you permitted people to criticize the regime. If you eased up on cultural controls, you permitted writers, artists, and performers to come out with cheeky new materials that implicitly rebuked the Communist model.

So you get rid of Stalin in image and structure. Then what do you do? Then does your Communist system start falling apart? As a matter of fact, that seems to be the case, but neither Westerners nor East Europeans understood this at the time. Such were the 1960s in East Europe, an unstable situation in which several regimes had de-stalinized but had not found a new, durable system to replace the Stalin model. This situation showed up in the culture of the period.

Culturally, it was an exciting time, for East European artists lived with an exquisite tension between defective, unpopular political and economic systems and a semifree ability to say they were unjust. In cinema, plays, and literature, East European writers outfoxed low-IQ censors by developing clever, indirect ways of saying things, sometimes by allegory, that scathingly criticized their regimes. It was as if they winked at their audiences to say, "You know what I mean," and the audiences winked back.

These writers played a major role in keeping the spirit of freedom alive. Some were unable to publish legally, but they distributed carbon copies of their stories, plays, and essays among circles of friends, who then passed them on. Some of these were published in the West in emigré journals and broadcast back on Radio Free Europe. In this way, impecunious and suppressed writers often achieved great recognition without ever having been published in their own countries. Some became moral heroes and political leaders, such as playwright Václav Havel of Czechoslovakia, who, before he became president, had scarcely any of his plays legally produced in Czechoslovakia.

ECONOMIC PROBLEMS OF SOCIALISM

The Communist systems of East Europe were doomed mainly because of their laggardly economic performance. For the sake of rapid, if lopsided, industrialization, the Stalin model introduced all manner of dislocations that eventually tripped up economic growth. A relatively short burst of industrial growth in the 1950s was followed by decades of slowing down and falling behind.

By 1950, little private industry was left in East Europe. Only some very small enterprises, employing chiefly family members, were left in private hands. Everything else was taken over by the state, although in some cases it was described legally as "socially owned," that is, owned by the society as a whole. Either way, when freedom came, unclear ownership left behind a difficult legacy of how to privatize firms in the 1990s (see Chapter 8).

There were a number of reasons for nationalization. First, it got rid of capitalists, and capitalists were the enemy. Capitalists deprived of their wealth and power were no longer a threat to the Communist regimes. Second, nationalization of industry gave enormous power to the Communists, increasing their control over society. What got built where, who got hired, who got apartments, and so on, all came under party purview. Third, nationalized industry was, under Stalin, presumed to be more rational and efficient than private enterprise. Although it sounds laughable now, some people honestly thought that socialism outperformed capitalism. They compared the economic decline of capitalist countries during the Great Depression of the 1930s with the rapid growth of the Soviet economy during the same period, the epoch of the Five-Year Plans. Instead of competing enterprises getting in each other's way and having their profits skimmed off by greedy capitalists, a rational, central plan would direct and coordinate all economic activity toward rapid growth.

And there was, to be sure, an ideological element to nationalization, at least at the public-relations level. By doing all the steps listed previously, the state takeover of industry would show both the local and the world's working classes that socialism was the wave of the future. According to Marxism-Leninism, big state-run industries were an advance over capitalism. Therefore, to have left industry in private hands would have been a sign of doubt and hesitation about the correctness of communism.

A final, and perhaps decisive, point that encouraged the nationalization of industry is that it placed all of East Europe's economy at Stalin's disposal, and he needed it. The Soviet economy was badly damaged by the war, and now a new Cold War was underway. Stalin was desperate for whatever resources he could get

Comecon

In 1949, a year after the Marshall Plan swung into action in West Europe, Stalin set up its eastern equivalent, the Council for Mutual Economic Assistance, called CMEA in the East and Comecon in the West. The Soviet Union, of course, had no aid to give, and in fact collected considerable reparations from its wartime foes of East Germany, Hungary, Romania, and Bulgaria. CMEA had little meaning until after Stalin. Under Stalin, there was much economic duplication and overlap between the various countries, what economists call *autarky*, that is, economic self-sufficiency.

Khrushchev refurbished Comecon as a planning agency that would assign each country production plans and quotas. This might be more efficient than autarky, but it also took away freedom of choice from member countries. Hungary, for example, built no cars, only buses. Hungary imported cars chiefly from Czechoslovakia, Poland, and the Soviet Union (in descending order of quality). Romania's Communist chief at the time, Gheorghe Gheorghiu-Dej, strongly objected to turning the Romanian economy into an adjunct of the Soviet economy and vetoed Romania's participation in Khrushchev's grand plan, although Romania continued as a Comecon member. Yugoslavia and Albania were not members of the CMEA.

his hands on, and state-run industries controlled by puppet states were a convenient mechanism for making East Europe deliver its goods eastward. A series of "joint companies," partly Soviet and partly local, were set up throughout East Europe, further cementing the East European economies to the Soviet economy. A free-enterprise economy would have largely faced west, for that is where the market and hard currency were (and still are). A state economy faced east and was oriented to Soviet needs.

This Soviet control over East Europe's economy was especially important with the outbreak of the Korean War in 1950. According to Khrushchev's memoirs, believed to be generally accurate, Stalin had not precisely ordered the North Korean invasion of South Korea; rather he had acquiesced to North Korean party chief Kim Il Sung's strong desire to unify his country under communism and Kim's conviction that the United States would not forcibly react to this. American analysts now believe that President Truman's strong reaction—not only in sending a large army to Korea but in greatly stepping up U.S. defense preparations worldwide—surprised and jolted Stalin and forced him to shift suddenly into a gigantic arms-building program. East European industry, especially the metallurgical capabilities of East Germany, Czechoslovakia, and Poland, were extremely valuable to the Soviet arms buildup and another reason these industries had to be state-run.

With the Korean War came forced industrialization in East Europe on the model of the Soviet Five-Year Plans of the 1930s. The largely agricultural economies of most of the region were rapidly redesigned to favor heavy industry, long a part of Stalinist thinking. Stalin and his helpers argued like this: Heavy industry, chiefly steel production, is the basis of all economic growth. Locomotives, machine tools, boilers, and so on, are all made out of steel. (Implements of war are also made out of steel.) The more steel you make, the sooner you lay the foundation for a thriving socialist economy, one that will leave capitalism far behind. This kind of economic reasoning, we now see, is extremely dubious—some of the fastest-growing economies are those oriented to consumer goods—but it was accepted without question by East European Stalinists: steel equals good. It is not for nothing, as the Russians like to say, that *stal* is Russian for steel and that Stalin means "man of steel." The results of forced industrialization were mixed. There was rapid industrial growth, but it was temporary, inefficient, environmentally damaging, and unrelated to consumer needs, and its products were of poor to mediocre quality.

In the revolts of several East European countries in the 1950s (discussed in the previous chapter) we see another thing that goes wrong with forced industrialization. It squeezes the population unmercifully, giving them little in return, until they rebel. The uprisings of 1953 in Pilsen and Berlin and of 1956 in Poznan and Budapest came when the industrial output of East Europe was probably showing its fastest increase. Little of it, however, went for consumer needs.

Collectivization of Agriculture

The collectivization of agriculture in East Europe, as in the Soviet Union, was the flip side of forced industrialization. Stalinist reasoning went like this: We are bringing millions of workers from the countryside into the urban areas for our new heavy industries. We are turning peasants into proletarians, who now have to be fed cheaply since we don't pay them much. We've got to squeeze more food at lower cost out of the countryside. Peasant farming is inherently inefficient; the acreage is too small and the techniques too primitive. (For much of East Europe, this point was generally accurate, and returning now to small peasant plots would be economic folly.) Besides, peasants are shrewd enough to know when they are being paid too little for their products; then they either stop growing or simply eat up what they have grown. We regard them as nasty little conservative individualists, and we will break them by combining smallholdings into big collective farms. Then we can get greater production with fewer workers and can make sure much of the crop is delivered to the state at a low price.

Collectivization in East Europe generally took place in the early 1950s. The farmers felt betrayed. Many had been given acres in the land reforms of the immediate postwar period. Estates owned by Germans and nobles had been confiscated and distributed to peasants. But now what the state had given the state took away by having small farmers give up their individual holdings to collectives. The difference between Soviet collectivization in the late 1920s and early 1930s and collectivization in East Europe in the early 1950s was that the latter was not nearly so brutal. For Soviet collectivization, Stalin practiced deliberate mass starvation, deportation, and sometimes the shooting of peasants. An estimated 6 million Ukrainians were starved to death to break their anticollective attitudes. In East Europe, the regimes generally pushed collectivization by taxing individual farmers heavily and by granting better deals on seed, equipment, and marketing networks, and offering improved health and living standards to those farmers who joined collectivized units. There was much grumbling but little bloodshed.

In Poland, where even Stalin understood that stubborn peasant resistance was simply too high, the regime let most farmers keep their holdings, but it tied them to state purposes by means of supply and marketing networks that effectively accomplished the same ends as collectivization.

THE LONG-TERM IMPACT OF SOCIALISM

In examining the net result of a socialist—or, if you prefer, Communist—economic system, we should get some things straight. First, a socialist economy does not spell instant catastrophe. The adoption of a Communist economic system one year does not lead to economic collapse the next. Instead, it slowly runs down. At the early stages of industrialization, a Stalinist approach produces impressive, rapid growth. It mobilizes all resources, including unemployed labor, and flings them into the construction of factories, especially those used in heavy industry. Historically, most of East Europe was at a low level of industrialization compared with West Europe. The exceptions in East Europe were certain areas of Bohemia and Poland that had inherited the industries of the earlier German and Austrian empires. By the late 1950s, all of East Europe (with the possible exception of Albania) had a considerable industrial plant and had greatly exceeded their prewar industrial output.

Second, what chiefly concerns us is not *absolute* economic growth, but *relative* growth. In almost every year, the economies of East European countries continued to grow. But, increasingly, starting in the 1960s, they grew at slower rates than the economies of West European countries. By the 1980s, the economies of East Europe were barely growing at all. This was a painful embarrassment for Communist regimes that had promised the economic collapse of capitalism and the arrival of material bounty through socialism. Everyone in East Europe knew that West Europeans lived better and were moving ahead faster. Even historically backward countries like Spain and Finland were moving into the ranks of prosperous, industrialized countries, and they were doing it without coercion and with improving living standards for their citizens. In the modern age, every country is looking over its shoulder to compare how it is doing with other countries. When East Europeans looked, it hurt. The power of this "jealousy factor" is not to be underestimated.

Bearing these two perspectives in mind, we can see that while the Stalinist model was industrializing rapidly, it was also introducing major distortions and

The Trouble with Statistical Comparisons

Communist countries do not measure their economies the way Western countries do, by Gross Domestic Product (GDP)—the sum total of goods and services produced in a year, usually expressed per capita. The East used material output only. And much of what was reported by the East was lies. Western economists, including a section of the CIA, tried to translate East-bloc figures into GDP equivalents, but they were little more than educated guesses and probably too high. But even accurate GDP figures would not tell the whole story. A socialist economy can have a growing GDP but put most of it into investment, thereby shortchanging consumption. This will give it a lower standard of living than a market economy with the same GDP. (A market economy lets consumer demand decide how much and where to invest.) Further, the centrally planned socialist investments may be poor: inefficient factories making junk products that few want. In a given year's economic statistics, these investments may look impressive, but in the long run they will be a drain on the economy and have to be propped up with state subsidies. With little reliable data, perhaps the best indicators were found by visiting and living in East European countries, thereby getting a subjective feel of how they are doing. Good subjective data beat inaccurate objective data.

To give you an idea of how wildly estimates could vary, here are per capita GDP estimates for East Europe in 1989, first those of the CIA, then those of the World Bank:

	CIA	World Bank
East Germany	$9,700	n.a.
Czechoslovakia	7,900	$3,200
Hungary	6,100	2,800
Bulgaria	5,700	2,400
Yugoslavia	5,400	2,500
Poland	4,500	1,800
Romania	3,400	2,300
Albania	1,000	n.a.

Notice how the CIA estimates are about double those of the World Bank. Why the huge difference? The CIA used "purchasing power parity" in its estimates, taking into account the lower cost of living. The World Bank did not, using instead nominal exchange rates to translate East Europe's economies into Western terms. Either way, East Europe was generally ahead of the Third World but behind the First World.

dislocations. It paid minimal attention to consumer needs. The Stalinist theory was to disregard consumer needs for at least one generation; this generation was to sacrifice so that future generations could enjoy a utopia. But what then will

Falling Behind

Hungarian economist Eva Ehrlich gathered data at four points in time to make one of the more sophisticated comparisons of relative economic growth in East and West Europe. American economist Paul Marer then calculated a series of two-country comparisons. Bear in mind that both countries are growing in absolute terms over time, but lower numbers mean that the East European country is slipping behind its Western counterpart. A 100 in the comparison between East and West Germany in 1937 (before Germany was divided), for example, means they were then equal in per capita GDP. A 70 in 1960 means that East German per capita GDP slipped to only 70 percent of West Germany's per capita GDP.

	1937	1960	1970	1980
East/West Germany	100	70	71	64
Czechoslovakia/Austria	90	91	78	70
Hungary/Italy	89	86	70	74
Poland/Spain	105	125	88	77
Romania/Spain	85	85	58	60
Yugoslavia/Greece	87	97	83	81
Bulgaria/Greece	82	122	100	110

In all cases except Bulgaria, the East European country in 1980 was further behind its West European counterpart country than it had been in 1937 or 1960. In some cases, there was a spurt of postwar industrialization in the East European country so that it kept or even improved its position relative to the Western country by 1960 (as in Czechoslovakia, Poland, Romania, and Yugoslavia) only to fall behind in 1970 and 1980. In 1960, some East Europeans could say, "Hey, we're doing pretty well compared with West Europe." Ten and twenty years later, no one could utter such a statement. In the growth race—with the possible exception of Bulgaria, which started from an extremely low level—West Europe beat East Europe.

motivate workers? If they are convinced that they are indeed building a utopia, they may be persuaded to sacrifice. This belief cannot last long, however. All a worker has to do is look around to see that, whatever they are building, it is not a utopia. They see dreadful corruption and unfairness, and they start demanding their share of rewards here and now, not waiting for some vague time in the future.

The system cannot deliver. Geared to heavy industry, it produces too few consumer goods to satisfy mass demand. Wages are held down drastically to prevent inflation, the problem that comes when too many złoty, koruna, or forint

The Diseducation of East Europe

Over the decades, fewer and fewer East Europeans attended universities, leading to a shortage of highly educated people, another of communism's legacies. Limiting student numbers was not generally the intent of East European regimes. Following socialist doctrine, educated and professional people were deliberately not well paid (unless they were also Communist party officials). In a system allegedly dedicated to the working class, the salaries of doctors and professors were kept at or below those of workers (who weren't paid very well either). This dissuaded many bright young people from prolonging their education. Instead, they went right into jobs requiring few skills. In some cases, not-so-bright people attended universities, producing what biologists call a "counter-selection," the opposite of skimming off the best and brightest. Years later, this showed up in inept medical care and lackluster scholarship. Education, like everything else, requires incentives, and East European regimes did not provide them.

chase too few goods. Some goods, even imported electronic treasures from Japan, are in shops, but few have the money to buy them. With such meager rewards, why work?

Lackadaisical work attitudes pervaded East Europe, made worse by the guarantee of jobs for all in a socialist economy. Communists always insisted that employment is a constitutional right more important than the bourgeois rights of free speech and a free press. If you can't eat, what good are other rights? Accordingly, economic enterprises were overstaffed and inefficient. Only Yugoslavia, with its experimental mix of socialism and a market economy, permitted unemployment (which grew to be quite huge). Inefficient enterprises were propped up for decades with government subsidies rather than let them go under, for that would mean both an admission of failure and unemployment.

In sum, workers had jobs, but they were poor jobs, with low pay and little chance of advancement. The jobs also put them in a position to judge for themselves the inefficiency of the system, the pervasive corruption, and the unfairness of the big rewards for the bosses and party people. As anger grew, work attitudes declined. This set up a vicious circle. With lackadaisical work attitudes, productivity was low. Discontented workers with inefficient, backward machines and factories turned out few products. With too few products on the market, workers had little to buy and therefore little incentive to produce more. Throughout the Soviet bloc, workers used to say, only half in jest, "We pretend to work, and they pretend to pay us."

The worst problem, found universally through the Soviet bloc, was (and still is) housing. With rapid industrialization came a major influx of workers from countryside to city, and this created a terrible housing shortage, one that continues to this day. Much urban housing in Poland and Yugoslavia had been blown up in World War II, so it was scarce to begin with. Regimes were reluctant to expend their precious resources on apartment construction, for that ate into their plans for industrial growth. The result was a monumental housing shortage, forcing whole families to live in one or two rooms and children to stay with their parents long after their school years. Trying to alleviate the shortage, regimes threw up gigantic prefabricated apartment blocks made of gray concrete slabs at the outskirts of most East European cities. Although small and unattractive by Western standards, East Europeans lucky enough to get the new flats after many years' wait felt triumphant.

In East Europe, in accordance with socialist doctrine, rents were extremely cheap—a few dollars a month—and tenure over an apartment nearly permanent. But there were hidden costs for this socialist benefit. It took years, sometimes decades, on a waiting list to get a small apartment. The money for apartments came not from renters but from the government budget. In effect, taxes went for apartments, so people paid for their cheap flats indirectly in the form of lower salaries. The unfairness with this system is that everybody paid, including people who weren't getting the new apartments. Furthermore, there was little money or incentive for state authorities to build quality new blocks or to maintain the old ones, which often looked shabby.

Perhaps the biggest problem with housing in East Europe was inflexibility. Once you had a flat, you clung to it. This made the system rigid. Instead of a flow of people in and out of apartments, changing as their job, number of children, and ability to pay dictated, you had people staying put forever and passing the apartment on to their children. Desperate East Europeans arranged complicated swaps of apartments in order to get their own rooms or to set up housekeeping as newlyweds. In effect, under a rigid socialist housing program, a "free market" in housing operated in a clumsy, inefficient fashion. Other problems come with housing rigidities. Industry cannot grow and expand if workers can't relocate because new apartments are so hard to find. With young people staying in the parental flat for an unusually long time, there is little incentive for them to work for a place of their own; they are simply not available. Crowding leads to horrendous child-parent fights, and a sense of despair settles over the younger generation, deepening the poor work attitudes.

Other shortages influenced economic growth in East Europe. Desirable consumer goods were scarce. In most of East Europe, few homes had telephones. Customers might have to wait years for a new car, often an obsolete model of an Italian Fiat made under license. Used cars often cost more than new cars, a sure sign of lagging supply. Parts and repair services were scarce, so drivers patched up vehicles themselves. By the 1970s, household appliances became fairly widespread, so homes had refrigerators and televisions. Once consumers had those, the really desirable items became imports from West Europe and Japan, for they were much more advanced in style and technology. Few serious photographers would use a painfully obsolete and poorly made Soviet or East German camera if they could help it; they were eager for new Japanese equipment, which might be brought back by someone who had visited abroad. When video cassette recorders caught on in the 1980s, millions of East Europeans craved them, but few were available; all were imported from Japan and South Korea. In short, what did East Europeans have to work for? Where were the incentives that prompt people to produce more and better goods?

The necessities of life were usually no problem in East Europe. Food and clothing were generally sufficient, although a higher proportion of an East European's budget went to pay for them than would a West European's. And East Europeans might have to wait in lines for them, really inflation in a disguised form. Instead of paying more for something as in Western-style inflation, you pay more for it by spending your time in line. During the 1960s (earlier in Yugoslavia), most East European regimes permitted farmers' markets, areas where producers could bring their foods into town to sell for whatever price they could get. Farmers might still have to deliver quotas to state enterprises, but beyond those they could grow for the market. State stores still monopolized most processed foods at relatively fixed prices. Certain basics, such as bread, were subsidized to sell at low prices. The trouble with subsidizing anything, including the basics of life, is that it encourages people to rely on them, rather than to raise their sights and work hard to obtain something better. Again, the incentive problem.

LOCKED IN A BLOC

Comecon, the East European trading bloc, had several weaknesses that limited its effectiveness, especially in comparison with West Europe's Common Market, or, as it now prefers to be called, the European Community. No East European currency was convertible; that is, it could not be exchanged for another currency except at set rates by state-run banks. You could not, say, buy Polish złoty in advance in New York for a trip to Poland; that was illegal (although some did it). If you were searched at the border, carrying złoty in or out, you could get in trouble. (Some Polish customs officials shrugged with indifference at smuggled złoty, but you were well advised not to try smuggling East German marks into the GDR; their border guards could be thorough.)

Trade accounts between East European Comecon members and the Soviet Union were kept in what were called "transferable rubles," though no rubles changed hands or crossed borders. Countries could accumulate ruble balances but could use them only for purchases of Soviet goods. Hungarian exports of machine tools to the Soviet Union, for example, could be used to purchase Soviet petroleum. Essentially, though, East European lands bartered among themselves: so many Polski Fiats for so many jars of Bulgarian fruit preserves. Such a system is not nearly as flexible as one based on convertible currencies, where trading

The Jealousy Factor

East Europe fell behind West Europe economically, but could the East European socialist systems have endured if their citizens hadn't *known* this? In other words, if they had been kept ignorant of the higher standard of living in the West, would they have been relatively content? Is it comparison with others and jealousy that make people discontent?

East European regimes tried to screen out images of the good life in the West, but, with the possible exception of Albania, they could not. By the 1960s, most East Europeans understood that they lived at a considerably lower standard of living than West Europeans. East European cultural groups performing on tour in West Europe and in the United States brought back stories and gifts of the material abundance capitalism had showered on Westerners. Could the regime have forbidden these cultural exchanges? Only if they wished to stay totally isolated, like Albania. The urge to travel, especially in the West, became an obsession with educated East Europeans. Some people lived to travel. They would carefully save up foreign currency—sometimes from blackmarket exchanges—for a low-budget trip every few years. Could the regime have forbidden travel to the West? Only at the cost of frustration and anger among the educated stratum of people that every regime depends on.

Group trips to the Soviet Union were easier to come by, but most East Europeans saw in the motherland of socialism a system that was poorer and more inefficient than their own. They were generally not impressed, and visits to the Soviet Union often had a negative impact on forming socialist attitudes. After a while, a feeling grew up in East Europe, especially among the more educated, that they had been not only economically deprived but also cut off from their natural ties to West Europe for the dubious advantage of participating in a backward socialist commonwealth of nations. Even hermetically sealed Albania leaked, as we learned when disturbances broke out there in 1990. It turned out that most Albanians all along were aware that they were being held in virtual slavery. In the long run, it was not possible to shield East Europeans from knowledge of the West, and this knowledge bred much discontent.

The tantalizing question remains: What if there had been no West to compare with? Suppose communism had actually triumphed and erected backward, inefficient regimes everywhere? The sources of change would still be present in Communist systems, but the whole thing would have happened much slower. Even without comparing themselves with those in capitalist nations, East Europeans could see gross corruption and inefficiency in their systems. Discontent would still have been high, as average people would still feel relative deprivation when they saw how the party elite lived. Comparison with the West helped things along, though; it served as a catalyst, a small but important chemical boost that speeds up a reaction that would take place anyway. The Cold War was not won by the West having more military might than the East (it didn't); it was won by the West outperforming the East in economic terms.

The Berlin Wall

Berlin, 110 miles inside East Germany, gave the Communist regime a problem shared by no other East European government: an easy escape hatch. Although divided into an East and West under the 1945 Allied agreements, Berlin remained open to free circulation. All a dissatisfied East German had to do was take a subway to a refugee center in West Berlin, and he or she would be flown out to a new life in West Germany, complete with West German citizenship. From the end of World War II until 1961, some 3 million persons fled through the Berlin escape hatch.

During the 1950s, the GDR was slowly bleeding to death. There were seldom fewer than a fifth of a million emigrating to the West every year, and they were the young, skilled, and productive. The West German *Wirtschaftswunder* (economic miracle) acted as a magnet, drawing East Germans to the West, where they knew they would get better jobs and a higher standard of living. The departure of these same people, on the other hand, severely hindered East Germany's economic growth.

In 1961, old-line Stalinist Walter Ulbricht, in consultation with Khrushchev, dammed the outflow by building the Berlin Wall, a chilling reminder of the GDR's inability to match West Germany's freedom and prosperity. East Berlin propaganda described the Wall as necessary to block "fascist" and espionage penetration from West Berlin, but the real motivation was economic, to stop the manpower loss to the West. When the manpower outflow to the West resumed in 1989—at first through Hungary and Czechoslovakia and then through the reopened Wall—East Germany was finished as a separate country. The Wall had given a temporary life span to a strange, artificial country.

partners use the income from the sale of their goods to buy whatever they wish from any country on the globe.

This arrangement sheltered the countries of the Soviet bloc from competing on the world market and producing world-class products. The various industries of the bloc were not supposed to compete—that was capitalism, messy and duplicative. Instead, they were to complement each other by each filling their assigned role in the plan. Quality did not enter into these planning considerations, just gross output. East Europeans figured, "The Soviets will buy anything. So why make it good?" Accordingly, there were very few East European goods (excepting Polish ham and Czech beer) of high enough quality to compete against products outside the Soviet bloc. This has now saddled East Europe with the monumental problem of how to make up for the lost decades and get back into international competition.

Stalin had originally ripped off the East European economies with unfair terms of trade that one-sidedly benefited the Soviet Union. Indiana University economist Paul Marer calculates that after World War II the Soviet Union sucked out some $14 billion from East Europe, about the same amount that the United States was

The Corruption Factor

Corruption grows at the interface of public and private sectors. The more such interfaces, the more opportunities for corruption. Their economies choked with controls, East Europeans learned that they could make life a little easier by paying off the controllers. East Europeans who knew the Soviet Union were quick to point out that the degree of corruption there was much higher. Compared with the Soviets, East Europeans considered their corruption a little harmless greasing of the wheels of commerce. Nonetheless, in East Europe everyone was looking for a deal and was not adverse to cutting a few corners to get it. No one suffered the least pangs of guilt, because all know the system itself was corrupt and not worthy of respect. This severely eroded any sense of civic duty or civic culture that makes democracy possible and is one of the problems communism has left behind for East Europe. It also meant that when the Communist regimes called for citizen support, no one stepped forward. Will they now step forward for the new democracies?

putting into West Europe with the Marshall Plan. In the 1950s, this changed. For one thing, the Polish October and Hungarian Revolution jolted the Kremlin into realizing that East Europeans had to get a better standard of living or there would be more revolts. The terms of trade eased. The Soviets supplied raw materials, particularly petroleum and natural gas, at favorable prices. With the oil price hikes of the 1970s, for a time Soviet petroleum prices to East Europe were way below world prices. And the Soviets took in payment East European products that couldn't make it on the world market. All this served to lock East European economies into the Soviet bloc.

Attempts to break out of this dependency on trade within the bloc were only partially successful. Poland, for example, in the 1970s borrowed a great deal of capital from the West (chiefly from West German banks) to invest in new factories and equipment that would turn out products for the Western market. Much of the investment was thrown away because of inefficient factories, corruption, indifferent workmanship, and the poor choice of products. For example, Poland produced heavy leather luggage in the 1970s when Western travelers had long gone to much lighter plastic and softsided luggage. Poland, which had counted on entering the world market, instead went deeply into debt. By the early 1980s, it was in technical default on its loans; that is, it could not pay, but its creditors, hoping to salvage something, pretended that it eventually would repay. In another example, Volkswagen invested in an East German factory to produce car engines. But their quality was not good enough for the Western market; they could be sold only in East Europe.

With the passing of each year, locked in their bloc, the economies of East Europe fell a little more behind, and it grew a little more embarrassing. By 1980, the per capita GDP of East Europe was roughly half that of the six original Common Market countries of West Europe, and the standard of living was surely less than half. For many East Europeans, including younger party members, this was a potent catalyst for change.

THE BEGINNINGS OF SYSTEM BREAKDOWN

It will be here argued that the East European upheavals that began in 1968 were qualitatively different from those of the 1950s. In 1953 and 1956 we saw the spontaneous anger of workers tired of being squeezed by rapid Stalinist industrialization. In Hungary, there was a considerable intellectual element added to the resentment. In the 1950s, these systems had been Communist only a few years. The Prague revolt in the spring of 1968 marked a more decisive and thought-out attempt to change the system by party people who had come to reject Stalinism.

In Hungary in 1956 we could glimpse the beginning of a split within the Communist party, but it was not the cause of the revolution. In Budapest, after the initial disturbances had broken out, people demanded a return to power of the relatively liberal Communist Imre Nagy, who then proceeded quickly to discard communism. By the mid to late 1960s, you were hearing in East Europe from party members seriously dissatisfied with socialism as it was presently constituted. For want of a better name, we might call them "liberal" Communists. As we shall explore in Chapter 7, they were to play a major if short-lived role in East Europe's unsteady march to democracy.

Prague, Czechoslovakia, 1968

In 1968, Czechoslovakia had been Communist for two decades and had the second best economy of the bloc (after East Germany), although since the early 1960s it had shown only sluggish growth. Much of East Europe had moved beyond its original Stalinist leaders of the postwar period, but in Czechoslovakia the old Stalinist hack Antonin Novotny still monopolized power as both party first secretary and president of the country. A malaise of stagnant politics and economics blanketed Czechoslovakia. Increasingly, discussions in party circles blamed Novotny and his associates for staying in power too long. In private conversation with foreigners, Czech and Slovak party members could be amazingly frank about their disgruntlement. This was not the socialism they had worked for or envisioned.

At the beginning of 1968, after much behind-the-scenes debate, the Czechoslovak central committee voted out Novotny as party leader and brought in the relatively liberal Slovak, Alexander Dubček. In March, Novotny also retired from the presidency. What happened during the next five months, the "Prague Spring," can only be described as wonderful. Quickly, under Dubček's leadership, the trappings of Stalinism fell away to reveal a vibrant and dynamic Czechoslovakia ready to join the democracies. Conservative Communists were ousted from the central committee to make room for a new breed of relative liberals. Censorship was ended and popular new television programs and newspapers revealed serious economic mismanagement and the misuse of police power. Some police officials, after being interviewed on television about torture, went out and hanged themselves. A New Economic Model brought in many elements of a free market. Delegations visited Yugoslavia to study the "self-managing" model of socialism. The newly freed labor unions volunteered "Days for Dubček" of unpaid work, something they wouldn't have dreamed of doing for Novotny. Czechoslovakia saw something it hadn't seen in decades: enthusiasm.

Did Dubček intend to dismantle communism? He never announced such intentions. Instead, in a parallel with Nagy in 1956, he said his country sought to build "socialism with a human face." But things moved faster than Dubček anticipated or perhaps even wanted. Like Nagy in 1956, Dubček found himself at the head of a swelling, joyous movement that embraced him as its hero. Conservative Communists both inside and outside Czechoslovkia, though, viewed Dubček and his program with alarm. If things kept going like this, they reasoned (correctly), Czechoslovakia would soon not be Communist. East Germany's Walter Ulbricht and Poland's Wladysław Gomułka feared the Prague Spring could spread. In the Soviet Ukraine, hard-line party leader Pyotr Shelest feared that the Ukrainian minority in Slovakia could spread news of the reforms into his fiefdom.

In June, Soviet party chief Leonid Brezhnev met with Dubček in Slovakia. Dubček pledged loyalty to the Warsaw Pact and Comecon but defended his reforms. Brezhnev warned him that the Soviet Union would intervene if any Pact member tried to restore a "bourgeois" system—that is, one in which non-Communist parties could compete with the Communists. Conservatives in the Czechoslovak party, in contact with the Soviet ambassador in Prague, continued to denounce Dubček and plot their own return to power. They finally persuaded Brezhnev, and on August 20, 1968, Warsaw Pact forces swept into Czechoslovakia to "save" socialism. The main forces were Soviet, but token Polish, Bulgarian, and East German troops were ordered to participate in order to show it was an all-bloc effort.

There was no armed resistance and little bloodshed. Two-thirds of the Czechoslovak Communist party central committee condemned the intervention. The population was near to unanimous in its condemnation and proudly placed pictures of Dubček everywhere. Dubček was arrested and taken to Moscow for a talking to by Brezhnev, but Dubček wouldn't back down. Brezhnev, knowing the world was watching, let Dubček return to office but greatly curbed his reforms. In April 1969, Dubček was formally ousted and made a minor forestry official in his native Slovakia with instructions not to speak to the media. Conservative Communist Gustáv Husák, also a Slovak, was named party first secretary and proceeded to purge reformist elements at every level. Husák called it "normalization," in effect, a partial return to the Stalin model but with greater attention to consumer needs. This brought a temporary improvement in the standard of living, but Czech

The Brezhnev Doctrine

One of the most interesting points of the 1968 Soviet invasion of Czechoslovakia was the way Soviet party chief Leonid Brezhnev rationalized it. Once a country had turned Communist, it would be against Marx's laws of history to let capitalists and imperialists sneak back in and take it over again. History proceeds only onward, to socialism. So, argued Brezhnev, if fools and traitors try to make a Communist country non-Communist, it is the internationalist duty of other Communist states to rescue their threatened brother. The Brezhnev Doctrine—it was so named in the West, not the East—in other words said, once Communist, always Communist.

Underneath the Marxist mumbo jumbo, the real meaning of the Brezhnev Doctrine was that the Soviet Union still evaluated East Europe as its protective shield against the West. A non-Communist Czechoslovakia, which is what the country would have soon become with Dubček's far-reaching reforms, would drop out of the Warsaw Pact or become an uncooperative member. Looking at a map, Czechoslovakia stretches like a dagger from Germany to Ukraine. Stalin seized Ruthenia in order to have a border with Czechoslovakia. Geopolitics rather than ideology provides a better explanation for the Brezhnev Doctrine.

enthusiasm for work, which flowered under Dubček, evaporated, and the economy slowed.

The seeds of Husák's later downfall, though, were planted. The liberal and reformist Communists who carried out the Prague Spring were either purged from the party or quit. Some joined with anti-Communist dissidents in 1977 to found Charter 77, an organization for civil rights that was rudely suppressed. Among the original 242 signers of Charter 77 were 140 ex-Communists. Charter 77, although many of its members were jailed, kept alive the spirit of opposition and served to produce the political seeds and the leadership for Civic Forum, which brought down the Communist regime in 1989.

Gdańsk, Poland, 1970

Within a few years of his elevation to power during the Poznan uprising of 1956, Gomułka had proved himself to be generally conservative. Under his relatively relaxed police and cultural controls, there was a great deal of intellectual ferment in Poland, all pointing in the direction of greater freedom. Gomułka, however, rejected suggestions for political and economic liberalization. Basically, Gomułka was afraid that such reforms could both weaken the party's control and bring Soviet intervention. Actually, he was right on both counts. But without economic reform, the Polish economy began to run down. The Prague Spring entranced Polish students. Discontent and disturbances grew in the late 1960s. Police beat and dispersed student demonstrators.

An example of the Communist use of anti-Semitism for political infighting came in Poland in 1968 from the man in charge of Poland's police. Brutish interior minister Mieczysław Moczar, leader of the party's conservative and nationalistic Partisan faction (so named because some had fought in the underground during the war), blamed the disturbances on Jews still serving the Communist regime. Moczar called their presence a "Zionist plot." Poland's Jews, by that time reduced to fewer than 30,000 and mostly elderly, were a handy scapegoat. Moczar attempted to use traditional anti-Semitic feelings as a lever to pry Gomułka from power so that he could take over himself. Brezhnev, fearing Moczar's nationalistic tendencies, backed Gomułka. Gomułka stayed in power; he purged Jewish officials and encouraged Jews to emigrate; most of the able-bodied did.

Such distractions did nothing for Poland's worsening economic situation. In December 1970, the desperate Gomułka government simultaneously raised prices and cut wages, and did this just in time for Christmas. Street demonstrations and violence broke out all along the Baltic seacoast in reaction to the price hikes. At the Lenin Shipyards in Gdańsk (formerly the German city of Danzig) on the Baltic, workers struck, occupied the shipyards, and refused to leave. Troops moved in, killing 45 and injuring nearly 1,200. Workers put up three giant steel crosses in Gdańsk to commemorate the massacre. As the protests started to spread, Gomułka, who suffered a stroke or heart attack upon hearing of the violence, resigned. His replacement, party administrator Edward Gierek, was no better.

The Rise of Solidarity

Like Gomułka, Gierek proved to be a temporary calmer-downer rather than a finder of long-term solutions. He was more responsive to worker demands. He even held an open dialogue when Baltic workers threatened another strike. Gierek blamed Gomułka, rescinded the price hikes, and boosted wages and fringe benefits. He allowed and recognized worker committees outside the officially controlled Communist unions. He eased out Moczar and his unsavory Partisans. All this was well and good, but it did nothing for the Polish economy.

Gierek's plan for the Polish economy, if indeed there was one, was to borrow heavily from the West for the purchase of modern imported technology, which would then be used to manufacture goods for export. It didn't work; in fact, it didn't work anywhere in East Europe. The Polish goods could not compete on the world market; some were completely the wrong product and were too expensive. The oil price hikes of the 1970s were reflected in higher costs for Soviet energy (which were still below world prices), and this increased costs for Poland's energy-inefficient factories. Poland, tied more than ever to the Soviet economy, produced much of its ships, locomotives, computers, and construction equipment for the Soviet rather than for the Western market. The foreign loans, much of them West

German, were largely wasted, and by 1980 Poland's international debt topped $20 billion, one of the highest per capita debts in the world.

Polish farm production stagnated, and food shortages started appearing. The regime, always unhappy about the largely independent Polish farmers, was still trying to encourage them to form larger units for greater productivity. Polish peasants, smelling a trick, continually refused; they saw no reason to cooperate with the regime.

In 1976, new strikes broke out, but this time with a twist that proved to be decisive. Worker discontent was one thing. Workers had specific demands related to the cost of living and their wages. The regime might be able to handle these demands by giving in a little, applying force here and there, and keeping the strikes isolated. Intellectual discontent was something else and had to be handled differently. Intellectual demands were not so specific or easy to compromise as worker demands, for intellectuals wanted not a few more złoty but major reforms. Although unstated, many of them wanted the end of the entire Communist system. They rejected the system not just on grounds of material deprivation, but also on moral and philosophical grounds. In Poland, intellectuals were sheltered and aided by the Catholic Church, which had been left largely autonomous by the regime. The Communists knew better than to take on the Polish Catholic Church. Intellectuals could be somewhat controlled by prison terms, by the loss of their jobs, by a lack of publishing resources, and by encouraging them to emigrate.

Revolutions, it has been said, must be based on the coming together of mass discontent and elite discontent, the numbers being provided by the workers and the brains being provided by the intellectuals. Kept separate, the two forms of opposition are weak and controllable. When the two streams of discontent form an alliance, however, they gain greatly in strength, sometimes enough to overthrow the regime. In Poland, numbers and brains combined effectively for the first time in East Europe, eventually leading to the first ouster of communism in the region.

The 1976 Polish strikes inspired a group of dissident intellectuals, with sociologist Jaček Kuron and historian Adam Michnik prominent among them, to form the Workers' Defense Committee, known by its Polish initials as KOR (*Komitet Obrony Robotnikow*). KOR investigated police brutality against strikers and offered legal aid for those arrested. In this way, intellectuals bridged the gap that had separated them from workers. Next, university students formed a Committee for Student Solidarity that published underground many antiregime pamphlets. Combining with KOR, they formed a "flying university" that held seminars and alternative courses in private apartments, free of the surveillance of Communist education officials.

By 1980, the ingredients were in place for a major antiregime movement that had both numbers and brains. The trigger came that year when the regime, in desperate economic straits, moved to raise meat prices. Worker opposition again flared at the Lenin Shipyards and quickly spread along the Baltic coast. Its leader was a modest but tough electrician, Lech Wałęsa, a man of little formal education

The Church Factor

Some observers of East Europe argue that it was ultimately the moral power of the Roman Catholic Church that brought down communism in the region. The church clearly played a major role in Poland, but less so in other countries. In some degree, to be sure, events in Poland helped spark unrest elsewhere in East Europe.

Crushed between the Lutheran Germans to their west and Eastern Orthodox Russians to their east, Catholicism came to define Polishness, especially when the Polish state was erased by partition for more than a century. "Good Catholic, good Pole" was the simple equation that preserved a sense of Polish nationhood. Even Stalin, who disparaged the Church's moral power with the cynical remark, "How many divisions has the pope?", knew better than to try to destroy the Polish Catholic Church. Provided it steered clear of direct political involvement, the Warsaw regime left the Polish Church wide areas of autonomy.

Some factors aided the Church. With the murder of Poland's Jews, redrawing of boundaries to exclude most Belorussians and Ukrainians, and expulsion of Germans, Poland after World War II had an almost completely Polish-speaking Catholic population, in sharp contrast to the complex mixture before the war. Philosophically, the dreary Marxism-Leninism propounded by the state-run media and schools soon wore thin and attracted few. In disgust at communism's materialistic theory of human nature, many Poles sought spirituality and dignity. Masses overflowed onto the street. Church periodicals and education were respected.

The crowning factor was the election in 1978 of a Polish cardinal, Karol Wojtyła, as Pope John Paul II, the first non-Italian pontiff in 456 years. The move electrified and inspired Poles. The Polish priest who for decades had never yielded a philosophical point to the Communists now expounded his principles on a world level. In 1979, John Paul II visited his native land and celebrated masses before huge crowds, generating a sense of society-wide solidarity that next year blossomed into the Solidarity movement. Lech Wałęsa and many of his supporters were serious Catholics who had long found solace and protection under the wing of the Church.

When the threat of Soviet military intervention in Poland loomed, John Paul II vowed he would return to Poland to stand with his countrymen. We do not yet know if his warning made the Kremlin rethink, but it is highly probable that the KGB, operating through its Bulgarian daughter service, ordered the unsuccessful assassination attempt on the pope in 1981. Moscow finally came to realize that philosophically and spiritually the pope indeed has many divisions.

but of firm Catholic and worker-rights convictions who had been fired from the shipyards in 1976 for his role in strikes. Worker committees soon banded together under the name Solidarity (in Polish, *Solidarnosc*), and the movement spread like wildfire nationwide in late 1980. Within a year, Solidarity had an amazing 7 million members, nearly a fifth of the Polish population. Eventually, it totaled 10 million.

In addition to the usual worker demands for more pay and less work, Solidarity demanded to be officially recognized as a legal trade union, something the Warsaw regime was reluctant to do, for it already had a puppet Communist union that it used as an instrument of control. The regime also understood that something as big and angry as Solidarity had more than worker rights in mind; it threatened their very rule. And, soon enough, Solidarity also began to demand worker self-management on the Yugoslav model, with elected committees in each factory to name directors and guide financial and production decisions. Solidarity, with its intellectual and Catholic input, saw itself as far more than a labor union. It was a movement to save Poland by introducing democracy. To calm the Soviets, at its first national conference in the fall of 1981, Solidarity said it had no intention of pulling Poland out of the Warsaw Pact.

The Soviet Union, then under the aging conservative Leonid Brezhnev, the same man who had invaded Czechoslovakia in 1968, did not trust Solidarity. The Gierek regime, unmasked as corrupt and incapable, was by now totally illegitimate in the eyes of its citizens. Communist party members were resigning in droves. A power vacuum was starting to build. Before Solidarity could fill it, the Polish army took over on December 13, 1981, reportedly with the Kremlin's approval. For Moscow, a Polish military takeover was cheaper and easier than the sending in of Soviet troops. The commander of Poland's armed forces, General Wojciech Jaruzełski, who began his military career in Polish units organized by the Soviet army in World War II, named himself Communist party first secretary and prime minister. Thousands of Solidarity activists were arrested, including Wałęsa. Strikes were put down by armed coercion. Solidarity went underground. Jaruzełski quietly offered a highly plausible argument: "Better me than the Russians." In 1992, the retired Jaruzełski went public with memoirs and interviews defending his role. He saw himself as a Polish patriot who saved a country that was on the brink of either civil war or Soviet invasion or both. By that time, many Poles reluctantly agreed with him.

Unable to rid itself of basically Stalinist systems, East Europe slowly fell behind. Increasingly, East Europeans sensed they were being deprived not only of the materially good life but the morally and spiritually decent life as well. Time was not on the side of the Communist regimes, none of which gained solid legitimacy among its citizens. Indeed, with time, complaints grew louder. By the time Gorbachev took power in Moscow, East Europe was ripe for change.

SUGGESTED READINGS

BATT, JUDY. *Economic Reform and Political Change in Eastern Europe: A Comparison of the Czechoslovak and Hungarian Experience.* New York: St. Martin's, 1988.

BEHR, EDWARD. *Kiss the Hand You Cannot Bite: The Rise and Fall of the Ceausescus.* New York: Villard, 1991.

BRADLEY, J.F. NEJEZ. *Politics in Czechoslovakia, 1945-1989.* New York: Columbia University Press, 1991.

BUGAJSKI, JANUSZ. *Czechoslovakia: Charter 77's Decade of Dissent.* Westport, CT: Praeger, 1987.

___________, and MAXINE POLLACK. *East European Fault Lines: Dissent, Opposition, and Social Activism.* Boulder, CO: Westview, 1989.

CARRÈRE D'ENCAUSSE, HÉLÈNE. *Big Brother: The Soviet Union and Soviet Europe.* New York: Holmes & Meier, 1987.

EKIERT, GRZEGORZ. *The State Against Society: Political Crises and Their Aftermath in East Central Europe.* Princeton, NJ: Princeton University Press, 1996.

HAVEL, VACLAV. *Disturbing the Peace.* New York: Knopf, 1990.

KAMINSKI, BARTLOMEIJ. *The Collapse of State Socialism: The Case of Poland.* Princeton, NJ: Princeton University Press, 1991.

MARER, PAUL. "The Economies and Trade of Eastern Europe." William E. Griffith, ed., *Central and Eastern Europe: The Opening Curtain?* Boulder, CO: Westview, 1989.

MICHNIK, ADAM. *The Church and the Left.* Chicago: University of Chicago Press, 1993.

OST, DAVID. *Solidarity and the Politics of Anti-Politics: Opposition and Reform in Poland Since 1968.* Philadelphia: Temple University Press, 1990.

REISINGER, WILLIAM M. *Energy and the Soviet Bloc: Alliance Politics after Stalin.* Ithaca, NY: Cornell University Press, 1992.

SKILLING, H. GORDON. *Samizdat and an Independent Society in Central and Eastern Europe.* Columbus, OH: Ohio State University Press, 1989.

SWAIN, NIGEL. *Hungary: The Rise and Fall of Feasible Socialism.* New York: Verso, 1992.

TARAS, RAYMOND, ed. *The Road to Disillusion: From Critical Marxism to Post-Communism in Eastern Europe.* Armonk, NY: M. E. Sharpe, 1992.

TISMANEANU, VLADIMIR. *The Crisis of Marxist Ideology in Eastern Europe.* New York: Routledge, 1988.

VALENTA, JIRI. *Soviet Intervention in Czechoslovakia, 1968: Anatomy of a Decision,* rev. and expanded ed. Baltimore, MD: Johns Hopkins University Press, 1991.

WEIGEL, GEORGE. *The Final Revolution: The Resistance Church and the Collapse of Communism.* New York: Oxford, 1992.

WESCHLER, LAWRENCE. *The Passion of Poland: From Solidarity to the State of War.* New York: Pantheon, 1984.

CHAPTER SEVEN

1989: The Gorbachev Factor

Many and learned are the studies examining the *internal* factors that contributed to the fall of Communist regimes in Central Europe. But if they focus only on the internal aspects, they may be seriously shortsighted; only by adding the great *external* factor of Soviet support and control do we begin to get a clear picture of why communism collapsed in Central Europe. The studies of internal factors, especially those focusing on political culture, religious and intellectual opposition, and mass discontent, are quite accurate, but they are studying constants, and how can a constant explain variation? Remember, these regimes never had a leg to stand on; most of their citizens had always disliked and many had hated them. They would have gladly chucked out the Communists in any year you care to name. But most of the time, they didn't try, because they knew it would bring Soviet tanks. Without Soviet tanks, these regimes would never have been installed. Without the return of Soviet tanks, at least three (East Germany, Hungary, and Czechoslovakia) and probably four (Poland) would have been swept away decades earlier. It was when the Kremlin changed its mind about East Europe that we get upheaval. To a certain extent, then, every student of East Europe should be a student of Soviet politics as well.

The Balkans, as usual, were a bit different. Here Soviet tanks had never needed to intervene, as local Communists, operating in backward economies and with less educated populations, managed to perfect dictatorships with little or no Soviet help. Three of the regimes (Yugoslavia, Albania, and Romania) in fact used anti-Soviet nationalism to help sustain themselves in power. But here, too, we see an external factor in the demonstration effect that the fall of Communist regimes in Central Europe had on their Balkan cousins. With a little time lag and with the clear vision that no one would come to its rescue, communism collapsed in the Balkans as well.

The Poisoning of East Europe

East Europe is the world's most polluted region, the result of four decades of Stalinist industrialization. The very heart of Europe, where Poland, Czechoslovakia, and East Germany border one another, is described by experts as an "ecological disaster." For Communists who were trying to boost industrial production, the environment counted for absolutely nothing. Capitalist countries have vastly better controls against pollution. This is because pluralist Western systems are responsive to protest by concerned groups; Communist systems aren't. Visitors had long noticed the terrible air in most East European cities, much of it from the unlimited burning of cheap brown coal, lignite. Most Western countries control the burning of lignite (named after Legnica, Poland, formerly Liegnitz, Germany), which produces little heat and much pollution, especially sulfur dioxide. Many East European cities have a distinctive, acrid smell from the burning of poor-quality coal.

The growth in number of private automobiles in East Europe made the air much worse by adding another acid, nitrous oxide. Soviet and East European motor vehicles are inefficient consumers of fuel and have no antismog devices. East European buses belch a thick, black diesel smoke that would get them banned in most Western countries. Depending on the terrain and winds, smog often extends far into the countryside that surrounds large East European cities. Many East European forests are dying from air pollution and acid rain.

In the 1980s, word began to leak out of serious health problems from environmental pollution in East Europe. Deaths from lung cancer in certain areas of Poland, Czechoslovakia, and Romania were extremely high. Chemical factories and power plants had no stack scrubbers, and they dumped their waste products into the ground, contaminating the water. Some areas are known to be dangerous for children and expectant mothers. In one particularly bad area, in Katowice in the south of Poland, people retreat to deep salt mines to give their lungs respite from the poisonous surface air. Environmental degradation by itself would have eventually forced major changes in the Communist systems of East Europe.

THE "LIBERAL COMMUNIST" INTERLUDE

The Prague Spring of 1968 marks the appearance of open splits in the ranks of the Communist elites of most East European countries, splits that eventually brought liberal Communists to power for very brief tenures. By 1990, liberal Communists had in turn been voted out of power by non-Communists in all but the Balkan countries. However brief their time in office, it will be argued here that these liberal Communists played an important role in bringing down Communist regimes.

At first the term "liberal" or "reform" Communist may sound a little funny. We can define a *conservative* Communist as one who wishes to generally preserve the Stalinist system and a *liberal* Communist as one who wishes to reform it in a more open and flexible direction. Historically, no Communist party has permitted formal factions, liberal or conservative. Informally, factions often formed around personalities and programs, but no group admitted this or attached a public label to themselves. That could have been fatal, for any identifiable faction could serve as a scapegoat, "an antiparty group," and get purged. So factions in ruling Communist parties were always low profile, discerned only by the diligent research of Western analysts. It is probably safe to say that all Communist parties contained factions just waiting to come out of the closet. In East Europe, over the course of a generation, liberal Communists increasingly stepped forward.

Already in the late 1950s, faint stirrings could be heard among some East European economists about the need to explore non-Stalinist alternatives. The limits and imbalances of the Stalinist model were slowly becoming clear, and growth was starting to slacken. Khrushchev's 1955 apology to Tito emboldened some East European thinkers to speak of developing their own paths to socialism. By the 1960s, criticism of the Stalinist system was widespread among economists and other intellectuals. Poland's Oskar Lange and Czechoslovakia's Ota Šik articulated ideas on economic liberalization and decentralization. Some East Europeans studied abroad, including in the United States and Yugoslavia, and brought back ideas for an economy that could combine socialism with free markets. The ruling conservative party elites rejected such notions, and the struggle between party conservatives and party liberals forms much of the history of East Europe from the 1960s to the ouster of communism in 1989.

Party conservatives feared—correctly, as it turned out—that anything but minor reforms could make the entire system fall apart and cost them their comfortable jobs and perquisites. Many party elites in East Europe lived quite well, some at a standard of living comparable to that of Western millionaires. The ideological argument offered by conservative ruling Communists (few of whom really cared about ideology) was that the form of socialism had already been determined and tested by time. New forms did not need to be developed because the system, essentially a somewhat modified Stalin model, works and is moving us along to an ever-improving socialism. Experiments can only wreck a working system. Increasingly, such arguments looked ridiculous in the face of stagnant growth, declining living standards, growing mass discontent, and a poisoned environment.

The interesting thing about the liberal or reform Communists is that they shared many of the perspectives of non-Communist intellectuals. Both knew the system had to change in a major way. Both saw that the economy was defective, that public morale was declining, and that environmental damage could soon become irreversible. Neither could accept the Soviet Union as a model for anything. The difference between the two groups was that the liberal Communists wanted to work within the system for major reform; most non-Communists wanted to chuck out the system. The liberal Communists were willing to grant autonomy to new political movements—for such causes as worker rights, protection of the environment, civil liberties, and so on—and to open a dialogue with them. Some liberal Communists could envision a mixed or hybrid system with the Communist party taking the leading role but sharing some power with non-Communists.

For as long as they could, conservative Communists rejected such notions and refused to budge, either politically or personally. Most of them became quite elderly in office, as Communist systems have no mechanism for the regular and orderly replacement of persons in power. The longer they stayed, the more they delayed. Their systems cried out for reform. Many younger party members along with nonparty intellectuals simmered in frustration. All the ingredients for major upheaval were present, but to move the systems of East Europe it took Soviet party chief Mikhail Gorbachev's conclusion that the Soviet Union could no longer afford its East European empire.

There were many and strong underlying factors that preceded Gorbachev's decisions: no regime legitimacy, mass discontent, religious and intellectual opposition, lagging economies, a split party, and growing foreign indebtedness. But these factors had been present for years or even decades. What suddenly made them operative in 1989? Why weren't Communist regimes thrown out in 1979? In 1969? Only one explanation fits: The regimes of East Europe liberalized and threw out the old conservative Communists because Gorbachev told them to. Specifically, during 1989 Gorbachev had personal meetings with nearly every Communist chief of East Europe, either in their capitals or in Moscow. His public statements indicated support for change with no Soviet interference in the process. He bluntly repudiated the Brezhnev Doctrine.

GORBACHEV'S NEW THINKING

Between 1986 and 1989, Soviet president and party leader Mikhail Gorbachev changed his mind about East Europe, turning from adherence to the Brezhnev Doctrine to benign indifference about East Europe's fate. By 1989, whatever East Europe wanted to do—even ousting Communist regimes—was acceptable to him. He told East Europe's party chiefs in 1989 that Moscow would no longer send tanks to support them.

The "New Thinking," a phrase Gorbachev used to describe his foreign policy, in the case of East Europe was actually forced on him and probably went farther than he wished. Did Gorbachev know what he was doing when he urged the conservative Communist leaders of East Europe to carry out major reforms? His chief interest had never been East Europe itself. He was preoccupied with saving the Soviet Union. East Europe mattered to him only insofar as it made that goal easier or harder to achieve.

It is likely that Gorbachev initially foresaw nothing more than the partial transformation of East European lands into some kind of liberal Communist or

The Debt Factor

Starting in the 1970s, most of the Communist regimes of East Europe played one last desperate card to try to keep from having to introduce market systems and political democratization: They plunged their countries deeply into debt, borrowing from the West in the vain hope that Western loans and technology would lift their slowing economies. By the end of 1988, the external indebtedness of East European countries, overall and per capita, was as follows:

	Overall (in billions)	Per Capita
Poland	$38.9	$1,000
East Germany	20.4	1,250
Yugoslavia	22.7	960
Hungary	17.7	1,800
Bulgaria	6.1	820
Romania	4.9	90
Czechoslovakia	2.5	400

Soon enough, East Germany didn't have to worry. Its big brother, rich West Germany, amply covered the GDR's external debt—most of it owed to West Germany—when they united in 1990. In fact, getting East Germany into debt with West Germany had long been, since the 1960s, Bonn's unstated strategy. The more dependent the GDR became on the Federal Republic of Germany (FRG), the easier it would be for West Germany to eventually swallow East Germany. It worked.

Romania's external debt had been cut to almost nothing by the end of the 1980s but at a terrible price. Ceausescu decreed that everything must go for export to pay off Romania's substantial debt, leaving nothing for consumption. Romanians were so materially starved that eventually they erupted in violence and murdered Ceaușescu. Czechoslovakia never got deeply into debt and didn't have to worry.

The other nations of East Europe, especially Hungary, had to worry. They had purchased a temporary pause in their economic decline and made life a little more comfortable for their citizens. Regimes had used foreign debt to paper over their deep economic problems. Then the loans came due, and many East European lands could not repay them. Their leaders stood unmasked as frightened fools. External debt was another reason the conservative Communist regimes of East Europe were pushed out of power.

"middle way" systems that brought in certain features of pluralism, democracy, and a market economy, but which held their overall structures under Communist

The 1989 Pattern

With many variations, the events of 1989 and 1990 in East Europe unrolled more or less like this in each country:

1. A group of liberal Communist officials, who were the seconds in command in the party structure, formed to quietly discuss ways to get rid of the conservatives who were still first in command.
2. This group of liberals was emboldened by Gorbachev's urgings to reform.
3. Anticommunist moral heroes stepped forward to lead strikes or protests, the regime would crack down, and this provoked more unrest.
4. The liberal Communists took this as their signal; they would step out of the closet and call for major reforms and democracy.
5. A phone call from the Kremlin would put Gorbachev on the side of the liberals; power then tilted to them.
6. The old Stalinist leaders would then resign or retire, and they were soon stripped of all their offices and even kicked out of the party.
7. The coalition of liberal Communists would then change the party's name from "Communist" to "Socialist" and promise free elections for early 1990.
8. In most of East Europe, new centrist parties would win the free elections; the Socialists (ex-Communists) would become small parties.
9. Gorbachev would then congratulate the new non-Communist government.

party control. He harbored the same mistaken presumptions concerning reform in the Soviet Union. Once liberalization got under way in both East Europe and the Soviet Union, it kept going farther and faster than Gorbachev had envisioned. The same forces that blew Communist regimes out of office in East Europe in 1989, blew his regime out of office in 1991. It is likely that Gorbachev had little or no overall plan, but merely improvised as events hit.

Early in his tenure—he came to power in 1985—Gorbachev did not sound at all flexible on East Europe. Addressing the 1986 Polish party congress, Gorbachev warned that "socialist gains are irreversible" and that the Soviet Union would make sure no one "undermined" the "socialist community." It sounded pretty much like the straight Brezhnev Doctrine. But during the next three years, Gorbachev changed his tune. His situation worsened considerably. With his marginal and ineffective economic tinkering, the Soviet economy declined. Food shortages appeared, and citizens complained bitterly. Non-Russian nationalities took advantage of his *glasnost* ("openness") program to publicize their demands for autonomy or even independence from the Soviet Union. Violence broke out in several areas.

Imperial Overstretch

The incredible changes in Gorbachev's policies are illuminated by Paul Kennedy's "imperial overstretch" thesis. Kennedy's massive and controversial 1987 book, *The Rise and Decline of the Great Powers*, argued that powerful nations are driven to expand until they overexpand, until their economy can no longer maintain their extravagant imperial costs, especially military commitments. The empires then slowly contract, sometimes collapse, from economic causes. Especially important to Kennedy's thesis is the imperial power's *relative* economic performance. Devoting so much of its economy to imperial and defense needs drains its economy so that, after some decades, smaller but more efficient economies start outperforming it. The imperial power's economy may still be growing, but not as fast as those of the upstart powers. Gradually, the empire it has built over many decades and at great expense becomes a drain and hindrance, pulling the imperial power down.

A storm of controversy erupted around Kennedy's suggestion that the United States might fit the pattern of imperial overstretch. But hardly anyone disputed Kennedy's contention that the Soviet Union fit the pattern very well. The collapse of communism in East Europe could have been scripted by Paul Kennedy.

Afghanistan, which the Soviets invaded in 1979, looked like a never-ending war. In 1986, the *mujahedin*, the Afghani anti-Soviet guerrillas, received U.S. Stinger missiles and started downing Soviet helicopter gunships; the tide of battle turned against the Soviets. In 1988, the Kremlin announced that Soviet troops would be withdrawn from Afghanistan; they were out by early 1989. Altogether, the Soviets had lost some 15,000 troops in Afghanistan (a number low compared to the 60,000 U.S. troops killed in Vietnam). Some observers suggest that the impossibility of victory in Afghanistan forced Gorbachev to change his mind about using Soviet military power to prop up Communist regimes in East Europe. There is no firm evidence for this, only an interesting coincidence in time.

The only bright spot on Gorbachev's international horizon was, curiously, the United States. President Reagan, who operated on the basis of gut instinct, met Gorbachev and decided he could be trusted. Reagan's harsh rhetoric about the "evil empire" of the Soviet Union ceased. Moscow made some important concessions leading to a treaty banning all intermediate-range nuclear forces (the INF treaty), which was signed in the White House in December 1987 and ratified by the Senate by the time Reagan visited Moscow in May 1988. Clearly, Gorbachev was calling off the Cold War. To really end it, however, he knew the Soviet Union could not retain firm control over East Europe.

Kremlin signals that East Europe could go its own way started in 1988. In his visit to Yugoslavia in March 1988, Gorbachev foreswore any "interference in the internal affairs of other states under any pretext whatsoever," and he further stated that all nations have the right to "their own roads of social development." It sounded like a replay of Khrushchev's 1955 visit to Belgrade. Later that same year, Gorbachev told the UN General Assembly that "freedom of choice" for all nations to decide their own path "is a universal principle which allows no exceptions."

In 1989 Gorbachev got stronger and more explicit about East Europe. The final communique of the annual Warsaw Pact meeting said "there are no universal models of socialism." Gorbachev urged the ministers to get in touch with their own peoples and traditions and make their economies work. He didn't specifically say to throw out socialism, but he publicly and repeatedly told the Communist regimes of the region to liberalize and democratize. He warned them that if they refused to move or went too slowly they would be overthrown. (Little did he realize he was predicting his own future.) And later, when they were overthrown, he cabled congratulations to the non-Communist successor regimes.

In short, sometime between 1986 and 1989—probably during 1988—Gorbachev decided to lift the Soviet hold on East Europe and let it go its own way, even if that meant the ouster of Communist regimes. He sacrificed the Soviet Eastern empire in order to join the West.

Domestically, Gorbachev avoided mention of the upheaval in East Europe. Perhaps he was embarrassed; perhaps he simply didn't care. One of his few references to East Europe came at the July 1990 party congress, when some hard-line Soviet generals complained about the loss of East Europe. Gorbachev sharply rebuked them: "Do you want the tanks again? Shall we teach them again how to live?"

Gorbachev gave a green light to sweeping changes in East Europe but only a cautious yellow light to modest changes in the Soviet Union. At home, Gorbachev wished to keep things under party and personal control. But the changes he had unleashed turned on him. What Gorbachev welcomed in East Europe, he tried to hold back in the Soviet Union, ultimately to no avail.

Particularly revealing is Gorbachev's adamant refusal to consider, in November 1989, parliamentary debate over deleting Article 6 of the Soviet Constitution, the clause that gave the Communist party a monopoly on political power. Harshly, almost brutally, Gorbachev squelched discussion on the matter. He even told Andrei Sakharov, the "conscience of Russia," then a member of the Congress of People's Deputies, to shut up and sit down. There was nothing moderate or liberal about Gorbachev at this time. The way Gorbachev saw it, a cohesive Communist party under his control was the indispensable tool for economic restructuring. To fragment political power and allow competing parties would dilute, distract, and ultimately block his design for a market socialist economy.

Ultimately and grudgingly, Gorbachev did relent, and Article 6 was repealed in early 1990. But Gorbachev continued to try to preserve the Communist party's monopoly on power. The repeal of Article 6 did not have the same rapid and decisive impact on the Soviet political system that similar repeals had had on East European regimes. What Gorbachev gladly granted East Europe he fought against and delayed in the Soviet Union.

By the time Brezhnev died in 1982, after eighteen years at the Soviet helm, the ship of state was dead in the water. By the time Gorbachev took over in 1985, all thinking Soviets knew the economy was bad and fast getting worse. Moscow's imperial commitments were costing a bundle. East Europe, figuring the expenses of stationing Soviet armed forces in those countries and economic subsidies, cost the Soviet Union an estimated $17 billion a year in 1970, which then grew to $40 billion a year in 1980. Subsidies to East Europe included selling petroleum and natural gas at below world-market prices and purchasing East European manufactured goods that could not compete on the world market. Soviet economic and military support for Third World client states such as Cuba, South Yemen, Syria, Angola, and Vietnam cost many billions more. The Soviet empire, with an inefficient, backward economic base, was severely overstretched.

As we considered earlier, precise figures on the size and condition of the Soviet economy did not exist; all were estimates, some foreign, some Soviet. The Soviets themselves issued no Gross Domestic Product figures, and the numbers they issued on other measures were dubious. Moscow got its GDP estimates from the CIA, which had a large section devoted entirely to measuring the Soviet economy. (In a sense, we subsidized the Soviet economy by making their GDP calculations for them.)

The measure the CIA looked for was the percentage of Soviet GDP devoted to defense. This figure measured the strain on the Soviet economy. For many years the CIA estimated that the Soviets spent roughly twice as much (about 12 percent) of their GDP on defense as did the United States (about 6 percent). In the mid-1970s, when George Bush headed the CIA, he cast a skeptical eye on CIA estimates. A "Team B" of outside academics with fierce anti-Soviet reputations was appointed to review and criticize the CIA's methods of estimating both the Soviet GDP and the portion of it devoted to defense. Team B argued that the CIA had overestimated the size of the Soviet GDP and underestimated Soviet defense spending. They thought Soviet defense spending was around 20 percent of the Soviet GDP. The CIA, bending with the political winds, adjusted its number upward to 16 percent, and for much of the 1980s this was the standard estimate.

At a 1990 Washington conference, however, two maverick Soviet economists said that everyone was wrong, that the Soviet GDP was smaller and the defense expenditures greater: some 25 to 28 percent of the GDP! This would be a crushing burden on any economy. Whatever figure you pick, 16 or 28 percent, the drain on the Soviet economy was enormous, stunting growth, depriving citizens of consumer goods—even necessities—and robbing them of any incentive to work. Later in 1990, Soviet foreign minister Shevardnadze used 25 percent as the portion devoted to defense. With costs like that, the Soviet empire was economically unsustainable. Brezhnev had been able to pretend that it was sustainable; Gorbachev, after four years in office to ponder the facts, could not. Trying to continue the imperial game could cost the Soviet Union everything.

> ***Hard Currency***
>
> Money that is freely traded and widely used and respected in world trade and tourism is called "hard" currency. Dollars, deutsche marks, and Swiss francs are instantly recognized and welcomed everywhere. Currencies that are either not convertible or are inflating so rapidly that few want them are called "soft." In world trade and tourism, no one uses Russian rubles, Polish złoty, or Mexican pesos. Sometimes the terms "dollars" and "hard currency" are used interchangeably, for the dollar is the most recognized hard currency.

Gorbachev actually worsened the Soviet economy. He announced early in his tenure a series of modest economic reforms under the grandiose title of *perestroika* (restructuring). These reforms did not go nearly as far as the earlier efforts of Hungary and China. Perhaps Gorbachev wished to go faster on economic reform, but he faced powerful conservative forces whose jobs and perquisites would be threatened by any major makeover of the economy in a market direction. Hesitation, improvisation, and outright mistakes characterized Gorbachev's economic program. By 1989, amidst glaring food shortages, Gorbachev knew that changes would have to go much farther and the Soviet budget would have to be drastically trimmed. Moscow had been operating at a mammoth budget deficit for many years and was printing money far in excess of the amount of goods people could buy, producing a monumental "ruble overhang" that in the 1990s erupted into wild inflation.

East Europe appears to have little concerned Gorbachev at this desperate stage. Said one Hungarian economist, "We were the last thing he was thinking about." Still, letting East Europe go its own way helped Gorbachev in several areas:

1. Soviet forces stationed in East Europe could be reduced and demobilized, saving on defense expenditures.

2. The pullback of Soviet forces in East Europe would assure the West that the Soviet Union posed no military threat and was therefore a fit partner for arms-control agreements. Arms cuts would further trim the Soviet defense budget.

3. By the same token, the Soviet Union would demonstrate its suitability for badly needed Western trade and investment, naturally on credit.

4. Moscow could also end its supply of subsidized raw materials to East Europe. If the East Europeans wished to purchase Soviet oil and natural gas, they could pay for it in hard currency at world prices.

Now, some policies logically flowed from the preceding points. The Brezhnev Doctrine had to be declared legally dead. Repeatedly in 1989 Gorbachev declared to East European Communist leaders, who came to him with fear in their faces, that he would not prop them up. To avoid mass anger and shore up their legitimacy, he advised them to undertake major reforms of a sort that went much farther than anything he had in mind for the Soviet Union. In many East European lands, the visiting Gorbachev was greeted by enthusiastic chants of "Gorby! Gorby!" He was seen as the liberalizing hero who was ordering the ossified local party gerontocracy to open up the system. And when East European liberalization led to the ouster of Communist regimes, Gorbachev said not a word against it and scarcely anything about it.

This does not mean that Gorbachev was necessarily delighted with the nearly clean sweep from power of party comrades from the Baltic to the Black Sea. More likely, he simply didn't have time or patience to care. Economic considerations far outweighed ideological considerations. Indeed, by this time probably no one east of the Elbe had any Marxist ideological considerations. And Gorbachev had warned the old East European leaders to liberalize before it was too late.

THE DOMINOES FALL

President Eisenhower first used the image of a row of falling dominoes in describing the Communist threat to Southeast Asia in the 1950s. The image fits East Europe better. In 1989, one domino after another toppled into the next. Once the toppling of the regimes started, it could not stop until communism was effectively finished in East Europe.

Poland

During the 1980s, things grew worse in Poland. Solidarity was decimated and went underground, but it stayed very much alive in the hearts and minds of Poles. The economy got worse, with annual growth rates near zero. General Jaruzełski, never popular to begin with, gained no followers. Approximately one-fourth of Polish Communist party members had quit the party in disgust. The Roman Catholic Church stood as a bastion of traditional and humane values; masses were full to overflowing and sermons were frequently pro-Solidarity and antiregime. Lashing out at the anti-Communist clergy, security police beat to death a leading priest (see box).

In 1987, the Jaruzełski government released the last of the Solidarity activists it had held in prison, some since 1981. It was intended as a goodwill gesture but earned the regime nothing. In 1988, new strikes broke out, again under the familiar banners of Solidarity, which was technically still illegal. Now the Jaruzełski regime was at the end of its tether. Economists worried that if the economy slipped much farther, Poland would become, in effect, a Third World country. Environmental poisoning was so bad that some biologists worried about the genetic degradation of the Polish people.

The Popiełuszko Factor

In October 1984, a pro-Solidarity Catholic priest, Father Jerzy Popiełuszko was abducted. Eight days later, amid a massive popular outcry, Poland's interior minister, General Czesław Kiszczak, announced with shame and regret that Popiełuszko had been taken by some of Kiszczak's own security police, beaten to death, and dumped in a reservoir. The three policemen involved said they acted under orders "from the top." Kiszczak and Jaruzełski denied issuing such orders, and they were probably telling the truth. Still, it was their regime that set the police against the church. The hated security police, who had been arresting and beating Solidarity activists for years, were repeatedly denounced from the pulpit.

The Popiełuszko incident shook the Jaruzełski government and deepened mass hatred toward it. Morally, the government did not have a leg to stand on. Five years later, when Gorbachev withdrew its Soviet prop, the Communist government collapsed. In the end, Father Popiełuszko triumphed.

In February 1988, General Kiszczak, the interior minister, called some of the very Solidarity people he had earlier imprisoned to meet with him for what became known as the "roundtable talks" to save Poland. The roundtable connoted meeting as equals. This was a major breakthrough, for it signaled the beginning of shared power. The Solidarity side was headed by Lech Wałęsa. The talks ended in April with the legalization of Solidarity and an agreement to hold semifree elections in 1989.

Kiszczak and prime minister Mieczysław Rakowski were playing a relatively liberal role—although their earlier actions in suppressing Solidarity gave few Poles much confidence in them at the time. In meeting with Solidarity leaders at the 1988 roundtable, they were treating them as equals and asking for their cooperation. They proposed a power-sharing arrangement: In new elections, Solidarity would get 35 percent of the seats of the legislature, the Sejm (pronounced "same"), with the larger part still reserved for the Communist and some small puppet parties. A new upper house, the Senate, would be wide open for free elections. The Senate would have the power to veto bills passed by the Sejm. In effect, Kiszczak and Rakowski offered Solidarity a partnership with right of veto.

Could this have been a long-term, stable solution? No. The reasons are explained in the box on "Fried Snowballs." It was an inherently temporary arrangement, although the Communist side may not have realized it at the time. Solidarity swept the Senate races so thoroughly that it clearly indicated the popular wave was with Solidarity. In *unopposed* contests for the lower house, many Communist candidates still lost, for voters could strike off their names in a negative vote. Some of the small parties previously controlled by the Communists in the Sejm—the Peasants party and Christian Democrats—were won over by Solidarity

The Contagion Factor

Related to the word "contagious," contagion in political science means the spread of ideas by copying. Economists call this the "international demonstration effect." Something happening in one country suggests to people of another to try the same thing. Contagion does not happen universally or automatically. If conditions are unalike, there will be no copying. But if conditions and attitudes are similar, as in East Europe in the late 1980s, what transpires in one land immediately inspires people in other lands.

and cut their ties to the Communists. When the Polish parliament convened after the elections in July 1989, Solidarity, occupying the opposition benches, was morally if not numerically stronger than the Communist party occupying the government benches.

In August 1989, the Sejm voted in General Kiszczak as the new prime minister, but everyone understood that he could not really govern without a popular mandate. To solve the impasse, General Jaruzełski, still president and still with the power to nominate the prime minister, named a Solidarity activist and Wałęsa aide, Tadeusz Mazowiecki (pronounced "mah-zov-yet-ski"), as prime minister. There was one more hurdle, as Communist leaders balked at supporting and participating in a Mazowiecki cabinet. But on August 22, Gorbachev held a 40-minute telephone conversation with Rakowski, after which the Communists announced "partnerlike cooperation" with Solidarity. At a key moment, Gorbachev had talked the Polish Communists into giving up power. On August 24, 1989, the Sejm confirmed Mazowiecki as prime minister by a vote of 378 to 4, with 41 abstentions. The Sejm was no longer the same; even most of the Communists voted for Poland's first non-Communist government.

Hungary

Poland was first, but Hungary was not far behind. Furthermore, Hungary did something extremely important for the unraveling of communism in all East Europe. In the summer of 1989, the liberal Communist government in Budapest decided to stop enforcing an East-bloc agreement to keep visitors from other East European countries from fleeing to the West through Hungary's borders. Thousands of East German "tourists" fled across the Hungarian border to Austria, starting a sequence of events that forced the East Berlin regime to change its personnel and policies. This led to the November 1989 opening of the Berlin Wall and, in short order, to the end of East Germany. Without East Germany to lock in Poland, the East bloc geographically could not hold together.

A change in Hungarian policy—abandoning its loyal role in the Warsaw Pact—marked the beginning of the end for the Warsaw Pact. How did this change

"Fried Snowballs": Is Reform Communism Possible?

Decades ago the Polish philosopher Leszek Kolakowski concluded that reformed communism was a contradiction in terms, about as likely as "fried snowballs." If you attempt to fry a snowball, it melts and disappears. Kolakowski subsequently despaired of Marxism and now teaches at the University of Chicago.

Events in 1989 and 1990 prove Kolakowski right. Throughout East Europe, reform Communists took power with the announced intention of liberalizing and democratizing. Within a few months, all had been replaced by non-Communist regimes. The crux of communism is control; the crux of liberalism is freedom. The minute you start liberalizing a Communist regime, you start dissolving it; you start frying snowballs.

A regime that attempts to control the economy, politics, society, culture, and even personal relations must fail. Leaders are simply not that smart, nor are the followers that obedient, so as to make society run like a well-oiled machine. Humans, Thomas Hobbes noted centuries ago, are not biologically programmed like bees to form perfect societies like hives.

In attempting to impose an impossible and undesirable system, the regime must apply a great deal of coercion and injustice. Humans, again as Hobbes noted, have long memories of the injustices that have been dealt them; their resentments do not fade with time. Permitted to express their views in newly uncensored and accessible mass media, people do so. The regime would like them to criticize the status quo moderately and nicely. Instead, long-smoldering resentments burst out, and then they criticize the regime for everything from economic calamity and political corruption to police repression and environmental degradation. They do not thank the liberal Communist regime for easing up; they want the whole Communist package out. Give them a free-speech inch and they take a democratic mile.

The irony is that the liberal Communist regimes that held power only briefly were composed of relatively nice guys, people (usually younger) within the party who had come to much the same conclusions as anti-Communist critics: that the decaying system had to change. As Alexis de Tocqueville wrote in his classic study of the French Revolution, "The social order overthrown by a revolution is almost always better than the one immediately preceding it." By admitting that things are wrong, the reform regime is also revealing its weakness and fear. The old, pre-reform regime could keep people cowed and silent; the new regime has let them speak. As Tocqueville observed, "The most perilous moment for a bad government is when it seeks to mend its ways." In a nutshell, reform communism is not possible. If attempted, its life is brief, about as long as a snowball in a frying pan.

come about? The official Budapest line is that it was merely implementing an agreement with Austria to drop border controls so that Hungarians and Austrians could visit each other freely. The East Germans discovered this hole in the Iron Curtain and bolted for it; there was no Hungarian intention to undermine the bloc. It may be a while before we get the whole story, but it is likely to have included money changing hands. West Germany—Hungary's biggest creditor—probably offered financially strapped Budapest some favors (new loans, a delay in repaying the old loans, personal gifts?) in return for opening its western border. Bonn's diplomacy long included economic carrots. In December 1989, West German Chancellor Helmut Kohl addressed the Hungarian parliament with his thanks for the "unforgettable days"—from May to November—that led from the Hungarian border opening to the Berlin Wall's opening.

For this sequence to have taken place, however, considerable change had been required in the Hungarian Communist leadership. In 1988, the now doddering Janos Kádár was dropped as party chief in favor of Karoly Grosz. Kádár was blamed for Hungary's economic woes, but the hard-line Grosz did no better. In 1988, for example, Grosz had police with sticks and tear gas break up a Budapest rally in favor of honoring Imre Nagy. Said Grosz of the idea: "Never." By 1989, however, Grosz had come under tremendous pressure to ease up. In February, amidst growing discontent, Hungary's parliament on the banks of the Danube legalized non-Communist political parties. Groups that had existed as "forums" turned themselves into parties. In March, 75,000 marched in Budapest to demand free elections and the withdrawal of Soviet forces from Hungary. The authorities did not stop them, and Gorbachev pledged not to interfere in East Europe.

In June 1989, a ceremony of great symbolic importance took place: the reburial, with full honors, of the 1956 hero Imre Nagy and four of his aides. A quarter of a million Hungarians attended, including government ministers. It was as if the Communist regime were admitting error and regret.

Hungarian relations with West Germany changed dramatically, almost as if Hungary were trying to please the FRG. In May 1989, Hungarian troops started tearing down the barbed-wire fence on their Austrian border, making it easier for East German "tourists" to flee. (Hungarian entrepreneurs attached small pieces of barbed wire to plaques to sell as "your piece of the Iron Curtain." People like that will surely succeed at capitalism.) In September, despite angry protest from East Berlin, very liberal Communist foreign minister Gyula Horn opened the Hungarian-Austrian border so that East Germans could simply drive across. Next spring, Horn was awarded West Germany's Grand Cross of the Federal Order of Merit, the highest honor Germany can bestow on foreigners. After the Hungarian elections in the spring of 1990, the very able Horn was out. He had served as foreign minister less than a year, but it was Horn who in large measure had unplugged the Iron Curtain.

While this was happening, reform Communists elbowed aside conservatives. In May 1989, liberal Communists such as Imre Pozsgay and Reszö Nyers, both Hungarian Politburo members, called for meetings with opposition groups and major economic liberalization. In June, they became part of a three-man collective party leadership, pushing Grosz aside.

In September 1989, the now liberal Communist government met with opposition groups to agree on holding multiparty elections in 1990. In October, the Communist party met to renounce Marxism and embrace democratic socialism. They changed their name to Socialist and made Reszö Nyers their new leader. He also became prime minister. In the spring of 1990, the Hungarian people elected a moderate anti-Communist coalition. Hungary's liberal Communists exercised power for only a few months, but they moved the system from Communist to free. Did they know what they were doing? Did they understand that they were ending the old system and putting themselves out of jobs? Probably not, but what difference does it make?

East Germany

During the first eight months of 1989 the neo-Stalinist regime of Erich Honecker was not about to put up with the kind of liberal and reformist nonsense that was ruining communism in Poland and Hungary. But by the end of 1989, Honecker was under arrest for stashing public money (obtained from trade with the West) in private Swiss bank accounts.

Like most East Europeans, East Germans were hungry for travel. The regime rarely let them travel to the West, fearing (correctly) that they wouldn't come back. By way of compensation, they generally let them visit other countries within the East bloc. Bloc governments agreed among themselves to impose the same border controls on East European visitors to their countries as they imposed on their own citizens. An East German vacationing in Hungary, for example, was not permitted to cross the border into Austria. That way the East German regime could be sure their citizens would return from vacation.

When Budapest decided that it no longer wished to act as enforcer of East German border regulations, word soon got out among East Germans that a vacation in Hungary could be an escape ticket to West Germany. Hungarian vacations became extremely popular. East Germans would go "camping" near the Austrian border, abandon their flimsy little Trabant cars, and walk across to freedom. Hungarian border guards didn't stop them. Thousands of others took refuge in the West German embassy in Budapest. By September 1989, over 13,000 East Germans had left via the Hungarian route. The East Berlin regime protested; Budapest shrugged. What started in Hungary spread to Czechoslovakia, which borders both East and West Germany. More than 17,000 fled via Czechoslovakia. As before the Berlin Wall went up in 1961, East Germany was again hemorrhaging. To staunch the flow, East Germany closed its border with Czechoslovakia. East Germans became madder than ever.

In September 1989, massive demonstrations broke out, centered in Leipzig. In October, Gorbachev visited to urge reform. He told Honecker: "Life punishes those who delay." East Germans greeted the Soviet president with the happy chant, "Gorby, Gorby!" By now 100,000 protesters were marching in Leipzig. Honecker ordered security police to get ready to fire on the Leipzig protesters—to copy the "Chinese solution" carried out the previous June in Beijing. But Egon Krenz, 52, and a much more flexible Communist, sensed catastrophe. As the Politburo member in charge of security, Krenz countermanded Honecker's order. (In another action that proved to be a calming factor, world-famous conductor Kurt Masur opened the Leipzig Gewandthaus concert hall for talks between the protesters and the party and police.) On October 18, Krenz became the new party chief and president. Krenz and his moderate assistants, trying to appease the population, in November allowed travel once again across the Czech border, and thousands crossed a corner of Czechoslovakia on the way to West Germany. By this time a million East Germans, led by a group of intellectuals calling themselves the New Forum, were in the streets demanding far-reaching democratization. The entire East German Politburo and cabinet, including the prime minister, then resigned.

In one last desperate act to restore some order and legitimacy, East Berlin opened the Wall to show citizens that there was no urgent need to flee, that they could go anytime they wished to and come back when they wanted to. Thousands poured into the West, and many did not intend to come back. At that moment, on November 9, 1989, East Germany effectively collapsed into the waiting arms of West Germany. Liberal Communist Hans Modrow became prime minister and named many non-Communists to his cabinet. In December, the country's parliament, the Volkskammer, voted to end the Communists' monopoly on power. The regime agreed to free elections in the spring of 1990. Honecker and five Politburo cronies were arrested for corruption. Their posh homes, country estates, and Swiss bank accounts (containing money skimmed from foreign-trade deals) were revealed on television. The public seethed with resentment. A very liberal Communist lawyer, Gregor Gysi, 41, became party chairman; he abandoned communism and changed the party name to Socialist. A few days earlier, amid revelations of the elite's opulent lifestyle, Egon Krenz resigned in embarrassment as president and as party chairman. He had been in power only 46 days, but much happened because he countermanded the order to fire on protesters.

The rest was an endgame until East Germany was officially absorbed by West Germany on October 2, 1990. The free elections of March 1990 produced a Christian Democratic-led East German government that fully agreed with its West German counterpart on the need for speedy unification. Too many East Germans were pouring into West Germany, straining the finances and housing supply of the welfare state. To get East Germans to stay put, West German Chancellor Helmut Kohl offered them a generous one-to-one exchange rate for their first 2,000 marks in July, making the *Westmark* the only currency and thus effectively unifying Germany economically. In 1990, then, East Germany ceases to exist and, by becoming part of unified Germany, loses its once-important status as an East European state. Now we study the eastern area of Germany as part of Germany, not as part of East Europe.

Czechoslovakia

Like East Germany, the Stalinist regime of Czechoslovakia was not going to give in to the tide of change. Prague held out longer, but the new leaders of December 1989 were non-Communists, some of whom had just been released from prison. In a parallel with Hungary, the old party chief Gustáv Husák, who had been in power since 1969 as a result of the Soviet invasion, was replaced in late 1987 with the younger—but not necessarily better—Miloš Jakeš (prounounced "yah-kesh"). As late as November 12, 1989, Jakeš was telling a Communist youth conference that the government would neither relinquish control nor stand for protests. Twelve days later, Jakeš was out.

The year 1989 began with thousands marking the twentieth anniversary of the death of Jan Palach, who had burned himself alive to protest the 1968 Soviet invasion. Protesters used the occasion to voice demands for human rights. The regime arrested some 800, including playwright Václav Havel, whom they sentenced to nine months in prison. He was paroled six months early, in May. As a founding member of Charter 77, a group formed in 1977 by intellectuals protesting civil-rights abuses, Havel spent more than five years in jail. In August, on the anniversary of the Soviet invasion, a Prague rally of 3,000 in favor of reform was broken up by the police, who arrested 370. In October, a protest by 10,000 was broken up.

Things really got rolling in November 1989. Early in the month, Moscow warned the Prague regime not to make the same mistakes as other East European regimes but to carry out major reforms before things worsened and got out of hand. It was another example of Gorbachev telling the old guard to give way. Jakeš, the obdurate fool, thought he could stand firm. Baton-wielding police broke up a student rally in Prague, injuring many. The brutality galvanized many Czechs into joining the new Civic Forum opposition group. In Slovakia, its counterpart, Public Against Violence, also mushroomed in size. On November 19, some 20,000 protesters marched in Prague. The next day, a quarter-million gathered to demand the government's ouster. On November 24, Jakeš quit, and was replaced by Karel Urbanek, a relative liberal. Alexander Dubček returned to Prague to the cheers of 300,000. A day later, half a million rallied in Prague and workers staged a two-hour general strike that brought Czechoslovakia to a standstill. By now, students and intellectuals had come together with the workers, a combination that made the regime tremble. At the end of November, parliament voted to end the Communists' monopoly on power.

In December 1989, the new, flexible prime minister, Ladislav Adamec (the c is pronounced "ts") named a cabinet of sixteen Communists and five non-Communists. This was not nearly enough for the citizens, and 150,000 marched in Prague to protest the cabinet. Three days later, Adamec quit, and was replaced by a young (43) and very liberal Communist, Marian Čalfa, who soon quit the party. On December 10, a sourpuss Husák, still the country's president, swore in a non-Communist cabinet and then resigned. At the end of the month, Dubček was elected speaker of parliament, which in turn elected Havel president of Czechoslovakia. Havel mused that nothing prepared him for the job as well as prison. In a month and a half, beginning with the student protest of November 17, communism in Czechoslovakia collapsed in what Havel called the "velvet revolution."

Bulgaria

In the Balkans, Bulgarians have long been known as followers of the Russians, the Slavic big brothers who liberated them from the Turks in 1878. Under the Communists, Bulgaria closely aped Soviet ways, including the reforms wrought by Gorbachev. The word *glasnost*—the same in Russian and Bulgarian—was widely used. When Gorbachev said to reform, the Bulgarian Communists reformed. In so doing, the Communists of Sofia were more clever than those of Prague. Seeing change coming, they jumped with it in late 1989. Perhaps for this reason, a liberal Communist party—now calling itself Socialist—was able to win a semifree election in 1990, but not a truly free election in 1991.

Todor Zhivkov, a classic Stalinist, had ruled with an iron hand for an incredible 35 years. Inspired by what was happening elsewhere in the bloc, agitation began to boil up in 1989. Some of the Bulgarian protests, though, were of a bizarre note: anti-civil rights. Bulgaria's poor and discriminated-against Turkish minority, estimated to number from 900,000 to 1.5 million (at least a tenth of the population), had been long hated as a dangerous foreign element and had been under great pressure to assimilate or leave. In the early 1980s, they were forced to take Bulgarian names and to stop speaking Turkish. In 1989, over 300,000 Bulgarian Turks were brutally expelled or fled to Turkey to live in squalor. This policy was just fine with most Bulgars, and it was one of the areas where the regime and people saw eye to eye. Trouble came when the regime indicated it would, under international pressure, *stop* mistreating its Turks. Some Bulgarians, using primitive fear images of a Turkish takeover, then rallied against the regime.

It was under these circumstances that younger and more flexible Communists, in telephone communication with Moscow, on November 10, 1989 (the day after the Berlin Wall was opened), replaced Zhivkov as party chief with the foreign minister, reformist Petar Mladenov, who also then became president. Mladenov named a reformist cabinet, gave up party leadership, changed the party name to Socialist, and led the party to a narrow victory in 1990. This election may not have been completely fair, but it must be said that many Bulgarians supported the party as the only force seemed to be able to hold the country together.

Romania

The last overthrow of a Communist regime in 1989 occurred in Romania, and it was by far the bloodiest. Several hundred people were killed by the Securitate,

Even Albania

Albania, as usual, lagged behind the rest of East Europe. The poorest and most backward country of Europe, trapped since the end of World War II in a hermetically sealed Stalinist dictatorship, in a slow process from late 1990 to mid-1991 had dumped its Communist regime. The brutal Enver Hoxha (pronounced *hod-ja*) ruled with an iron hand from 1946 until his death in 1985. Few visitors got into Albania, and even fewer Albanians got out. Fearful of Yugoslav takeover and scornful of Khrushchev's reforms, Albania adopted an absurd Maoist position and held it even after Beijing abandoned Maoism in favor of growing ties with the West.

A Hoxha assistant, Ramiz Alia, took over as president in 1985, vowing to keep Albania on its pure socialist course. But news of the upheavals elsewhere in East Europe penetrated Albania from Italian and Yugoslav television, and public discontent stirred. Alia, who in retrospect was a liberal Communist, announced some cautious reforms, but this just whetted Albanians' appetites. In late 1990, students mounted violent protests, and Alia announced bigger reforms, including a market economy and legal opposition. Two professors immediately founded a Democratic party. In 1991, tens of thousands of lean, desperate Albanians fled to Italy and Greece, where they were not particularly welcome.

In 1991, Alia held elections. They were not completely democratic, thanks to the Communists' hold on the countryside, and the Communists won a majority of seats in parliament. Tellingly, Alia personally lost his seat to a Democratic candidate. Under the pressure of strikes and street demonstrations, the Communist government resigned in June 1991 in favor of a national unity cabinet that prepared for new elections in March 1992. This time the Democrats won, with 65 percent of the vote to the Socialists' (as the Communists now called themselves) 26 percent. Cardiology professor (and former Communist party member) Sali Berisha took over as president to begin a difficult process of opening up the hermit republic as the economy collapsed. Albania shows rather neatly the impossibility of a Communist regime easing up a little, for when they do, the people demand more, much more.

the security police, in December before the tyrant Nicolae Ceauşescu, in power 24 years, was overthrown and executed by his own military. Why was Romania bloody and the other East European overthrows of communism not? The clue here is that Romania was not closely tied to the Soviet Union; its leaders and party did not follow the Kremlin line. Accordingly, Gorbachev had no input or leverage with the extremely brutal Ceauşescu regime.

Ceauşescu, who came to power in 1965, soon took Romania on an independent course. He resented Romania's economy being subjected to Comecon. In 1968, Romania (along with China) denounced the Soviet invasion of Czechoslovakia; after all, they might be next. Internally, though, Ceauşescu was a complete

Stalinist. He kept Romanians oppressed and poor in order to wring out every bit of industrial production. He ordered the historic heart of Bucharest torn down to make way for monstrously distasteful architecture, including the immense House of the Republic, his personal palace. He ordered ancient villages razed and forced their inhabitants to relocate to prefab apartments elsewhere. To pay off Romania's foreign debt, he sweated workers and lowered living standards. Food was hard to find. Heat and electricity were often off. Demanding a high birthrate, Ceauşescu outlawed abortion. Unwanted children, though, were housed in unheated zoolike conditions until they died. Romania's backward medical system gave unnecessary blood transfusions to newborns; hundreds of babies got AIDS from unscreened donors and slowly died.

The Hungarians of Transylvania triggered the Romanian uprising. Ceauşescu was especially intent on razing Hungarian villages and moving ethnic Magyars away from border areas. In early 1988, ethnic Hungarians fled from Romania across the border into Hungary, which for them was relatively free and prosperous. A Hungarian Calvinist pastor, Reverend Lászlo Tökés, in Timişoara began to denounce the repression of Hungarians in Romania. The Securitate tried to arrest Tökés on December 15, but demonstrators—of all ethnic groups and religions—encircled his church to protect Tökés. The next day, the Securitate opened fire on the Timişoara demonstrators, killing hundreds, who were buried in mass graves. Ceauşescu gave orders to shoot any protester anywhere and then flew off to visit Iran. But the protests spread. Ceauşescu returned quickly and called the protesters "fascist, reactionary groups." On December 21, Ceauşescu staged a rally but was shouted down by protesters in Bucharest. Romanian television broadcasted nationwide the look of shock on his face. At that moment, the "hero of the Carpathians" was finished. The next day the regular army, which always resented the Securitate, joined in to protect the revolution; they battled Securitate snipers. Altogether, several hundred Romanians were gunned down by the Securitate. Ceauşescu and his wife Elena were captured, given a quick, secret military trial, and executed by firing squad on Christmas Day 1989.

The old Communist elite, including relatively liberal Communists, some of whom had been under house arrest for criticizing Ceauşescu, formed a Council of National Salvation and pledged democracy. The Council named Ion Iliescu president and Petre Roman prime minister. Many observers, both foreign and Romanian, quickly noticed a contrived element to the Romanian revolution. The new leaders, who now called themselves socialists, blamed everything on the Ceauşescus (who were now conveniently dead) while they staffed the new regime with holdovers from the old. Bucharest intellectuals and students demanded total ouster of ex-Communists from power, but Iliescu stood firm and was confirmed in office in rigged elections. The clean sweep of Communists from power that took place in Central Europe, from Hungary north, was delayed in the Balkan lands of Romania, Bulgaria, Yugoslavia, and Albania, where many ex-Communists retained power under different guises.

SUGGESTED READINGS

BANAC, IVO, ed. *Eastern Europe in Revolution.* Ithaca, NY: Cornell University Press, 1992.

BERMEO, NANCY, ed. *Liberalization and Democratization: Change in the Soviet Union and Eastern Europe*. Baltimore, MD: Johns Hopkins University Press, 1992.

BRUMBERG, ABRAHAM. "Poland: The Demise of Communism," *Foreign Affairs: America and the World, 1989/90.* 69 (Winter 1990), 1.

CODRESCU, ANDREI. *The Hole in the Flag: A Romanian Exile's Story of Return and Revolution.* New York: Morrow, 1991.

DAWISHA, KAREN. *Eastern Europe, Gorbachev, and Reform: The Great Challenge,* 2nd ed. New York: Cambridge University Press, 1990.

DEBARDELEBEN, JOAN, ed. *To Breathe Free: Eastern Europe's Environmental Crisis.* Baltimore, MD: Johns Hopkins University Press, 1991.

ELSTER, JON, ed. *The Roundtable Talks and the Breakdown of Communism.* Chicago: University of Chicago Press, 1996.

GARTON ASH, TIMOTHY. *The Magic Lantern: The Revolution of '89 Witnessed in Warsaw, Budapest, Berlin, and Prague.* New York: Random House, 1990.

_____________. *The Uses of Adversity: Essays on the Fate of Central Europe.* New York: Random House, 1990.

GILBERG, TROND. *Nationalism and Communism in Romania: The Rise and Fall of Ceausescu's Personal Dictatorship.* Boulder, CO: Westview, 1990.

GLENNY, MISHA. *The Rebirth of History: Eastern Europe in the Age of Democracy*, rev. ed. New York: Penguin, 1995.

HOLMES, LESLIE. *The End of Communist Power.* New York: Oxford University Press, 1993.

JOPPKE, CHRISTIAN. *East German Dissidents and the Revolution of 1989: Social Movement in a Leninist Regime.* New York: New York University Press, 1995.

MASON, DAVID S. *Revolution in East-Central Europe: The Rise and Fall of Communism and the Cold War.* Boulder, CO: Westview, 1992.

POZNANSKI, KAZIMIERZ Z. *Poland's Protracted Transition: Institutional Change and Economic Growth, 1971-1993.* New York: Cambridge University Press, 1996.

STOKES, GALE. *The Walls Came Tumbling Down: The Collapse of Communism in Eastern Europe.* New York: Oxford University Press, 1993.

TOKÉS, RUDOLF L. *Hungary's Negotiated Revolution: Economic Reform, Social Change and Political Succession.* New York: Cambridge University Press, 1996.

WALESA, LECH. *The Struggle and the Triumph: An Autobiography.* New York: Arcade Publishing, 1992.

WHEATON, BERNARD, AND ZDENEK KAVAN. *The Velvet Revolution: Czechoslovakia, 1988-1991.* Boulder, CO: Westview, 1992.

CHAPTER EIGHT

The Struggle for Democracy

Most of Central Europe won the struggle to build working democracies; most of the Balkans has a way to go. With this we return to a theme discussed in Chapter 1, the differences between Central Europe and the Balkans, for it is important to current politics. The "East Europe" of the Cold War has fractured into Central Europe (from Hungary north) and the Balkans (south of Hungary). A key difference between the two is that Central Europe developed intellectual and ideological opposition to communism well before 1989; the Balkans did not, at least not in any organized sense. In Poland, Czechoslovakia, and Hungary anti-Communist catchall parties or movements took over in 1989 with a unity of purpose that said, "Sweep the package out!" Later, of course, these catchalls quarreled and broke up over the pace and pain of privatization and in Hungary and Poland lost elections to Socialist parties composed of some of the more liberal of the ex-Communists. But in Central Europe the anti-Communist catchalls were in power long enough to launch irreversible economic, legal, and bureaucratic reforms that broke the power of the old Communist *apparat*.

The Balkan countries, with no anti-Communist movements antedating the overthrows of late 1989—after Central Europe had carried out its revolutions—had little intellectual or organizational bases. Once formed, the Balkan movements were terribly weak, and some were hastily renamed Communist fronts. The hold of the Communist party, especially in the countryside and in the powerful *apparat* permitted not-so-ex-Communists to cling to power as newly proclaimed "Socialists," unwilling and unable to "sweep the package out." They were the package. Iliescu in Romania, Gligorov in Macedonia, and Milošević in Serbia carried on in much the same style as the previous Communist regimes. They were supported by a mafia of old apparachiks, often now dubious "businessmen."

The new Central European governments, still imbued with a certain anti-Communist passion, were willing to bite the bullet on rapid economic privatization. The exception here was Slovakia, where founding prime minister Vladimir Mečiar broke Slovakia away from the Czech Republic in part to avoid rapid privatization. In the Balkans, anti-Communist passion was confined to a handful of intellectuals with no mass movements behind them, their weakness to this day. The old *apparat* easily overrode them and stayed in power a few years longer.

Thus in the Balkans, regimes pursued policies of temporizing, of talking of economic liberalization but not doing it. A clean break with the Communist past would have cost Balkan regimes the support of the old apparatchiks and stirred up mass discontent over unemployment. Accordingly, many state-owned industrial dinosaurs continued to get state subsidies that fueled inflation. Some regimes claimed they sought "third ways" between capitalism and socialism. Such paths are illusory, and after a while these regimes crashed. Meanwhile, the Central European lands (perhaps without Slovakia) will join West Europe.

THE CATCHALL PARTIES SPLINTER

The parties that first ousted the Communists in Central Europe were broad catchalls. These were the parties or coalitions of several parties, often grouped around heroic figures, that sprang up to lead opposition to the Communist regimes in 1989 and earlier in the case of Poland. Vaguely center-right, they claimed to stand for just about everything and did not offer a clear program, only a sense of renewal and a fresh start. Typically these catchall parties or alignments contained Christian democrats, chauvinistic populists, free-market liberals, nostalgic agrarians, and frightened industrial workers. Some of these groups were organized as parties, others merely as "wings" within the catchall party. Often they were at odds with each other.

Poland's Solidarity, for example, which resoundingly won the contested seats in semifree 1989 elections, enrolled some 10 million Poles of all walks of life. Likewise, Hungary's Democratic Forum, Czechoslovakia's Civic Forum and Public Against Violence (the Slovak branch), and Bulgaria's Union of Democratic Forces (which was formed only after the Communist regime was ousted) were all extremely broad catchalls, united in little but opposition to the Communist regimes.

These broad catchalls soon fell apart. Often unnatural alliances, hastily and poorly organized, the catchalls were unable to merge their divergent factions or constituent parties into a cohesive single party. The hardships brought on by the economic restructuring implemented by free-market liberals, who generally got the economic ministries of the new governments, soon caused factions or successor parties to emerge, complain, and separate. Even Poland's Solidarity, which seemed to be so well organized and cohesive during its struggle with the Communist regime, quickly broke up in the new conditions of political freedom coupled with

The Great Backlash

Democracy and market economics are fairly closely related: where you find one you usually find the other. But the transition to them is difficult, for the two can get in each other's way. If you are instituting painful economic reforms, in which many people suffer from unemployment and inflation, they will use their new-found democratic tools to vote against you and your well-intentioned reforms. In this way, Polish voters "thanked" the marketeering reformers who had paved Poland's way to rapid growth by booting them out. This was the great voter backlash that hit Central Europe in the mid-1990s, after the initial waves of economic reforms.

East Europeans, like many voters (including U.S.), hold contradictory views. Most of them say they want free markets, but in the next breath they also say they want government welfare and limits to the profits of capitalists. They want the bounty of free enterprise but none of the pain and inequality. Used to a complex welfare state with generous retirement plans under the Communists, many citizens found themselves quickly poorer under capitalism. Inflation, for example, drastically shrunk the value of pensions.

This did not mean the Socialist governments reversed the drive to capitalism; they merely tried to build a better social safety net. In this regard they are like the Socialist and Social Democratic parties of West Europe. In time, East Europe's politics may resemble West Europe's and revolve around the question, "How much of a welfare state should we have and can we afford?"

economic hardship induced by the "shock therapy" marketization of Finance Minister Leszek Balcerowicz. Its successor parties now include the center-liberal Democratic Union of former Prime Minister Tadeusz Mazowiecki (and most Solidarity intellectuals); the pro-business Liberal Democratic Congress; the Christian democrats of Catholic Action; the pro-Wałęsa Center Citizens' Alliance; the Peasant Alliance; and two worker-oriented parties with Solidarity in their name. Solidarity, the people's choice in 1989, had by the elections of 1991 split into two main and several smaller parties, none of which had a strong following. By the 1993 elections, won by the Democratic Left Alliance, Solidarity was a shambles.

Likewise, in the early to mid-1990s the Hungarian, Bulgarian, Czech, and Slovak catchalls were showing signs of decline and division. In the 1994 elections, the governing Hungarian Democratic Forum declined drastically. The Bulgarian UDF also splintered and in 1995 lost to the Socialists. In the 1992 elections, the Czech and Slovak catchalls virtually disappeared. Even Romania's Communist-descended National Salvation Front split in the 1992 elections as its leading personalities strove for predominance.

East Europe's Election Rules

There are basically two types of electoral systems: proportional representation (PR) and single-member districts (SMD). PR sends deputies to parliament in (more or less) proportion to the percent of the vote they have won. SMD is the familiar British and U.S. system in which a district sends one person to parliament, whoever wins the most votes (a plurality rather than a majority). The French variation uses SMD with two rounds, the first requires a winner to get a majority, a runoff a week later requires only a plurality. The postwar German pattern combines PR and SMD. The Swedish variation uses PR in districts and then evens up numerical discrepancies from party totals with a nationwide PR list. One finds combinations of these systems, which are changed from time to time, in East Europe.

	Deputies in Assembly	Electoral System	Percent Threshold
Albania	140	100 SMDs with runoff plus 40 PR	4
Bulgaria	240	PR in 31 districts	4
Czech Republic	200	PR in 8 districts plus nationwide PR	5
Hungary	386	176 SMDs with runoff 152 PR in 19 counties 58 PR nationwide	4
Poland	460	PR in districts for 391 plus 69 PR nationwide	5
Romania	387	PR in districts plus PR nationwide	3
Slovakia	150	PR in 4 districts plus SMDs	5

Albania and Slovakia, for example, use variations on the German combination of SMDs and PR. The Czech Republic, Poland, and Romania use PR at two levels, most district but some nationwide. Bulgaria uses classic PR in districts. Hungary uses a combination of everything.

The "percent threshold" indicates the minimum percentage of the popular vote a party needs to obtain any PR seats. The higher the threshold, the more small parties are kept out of parliament. Although some consider this unfair, a parliament with too many parties often has trouble forming cabinets, which usually consist of several parties. As a general rule, the more parties in a coalition cabinet, the less stable it is, as one or more parties may walk out over a political issue. This undermines the ability to govern and with it hopes for democracy.

Some observers regretted the breakup of these early catchalls, as if a chance at electoral and political stability had been lost. But there was always a contrived element to them, and they could retain cohesion only as combatants in the final overthrow of a decaying authoritarian system. Under more normal circumstances, faced with governing responsibility in the midst of economic decline, it was inevitable that their components would reassert themselves. Eventually, they will learn to put aside their differences over personality and policy, reunite, and achieve electoral victories.

A MODEL EAST EUROPEAN PARTY SYSTEM

To represent an ideal-typical Central or East European party system we might divide it into those parties that spun off from the original catchall and those who had an existence independent of the catchall. In time, the origin of parties—inside or outside the catchall—may not matter, but for the present we gain some clarity by dividing them in this way. Accordingly, our spectrum of political parties would have two axes, the conventional horizontal left-right, plus a vertical axis of former catchall and parties of independent origin:

Former catchall

worker   liberal   Christian   agrarian   populist

LEFT   **CENTER**   **RIGHT**

Communist   socialist   social democrat   nationalist

Independent origin

Any such graphic is an approximation and bound to oversimplify the complexity and nuances of party systems, especially the rapidly changing ones of Central Europe and the Balkans. We may have trouble deciding, for example, whether a Catholic, peasant, or populist party is most right or only center-right, as they will mix their appeals. In some areas, such as farm-price supports, agrarian parties may demand the sort of government intervention that puts them to the left of free-market liberals. On other questions, the agrarians may be the most-rightist element, as were the Hungarian Smallholders on the subject of Hungarians living outside of Hungary. The ex-Communist parties may fan nationalist flames as a way to discredit and destabilize the system, as in Slovakia and Bulgaria.

There may also be an independent peasant party, in the case of Poland a Peasant party that had earlier been under the control of the Communists, now cooperating in a governing coalition with the Democratic Left Alliance. This party would probably be considered leftist, whereas most peasant parties are on the right or

Poland

Two Polish elections illustrate the swing to the left in Central Europe. In November 1995 Lech Wałęsa, the hero and head of Solidarity, was voted out of the presidency. Amazingly, in his place Poles elected by 52-48 percent a young, polished ex-Communist, Aleksander Kwaśniewski, the leader of the new Democratic Left Alliance (DLA), Poland's largest party, which had won 20 percent of the vote in 1993 parliamentary elections and 171 (37 percent) of the seats.

What had happened? The Polish economy was doing quite well, but the unemployed and other economic losers resented the newly rich capitalists. Governments changed too often; cabinets lacked stability. Wałęsa disliked many of his prime ministers, whom he did not choose; they were thrust on him by parliament. Wałęsa, a gruff and poorly educated man, failed to found a viable political party; he thought he was above parties. The massive Solidarity catchall fragmented into some 15 small parties, few of which cleared the electoral threshold. And the Catholic Church, now calling the shots on education and abortion, earned the anticlerical resentment of many educated Poles, especially women.

The two elections did not mark a return of communism, however, as the DLA is social democratic and in favor of a market economy and joining NATO. The DLA merely sought better welfare guarantees for economic losers. The 1993 election also greatly simplified Poland's party system; a new 5 percent threshold allowed only six parties into parliament, in contrast to the 29 parties in the *Sejm* after the 1991 elections, an example of the impact of electoral laws. Poland's new electoral system deliberately overrepresented the large parties at the expense of the small ones, a step urged by President Wałęsa to promote stability.

The Polish Peasant party (which had been a puppet party under the Communists) came in second in 1993, with 15 percent of the vote and 29 percent of the seats. With two-third's of the Sejm's seats between them, these two parties formed the governing coalition. The best the non-left could do in 1993 was a Solidarity successor, the free-market Democratic Union, which won less than 11 percent of the vote and 16 percent of the seats, as Poles blamed it for the pain of (successful) economic transformation.

The only other parties to make it into parliament in 1993 were President Wałęsa's vague and hastily organized Non-Party Bloc with 5 percent and 16 seats, the leftist Solidarity-spinoff Union of Labor with 7 percent and 41 seats, and the nationalistic Confederation for an Independent Poland with 6 percent and 24 seats. The third-place winner of 1991, the prochurch Catholic Action, was voted entirely out of parliament. The most Catholic country in the world thus had no deputies from a Catholic party. Poles are Catholic but not necessarily clerical. To win in the future, Poland's center-right must unify into one party, the prescription for many other countries in the region.

even far right. On the left, Communist here means the unreconstructed types, often still calling themselves Communist, whose parties drew few votes. Socialist here means the liberal ex-Communists, now democratic and welfarist, who often became the largest and sometimes governing party.

THE RETURN OF THE LEFT

Poland and Hungary returned ex-Communists to power in free and fair elections. This should not bother us. Much of the Balkans took years longer to get not-so-ex-Communists out of power, and elections were often unfair. This might bother us. The Polish Democratic Left Alliance and Hungarian Socialist party really are democratic socialist parties of the West European type. True, some of their adherents and voters may be old-style Communists, especially connected with the old Communist trade unions, but most of their voters and party leadership are democratic, pro-market economics, and pro-West. They want to join NATO as much as the anti-Communist catchall parties that proceeded them. The chief difference between them and the now-fractured catchalls: the socialists want a better and higher social safety net for those unduly harmed by the rapid economic transition. This is essentially the same policy followed by West European left parties and illustrates a tendency of Central European politics to resemble West European politics.

Every country has a left. In West Europe, the combined vote for left parties (Socialist, Social Democratic, Labor, Communist) generally totals between one-third and 40 percent. Should Central Europe be much different from West Europe in this regard? The question is what kind of left, democratic and moderate or totalitarian and revolutionary? West Europe, operating in a context of electoral competition, chose the former. Central Europe, trapped behind Soviet bayonets, had the latter forced on them. With the bayonets gone, Central Europe developed a "normal" political spectrum of parties on the left, right, and center. The Balkans took longer to accomplish this.

And in East Europe there are good reasons for more than a few citizens to vote for a left party. The region has seen an explosion of inequality. Some sharp characters, often with ties to the old Communist structure, got rich. Some were able to convert the state enterprises they used to direct into their personal private property. Others knew exactly which properties to buy when they came up for privatization. And some, to be sure, earned money the old-fashioned capitalist way, by founding new businesses. The main boulevards of the capital cities are now lined with smart shops and clogged with late-model cars (many freshly stolen in Germany). But many other citizens, especially ordinary workers and retirees, suffered. Their wages and pensions lagged behind inflation; no smart clothes and cars for them. The socialist parties of East Europe simply did the natural, political thing: they appealed to a large, worried section of the electorate and won big.

Romania

Romania's elections (both parliamentary and presidential) of late 1996 were a good sign that Romania, after a seven-year delay, was finally shedding its Communist past and starting to catch up with its Central European neighbors. In both 1996 elections, a coalition of democrats finally ousted the "Party of Social Democracy," the ex-Communist holdovers who had taken power in a fast shuffle at the end of 1989. In contrast to earlier Romanian elections, those of 1996 were free and fair.

The biggest vote went to the Democratic Convention, a center-right catchall of dissidents and intellectuals headed by geology professor Emil Constaninescu, who became Romania's president. In the French-style presidential race, incumbent President Ion Iliescu had edged out Constantinescu 32-28 percent in the first round. A runoff (required if no one wins an outright majority in the first round) two weeks later gave victory to Constantinescu, 53-41 percent.

The Democratic Coalition, though, did not win enough parliamentary seats to govern alone, so it formed a coalition with the smaller Democratic party, a centrist group led by (probably well-reformed) ex-Communist Petre Roman, a clever and popular politician. The election's issues: slow economic growth and corruption. The ruling coalition's great challenges: privatization, currency stability, and foreign investment.

Even in the Czech Republic in 1996, the Social Democrats and Communists (unreconstructed) scored major electoral gains, but not enough to form a government. The Czech pattern was the same as in Poland and Hungary; it just didn't go as far; the Czech conversion to a market economy went well, with little inflation or unemployment. In Central Europe, with perhaps the exception of Slovakia, there was a sort of natural swing to the left.

In the Balkans, the left clung to power for many years. Here, instead of an anti-Communist catchall ousting the old regime, elements of the old regime turned themselves into a fake catchall to preserve their wealth and power. The clearest examples of this were Serbia and Romania. Bulgaria is a bit like Central Europe with a time delay: in 1991 the UDF ousted the Bulgarian Socialist party (BSP); the BSP bounced back in 1995 but lost the presidency in 1996. Albania saw the electoral triumph of the Democratic party in 1992, but by 1996 it behaved in a most undemocratic fashion in winning what all observers called rigged elections.

EMERGING PARTY SYSTEMS

Party systems contribute a lot to the stability of democracy. The right party system—one without too many parties and in which competition follows certain rules of the game—can make democracy work. An out-of-control party

The Czech Republic

In 1996 the Czech Republic experienced the same lurch to the left that had earlier hit Poland and Hungary. The Czech resurgent left, however, was not strong enough to form a government, and Václav Klaus, a militant free-marketeer, continued as prime minister. Czech economic stability was the best in East Europe: rapid privatization, excellent growth, low inflation and unemployment, a solid currency (the *koruna*, crown), and budget surpluses. But Klaus governed with a quarrelsome three-party center-right coalition. Chief problem: Klaus's bossy arrogance.

Klaus's Civic Democratic party was still first with 30 percent of the votes but fell from 72 (out of 200) seats to 68, and the coalition parties as a whole declined to 99 seats, just under half. The left increased, the Social Democrats to second place with 26 percent and 61 seats and the Communists with 10 percent and 22 seats. Result: a minority government headed by Klaus but one that depended on the cooperation of the Social Democrats, headed by Miloš Zeman, who favored a "socially and ecologically oriented market economy." Chief problem with cooperation: the arrogant Zeman dislikes the arrogant Klaus.

The 1996 Czech elections showed some positive signs. Several small parties (accounting for 11 percent of the vote) failed to clear the 5-percent threshold, and the number of parties in parliament fell from eight to six. In time, Czechs may learn to not waste their votes on small parties. With further consolidation, the Czech Republic could resemble Germany with a large pro-capitalist party facing a moderate welfare party.

system—one with too many parties and in which competition turns extremist—can wreck what on paper seems to be a fine democracy. West Europe, over time and with some pain, evolved party systems that support stable democracy. East Europe is now engaged in this process.

West Europe's parties were usually founded on underlying social cleavages over region, religion, language, and social class. Various sectors discovered they could get much farther if they joined together in one party. For example, the landed aristocracy discovered that it had certain interests in common with the urban bourgeoisie, and this produced a conservative party. Over time—in most of West Europe after World War II—the polarizations and passions of the early stages of democracy faded, and systems of moderate competition emerged, often in the form of "two-plus" (two big and a few small) party systems.

Things can go wrong with this gradual march to stable democracy, however. If too many parties, some of them extremist, compete, they tend to engage, in the words of political scientist Giovanni Sartori, in a "politics of outbidding" that produces "center-fleeing tendencies" that may collapse the democratic system. Germany and Spain in the 1930s fell into this pattern.

Slovakia

Slovakia emerged from the 1993 "velvet divorce" far less democratic than the Czech Republic. The split between Prague and Bratislava (the Slovak capital) was largely the fault of Slovak Prime Minister Vladimir Mečiar, an ex-Communist and ex-boxer with an authoritarian streak. Not wishing to share power with Prague or privatize so fast, Mečiar engaged in a nationalistic politics of outbidding with other Slovak politicians that led to a split only a minority wished. Unlike the Yugoslav situation, few Czechs lived in Slovakia and vice versa, and separation was peaceful. Bratislava stalled on privatization, but once enterprises came into private hands (many of them Mečiar's friends and supporters), Slovakia enjoyed some of the region's fastest economic growth (7.4 percent in 1995) and best trade surplus (4 percent of GDP).

Mečiar's Movement for a Democratic Slovakia (a remnant of the original Public Against Violence catchall) won 35 percent of the vote and 61 (out of 150) seats in 1994. Mečiar's party formed unsteady coalitions while Mečiar himself tried to ban critical media comments, opposition rallies, and the use of the Hungarian language by Slovakia's sizeable (11 percent) Magyar minority. He called gypsies a threat to the white race, a view many in the region share. Mečiar apparently used Slovak security police in an ugly conspiracy to unseat Slovak President Michal Kováč. A 1996 electoral law changed the system from PR to a mix of PR and SMD calculated to both dilute the Hungarian vote and give Mečiar's party a majority of seats with only a minority of the votes. Considering Mečiar's authoritarian drift, some observers compare Slovakia with Croatia and other Balkan lands. Slovakia's hope: several democratic opposition parties have allied in preparation for the 1998 election.

East Europe, unfortunately, does not have the time to gradually develop parties and party systems. With the collapse of Communist regimes, competitive elections were thrust on most countries of the region in 1990. Instead of patiently building party strength and gradually obtaining electoral success and parliamentary seats, East Europe's parties had to suddenly contest elections with little practice, organization, or political skill. In many cases, East European parties had no clear social bases, and East European voters had little party identification. Instead of gradually incorporating the traditional cleavages of center versus periphery, state versus church, and owner versus worker into a party system as in West Europe, East European voters tumbled into a confusing, unfocused situation in which the only fixed pole was the old Communist regime, repudiated by most voters.

The gradual evolution of social cleavages and party systems typical of West Europe had been frozen by Communist control of East Europe, and this left East European politics unstructured and volatile in the post-tyranny era. Will the East

Europeans be able to compress the historical experiences of West Europe into a stable, modern party system? Or will East European politics resemble the tumult, extremism, and authoritarian results of the region's short experiment with freedom and democracy that we considered in our chapter on the interwar years? Gradually, East European party systems seem to be settling down and, in Central Europe earlier than in the Balkans, becoming like West European systems.

FOUNDING ELECTIONS

The first elections after a long tyranny are bound to be strange. In the flush of freedom, too many parties, many without clear electoral support, insist on competing in elections. All fancy themselves the saviors of the nation. The first free elections have been called "founding elections," gropes in the dark that trim down the number of parties, persuade some parties to merge with others or to simply go out of business, and teach politicians about the shape of the electorate, their likely constituency, and how they may best communicate with it.

Furthermore, citizens casting a free ballot for the first time often don't know what to do with it. Party identification—the psychological anchoring of voters to parties they know and prefer—is extremely low. Many voters are totally ignorant as to which party stands for what. This is particularly true when too many parties run. Especially in rural areas, where the old party bosses still hold sway, people often vote the way they are told. This was true of Spain in the 1880s (*caciquismo)*, Brazil in the 1920s (*cornelismo*), and Romania in the 1990s. It may take several elections for voters, especially rural voters, to learn they can ignore the local boss and use their ballot as a tool for expressing their interests and preferences.

First-time elections produce party systems with far too many parties. In the 1990 and 1991 elections, Hungary, Bulgaria, and Czechoslovakia each fielded a dozen or more parties. In the 1991 Polish elections, 67 parties entered Poland's first fully free elections after the partially competitive elections of 1989. The electoral systems of each state, variants of proportional representation, are partly to blame for the plethora of parties, at least for first-time elections. Eager new politicians, operating in an environment of nearly zero knowledge about their electorates, are rarely discouraged by electoral-law thresholds, be they high or low. The thresholds may consist of either a minimum percentage a party must obtain to win any seats in a proportional-representation system (for example, the 5 percent minimum in Germany and the Czech Republic, 4 percent in Sweden and Bulgaria) or by establishing single-member districts with either a simple plurality winning on the first round (Britain, U.S.) or in a runoff (France). Poland, happily, introduced a nationwide threshold of 5 percent for its 1993 elections, and only six parties made it into the *Sejm* compared to the 29 (11 with only one seat) in 1991. After the first-time elections, as data and opportunities become clearer, higher thresholds in the electoral system may help hold down the number of parties, although they by no means bar the rise of new parties (for example, the Greens in Germany and

Sweden, antitax parties in Denmark and Norway, and regionalist parties in Spain).

More to blame than the electoral system in first-time elections is the fact that new parties and inexperienced politicians all think they enjoy broad support and have a chance at entering parliament or even forming a government. They tend to disbelieve survey research that shows them irrelevant. If Spain and West Europe generally offer any guidance, the number of parties is likely to decline after a few elections, as many discover they have no electoral support, a process accelerated by increasingly credible surveys of political opinion. At that point, electoral laws can help, as higher thresholds convince marginal parties to merge or fold, a process now well underway in Central Europe.

NATIONALIST OUTBIDDING

As noted, too many parties can lead to a "politics of outbidding." Virtually all the countries of the region have rightwing and nationalist parties. All the catchalls discussed earlier contained populist elements that tended to chauvinism. Some of them departed from the catchall and engaged in a politics of outbidding with other, sometimes more extreme right-wing parties. The result is that several political figures in East Europe are playing nationalist cards. In East Europe, nationalism is closely linked to anti-Semitism.

There are several highly nationalistic Polish parties—the Confederation for an Independent Poland, Catholic Action, and the personal vehicle of the demagogic Stanisław Tyminski, Party "X"—some of them anti-Semitic. There are fewer than 15,000 Jews left in Poland, most elderly, but alleged Jewish influence serves for some Poles to explain Poland's economic hardships. One Polish wag responded to the inconsistency of anti-Semitism without Jews by saying, "Why not? We have traffic jams without cars." Anti-Semitic outbidding began in the 1990 Polish presidential contest, as some Wałęsa supporters cast doubt on the "Polishness" of several of Mazowiecki's advisors. Some poorly informed voters even accused Mazowiecki—a Catholic intellectual who worked under Church aegis for many years—of being Jewish. In the 1991 parliamentary elections, Tyminski imputed Jewish characteristics to mainstream parties, including those supporting Wałęsa. What goes around comes around.

Some Hungarian politicians also played the anti-Semitic card. Hungary has 80,000 Jews (0.8 percent of Hungary's total), chiefly in Budapest—and several Jews were prominent in the Alliance of Free Democrats (AFD), including its founding chairman, philosopher Janos Kis. Although Alliance figures took the lead in toppling the Communist regime, some candidates of the Hungarian Democratic Forum depicted the AFD as essentially Budapest Jews who had recently converted from communism. The 1990 elections were almost a replay of interwar Hungarian politics, which were dominated by an urban-populist split that was always won by the populists. The populists—representing rural, Catholic, and peasant

Hungary

Hungary's third free elections, in 1994, showed a pattern similar to Poland: the resurgence of the left. The Hungarian Socialist party won a third of the PR ballots and took 209 seats, an outright majority of parliament. Socialist leader Gyula Horn became the new prime minister. A liberal Communist, as foreign minister in 1989 Horn had opened the border with Austria, a crack that brought down the whole Communist edifice in East Europe. Rather than govern alone, the Socialists formed a coalition with the (classic) liberal Alliance of Free Democrats, who came in second with 20 percent of the PR vote and 70 seats. The wise move showed Hungarians and the world that the Socialists really were a market-oriented, non-Communist party that could be trusted. The policies of the Socialist-led government differed little from those of its predecessor.

Hungary's electoral system for the 386-member parliament is extremely complex and confusing; few Hungarians can explain it. First, 176 members are elected in single-member districts. If no one gets more than half the votes, a French-style runoff among those who got at least 15 percent are held two weeks later. For another 152 members, Hungary uses classical proportional representation (PR), with multiparty lists in each of its nineteen counties. Citizens choose one party, and seats are awarded proportional to voting strength. The remaining 58 seats are parceled out on the basis of how parties had done at the first two levels. The complexity of this voting system is one reason Hungarian voter turnout is not high. As with most electoral systems, it deliberately overrepresents large parties at the expense of small ones.

What happened with the original catchall party that governed Hungary for four years, the Hungarian Democratic Forum? In a parallel with Poland's Solidarity, the HDF made several inept moves, splintered, and suffered a backlash over economic restructuring, which left many Hungarians poorer. The HDF got only 12 percent of the PR vote and 37 seats. Several small parties, some with extreme nationalist orientations, failed to win any seats. Unlike Poland, there was no anticlerical backlash in Hungary, as the Hungarian Catholic Church has no monopoly on religious life and had few political demands.

The big disappointment of the 1994 elections were the Young Democrats, known by their Hungarian initials as *Fidesz*. Until 1993, Fidesz membership was limited to those under 35 (although anyone could vote for it). This gave Fidesz a fresh and somewhat cheeky image. With an orange as its symbol (sometimes with a smile on it), Fidesz was the most free-market and socially open of all Hungarian parties. Support for Fidesz grew in the early 1990s, but then things went wrong. Fidesz officials were found misusing party funds; they no longer looked so clean and fresh. Their free-market doctrine began to ring hollow among unemployed younger Hungarians. Fidesz won only 7 percent of the PR votes and a mere 20 seats. It was a clever idea, but even youths grow old.

viewpoints—outnumber, detest, and routinely triumphed over the liberal intellectuals of Budapest. The 1994 electoral victory of the Socialists covered over the split but did not end it.

Hungary's potentially dangerous national question concerns the 3 million ethnic Hungarians in neighboring Slovakia, Yugoslavia, and Romania and introduced an outbidding tendency in domestic politics. The parties of the right focused concern on the lost brothers; some politicians mentioned possible changes in borders. Refugees from Romania and the fighting in Yugoslavia kept this issue alive and forced politicians to pronounce themselves in favor of doing something—no one knew what—to help. The populist wing of the Hungarian Democratic Forum (which later left the HDF) stressed this issue in bidding against the Smallholders, who are perhaps the most extreme in this regard. Language rights for the Magyar minority in Slovakia are closely followed in the Hungarian media and are a source of Hungarian-Slovak tension. Hungarian concern over the 400,000 ethnic Magyars in Serbia's Voivodina was a worrisome factor in Budapest's foreign policy.

Several Romanian parties at first played a nationalistic politics of outbidding with each other, chiefly over the Hungarian minority in Transylvania, 1.6 million people who have been under pressure for decades. In the (not completely fair) 1992 elections, 15 percent of Romanians voted for one of six extreme nationalist parties. The (ex-Communist) Social Democrats emerged as the largest party but short of a majority, so they formed a coalition with the hysterically anti-Hungarian National Unity party, the hysterically anti-Semitic Great Romania party, and the Socialist Labor party (unreconstructed Communists, extremely nationalistic). Catering to chauvinist sentiment, the Bucharest government rehabilitated World War II fascist dictator Ion Antonescu, complete with statue and laudatory media portrayals. Romania is possibly the most nationalistic country in Europe.

Bulgarians take out their frustrations on their Muslim minority, a substantial million or more, some 13 percent of the population. Bulgaria was freed from the Ottomans only in 1878 (formal independence was declared only in 1908) and still fears Turkish reconquest, in which the local Turks and Bulgarian Muslims, now severely discriminated against, would serve as a fifth column. Forbidden to openly organize an ethnic or religious party, Bulgarian Turks and Muslims vote massively for their Movement for Rights and Freedoms (MRF). The renamed Communists, the Bulgarian Socialist party, won the 1994 election in part by attacking the MRF as a sinister threat.

The politics of nationalist outbidding pulled Czechoslovakia apart. Several Slovak parties goaded each other into ever-stronger stances on Slovak autonomy, then to sovereignty, and finally to independence. Surveys showed most Slovaks never favored outright independence, but the debate among Slovak politicians escalated to separation. The Christian Democrats of former Slovak Prime Minister Jan Čarnogurský were always somewhat nationalistic but not necessarily separatist.

Bulgaria

Bulgaria has lagged behind Central Europe but has done better than some of its Balkan neighbors. In 1990, the Bulgarian Socialist party (BSP, the renamed Communists), by not allowing sufficient time for other parties to campaign, by their control over the countryside, and by some outright rigging, won a majority of seats in a 400-member Grand National Assembly, which wrote a new constitution.

Bulgaria's elections for a new 240-member parliament in 1991 were its first free and fair elections. An anti-Communist catchall, the Union of Democratic Forces (UDF), won with 34 percent of the vote and 111 seats, nine seats short of half. (In a separate election, philosophy professor Zhelyu Zhelev, head of the UDF, won the presidency, but this is not a powerful office.) Small parties, some of which had splintered off from the UDF, fell under 4 percent and got no seats. The Socialists, however, were a very close second with 33 percent and 106 seats. The only other party to make it into parliament was the Movement for Rights and Freedoms (MRF), which everyone understood represented ethnic Turks and Bulgarian Muslims, even though openly ethnic and religious parties are illegal. The MRF won 8 percent and 23 seats and formed a shaky coalition with the UDF that changed prime ministers frequently and made little progress in privatizing.

Bulgaria suffered economic decline. Subsidies for still state-owned industries fed inflation, lawlessness grew, and workers, farmers, and the elderly suffered. The result in 1994 elections was a BSP-majority parliament that named bright, young ex-Communist Zhan Videnov prime minister. He did not favor the free market, and the Bulgarian economy declined worse. "You can't get a country more bankrupt than Bulgaria," said a Western banker in 1996. Many Bulgarian ex-party people got rich, many through corruption. A former prime minister and leading member of the Socialist party was shot dead outside his house, probably over who would get what part of the spoils. The result: in late 1996 Bulgarians elected the UDF's Petar Stoyanov president with more than 60 percent of the vote (against the BSP's Ivan Marazov). By now the Bulgarian economy was a basket case that cried out for reforms. This will be difficult, for the largest party in parliament is still the BSP. The lesson, slow to penetrate in the Balkans: he who delays economic reform suffers economic decline.

Current Prime Minister Mečiar played the nationalist card without restraint on his way to power, pushing Čarnogurský and other Slovak politicians to match or outdo him. The worsening economic situation, in which Slovak unemployment was double the Czech rate, bolstered the nationalists' arguments. The result was a nonviolent "velvet divorce" that only a minority wished. The most hideous nationalist outbidding occurred in Yugoslavia, where (as we shall explore in greater detail in Chapter 9), two of the country's most hysterical nationalists, Serbia's Milošević and Croatia's Tudjman, were elected on chauvinistic platforms in 1990, paving the way for Yugoslavia's breakup in 1991. Calmer voices were shouted down, and moderates suffered possible electoral fraud. Yugoslavia should remind nationalists of where their policies can lead.

CABINET INSTABILITY

Another problem with too many parties in parliament is the difficulty this makes in forming and sustaining a cabinet. In parliamentary systems—the standard in most of Europe—a cabinet (also known as the "government," what Americans call an "administration") is formed only with the consent of a majority of the legislature. If it lacks a majority, it will soon fall on a vote of no confidence; that is, a majority will vote against it. This is almost the opposite of the U.S. separation of powers; European countries have more nearly a fusion of powers. The European system can work fast and well if a single party wins a majority of seats in parliament; its leaders name the cabinet and bills they want and get them.

But this is rarely the case. In most European countries, one party doesn't win enough seats to govern alone; several parties must form a coalition that commands a majority of the parliament. The more parties in this coalition, the less stable it tends to be. If one or more members of the coalition don't like the prime minister's policy, they walk out of the coalition or threaten to do so. Perhaps they represent only 2 percent of parliament, but it may be the crucial 2 percent that drops the coalition from 51 percent to 49 percent. Accordingly, much of the effort of a prime minister is in holding the coalition together. To do this, he or she usually must avoid radical new policies that one or more coalition parties might oppose. Such systems, then, often resist change and end in what the French call *immobilisme*, getting stuck over a major policy issue. Even a small party can block a proposed change. Italy and Israel are often examples of this.

Poland in the early 1990s had five- to seven-party coalition cabinets. And, sure enough, they produced instability and immobilism. In June 1992 Poland got its first woman prime minister, 46-year-old law professor Hanna Suchocka of the Democratic Union. She put together a seven-member coalition but could hold it together for less than a year even by avoiding and compromising on some of the tough privatization questions. Privatization was an issue that angered Catholic nationalists in the coalition. Hungary, with just a three-party coalition, experienced difficulties in deciding what to do with lands the Communists had seized decades ago from their owners. Should they be returned to the children? The Smallholders thought so, but many doubted that tiny peasant holdings would be productive and efficient. Even in Bulgaria, where a 4-percent threshold had eliminated over 30 parties, the Union of Democratic Forces lacked a parliamentary majority and depended on the support of the small ethnic Turkish party, whose support was not always forthcoming. Considering the magnitude of the problems to be faced, we may expect many East European cabinets will continue to suffer from instability and immobilism.

THE KEY ISSUE

The main political issue, around which East European politics polarize, is over the pace and pain of economic reform. Everyone wants prosperity on the West European market model, but some approach the problem with the naiveté of a cargo cult: They see the results but don't grasp what makes the thing work. The (classic) liberals, such as Balcerowicz of Poland and Czech Prime Minister Václav Klaus, demand rapid marketization and privatization. If marketization—freeing prices to find their own level with few or no fixed prices or government subsidies—is painful, privatization is worse.

Privatization—turning previously socially or state-owned industries over to private owners—cannot be accomplished without at least some unfairness, but it must be done. Polish economists who participated in the shock therapy argue that failure to privatize quickly was a major error. Don't worry about unfairness, they say; just get it done fast so as to unleash restructuring and investment. To marketize while stalling on privatization prolongs and deepens inflation, the problem in most Balkan countries.

Economically the free marketeers were right, but politically they got a backlash. Few citizens understand the fine points of the Chicago or Harvard schools of economics. Privatization means that some new entrepreneurs do extremely well while employees of money-losing state industries see their salaries eroded by inflation. Such people turn bitterly resentful and receptive to demagogic solutions. Selling industries to foreign capitalists stirs nationalist anger. (Some factories should simply be given away for the sake of the new investment and technology the foreigners would bring.) Many citizens feel the country is being "sold for a dollar." Throughout the region, ex-Communists gained control of enterprises, often unfairly. A Czech device, soon adopted by most governments of the region, of giving citizens coupons with which to buy shares as state industries are sold off ("coupon privatization," sort of enrolling everyone in mutual funds) theoretically spreads the wealth, but still leaves winners and losers. The possibilities of privatization turning into political resentment that can be harvested by demagogic politicians are obvious, and such demagogues are just as likely to be found on the left as on the right.

TO PUNISH OR TO START ANEW?

Another issue in East European politics is whether to root out and punish the officials of the old Communist regimes. Many citizens had hard feelings, especially

Economic Decline and Recovery

In most of Central Europe after 1989, economies plunged downward but in a few years recovered. Most Balkan lands just kept declining. The reason for the difference is not hard to find. A 1996 World Bank study of 26 East European and ex-Soviet economies found that those who freed and privatized their economies sooner showed faster growth.

Poland, under the guidance of the U.S.-trained Finance Minister Leszek Balcerowicz and with the advice of Harvard economist Jeffrey Sachs, marketized almost overnight, at the start of 1990, in what was called "shock therapy." Indeed it was; some thought the shock would kill the patient. Polish inflation soared and industrial output dropped. Within two years, however, things started looking up. Inflation slowed, the *złoty* traded freely on currency markets, and output and exports grew, giving Poland the fastest percentage GDP growth in all of Europe. (Granted, that's starting from a pretty low base.) Some Poles made a lot of money quickly while others fell behind, contributing to the voter backlash in favor of the Socialists in the 1993 and 1995 elections.

Czechoslovakia tried much the same thing, but many Slovaks didn't like it, and Slovak politicians made it one of their grounds for divorce. Hungary had a head start on the process, having cautiously edged into market and private enterprise with the New Economic Mechanism of the 1970s. Overall, the Czech Republic has the best record for low inflation and unemployment and rapid privatization of all East Europe.

The Balkans, as usual, lagged. Romania and Bulgaria, under not-so-ex-Communist rulers, privatized either haltingly or not at all. To be sure, these were always some of Europe's poorest countries, but now their economies deteriorated until their voters revolted. That is one of the lessons of the modern world: you can't fool the economy or the people for long. If you don't put food on the table, they'll vote you out. Propaganda and secret police can no longer keep people isolated and docile.

Published economic statistics are deceptive, because much of the economy is off the books to avoid taxes. There are few reliable figures for ex-Yugoslavia and Albania. The best figures for 1994 per capita GDP at purchasing-power parity (which figures in the relative cost of living in each country) was reckoned at:

Czech Republic	$7,910
Slovakia	6,660
Hungary	6,310
Poland	5,380
Bulgaria	4,230
Romania	2,920

In comparison, the average for the 15 members of the European Union (West Europe) was $18,170 and for the United States was $25,000.

about the security police, who had spied on people, ruined their careers, and sent dissenters to prison. Crooked Communist officials had feathered their own nest for many years, in some cases stashing money abroad. A giant network of informers had reported to the security police on their friends. Many wanted to open the "poison files" and find out who exactly did what. The term for this, coined in Prague, was the Latin "lustration" (related to illustration), the making of things clear in a purification rite.

The trouble was, where would lustration stop? Suppose an official had just been doing his or her job, had not informed on anyone, and hadn't even been an enthusiastic party member? Should he or she be punished? Suppose an informer had just given the security police occasional snippets of irrelevant information designed to keep the police off track? He or she would still be listed in the files as an "informer." Lustration could potentially ruin thousands of innocent people in its pursuit of dozens of seriously guilty ones.

This process went farthest in former East Germany, where miles of files were opened. It was found that dissidents had informed on other dissidents, husbands on wives, friends upon each other. It was horrifying and ruined many relationships and a few political careers. Things didn't go so far in the Czech Republic; President Havel was against recrimination and in favor of a new beginning. President Wałęsa in Poland likewise opposed and defeated a lustration law. But the issue still smolders and was one of the arguments of Hungarian rightist Istvan Csurka: ex-Communists are still in high places; we must smell them out and punish them. Except for those accused of specific crimes, East Europe is probably well advised to avoid mass lustration and to get on with building a new economy and society.

THE RIP VAN WINKLE EFFECT

The newborn party systems of East Europe bear striking resemblance to those of the interwar years, almost as if the region had woken in 1990 from a sleep of more than half a century. The earlier period was characterized by extreme fractionalization of the party system, difficulty in forming and maintaining coalitions, immoderate ideological fighting, and general chaos that mostly ended in authoritarian rule. Some of these parties revived briefly after World War II, only to be crushed by the Communists. In a few cases, the interwar parties reappeared in post-Communist East Europe, at least in name.

The Polish *Sejm* in the early 1920s was home to thirty-four parties. Unable to stand the squabbling and paralysis, Jozef Piłsudski, the founder of modern Poland, seized power in a coup in 1926 and established a military dictatorship. The Czechoslovak parliament contained at least thirteen parties, not counting independent deputies. Forming a Prague government required the participation of four to six centrist parties, but these coalitions were moderately effective, and the

Albania

Albania, like most Balkan countries, had trouble establishing democracy. In 1992 the Democratic party ousted the (formerly Communist) Socialist party with 62 percent of the vote and 92 (out of 140) seats in Albania's parliament. But in the 1996 election the government used its control of the mass media, massive fraud, and intimidation. In protest, most opposition parties withdrew from the election, leaving the Democrats free to claim 101 seats. Police beat protesters. President and Democrat leader Sali Berisha, himself a former Communist, tried to get a new constitution in 1994 that would have given him more power; it was rejected in a referendum. In 1995 Berisha pushed through a "genocide law" prohibiting senior members of the old Communist party from running in elections until 2002. This conveniently got rid of 70 opposition figures. Berisha also controls radio and television and the revived Sigurimi security police, now called SHIKU. Although cooperating closely with the United States on regional security, Albania stayed very Balkan in its domestic politics.

system did not break down into authoritarianism. Interwar Hungary, on the other hand, was authoritarian almost from its founding. Under the regency of Admiral Horthy, party formation and elections were limited and controlled, but some ten parties existed, with half a dozen in the Diet at any one time. Bulgaria's last free elections in 1931 produced a National Assembly of nine parties, not counting independents. A 1934 military coup led to a royal dictatorship that lasted until 1944.

Might the past to some degree predict the future? Certain continuities echo over the decades. Many Poles, including Lech Wałęsa, hold a very positive image of Marshal Piłsudski as the savior of Poland. Wałęsa's exasperation with extreme multipartism, a fragmented parliament, and cabinet instability was pushing him to what Poles call "the presidential solution," a redrawn Polish presidency with de Gaulle-type powers. Wałęsa was voted out before he could obtain such powers. Between the wars, many Slovaks resented rule from Prague and flocked to the clerico-fascist banners of an independent Nazi puppet state. The Hungarian urban-populist split that characterized interwar politics continued remarkably intact.

Almost everyone understands that East Europe's chances for economic survival and prosperity depend on a relationship with the European Union, and the EU does not automatically accept all applicants. Indeed, for selfish economic reasons, Brussels is slow and cautious on expanding membership. Applicants must be politically democratic and have a prosperous market economy; the EU can't afford any more poor members. Extremism of any sort would kill the chances of membership or association with the EU and discourage foreign investment. Capitalist interest in East Europe covaries with the probability of a given country's entrance into the EU. The really big investors are not so much interested in the Polish or Hungarian market as they are in using low wages to produce for a European-wide market ("Belgian productivity at Filipino wages").

The international context is not completely favorable for East Europe. Slow growth and a shortage of investment capital in the West means western investors are unlikely to ride to the rescue in large numbers. The genocidal horrors of ex-Yugoslavia could fan nationalism throughout the region. West Europe and the United States did not respond strongly or quickly; they do not define themselves as the stabilizers of East Europe.

Aspects of polarized pluralism are at work in East Europe and have produced center-fleeing tendencies that have already led to the breakup of one country. The economic strains of marketization and the jealousies aroused by privatization put regimes and party systems under incredible pressures. But many East Europeans understand the difficulties they face and are prepared to stay with nonextremist parties. In a situation ripe for demagoguery, only in Slovakia and ex-Yugoslavia did elected demagogues take power. The past does not necessarily predict the future.

SUGGESTED READINGS

BALCEROWICZ, LESZEK. *Capitalism, Socialism, Transformation*. New York: Oxford University Press, 1995.

BERGLUND, STEN, AND JAN AKE DELLENBRANT, eds. *The New Democracies in Eastern Europe: Party Systems and Political Cleavages*, 2d. ed. Brookfield, VT: Edward Elgar, 1994.

BLEJER, MARIO, AND FABRIZIO CORICELLI, eds. *The Making of Economic Reform in Eastern Europe*. Brookfield, VT: E. Elgar, 1995.

BROWN, J.F. *Hopes and Shadows: Eastern Europe after Communism*. Durham, NC: Duke University Press, 1994.

CAMPBELL, JOHN L., AND OVE K. PEDERSON, eds. *Legacies of Change: Transformations of Postcommunist European Economies*. Hawthorne, NY: Aldine de Gruyter, 1996.

GALLAGHER, TOM. *Romania After Ceauşescu: The Politics of Intolerance*. New York: Columbia University Press, 1995.

HOFFMANN, EVA. *Exit into History: A Journey Through the New East Europe*. New York: Viking, 1993.

LEFF, CAROL SKALNIK. *The Czech and Slovak Republics*. Boulder, CO: Westview, 1996.

MILLARD, FRANCES. *The Anatomy of the New Poland: Post-Communist Politics in Its First Phase*. Brookfield, VT: E. Elgar, 1994.

NAGORSKI, ANDREW. *The Birth of Freedom: Shaping Lives and Societies in the New Eastern Europe*. New York: Simon & Schuster, 1993.

OLSON, DAVID M., AND PHILIP NORTON, eds. *The New Parliaments of Central and Eastern Europe*. Portland, OR: Frank Cass, 1996.

PLASSER, FRITZ, AND ANDREAS PRIBERSKY, eds. *Political Culture in Central Europe*. Brookfield, VT: Avebury, 1996.

PRIDHAM, GEOFFREY, AND PAUL LEWIS. *Stabilising Fragile Democracies: New Party Systems in Southern and Eastern Europe*. New York: Routledge, 1996.

RAMET, SABRINA PETRA. *Social Currents in Eastern Europe: The Sources and Consequences of the Great Transformation*, 2d ed. Durham, NC: Duke University Press, 1995.

ROSENBERG, TINA. *The Haunted Land: Facing Europe's Ghosts after Communism*. New York: Random House, 1995.

TARAS, RAYMOND. *Consolidating Democracy in Poland*. Boulder, CO: Westview, 1995.

CHAPTER NINE

The Horrors of Yugoslavia

THE OBVIOUS CULPRIT

Many observers of Yugoslavia blame its recent horrors on Serbia in general and its president, Slobodan Milošević, a thuggish authoritarian manipulator and opportunist, in particular. He deserves plenty of blame but hardly explains the whole situation. Others, often those who know little about Yugoslavia, blame centuries of ethnic hatred; when the Communists lost their grip ancient angers erupted anew. There is hatred, to be sure, but it is not ancient and is not a complete explanation. Forgotten by many in all this is the obvious culprit: Yugoslavia's President-for-Life Josip Broz Tito. To put it mildly, Tito built his postwar Yugoslavia poorly, leaving it ripe for disintegration, the signs of which appeared long before his death in 1980.

Tito built a contrived, artificial system that seemed almost designed to rip itself apart (see box). Superficially, Yugoslavia looked like the mildest and most-reformed of the Communist countries of East Europe. Closer up, Yugoslavia was a shambolic, improvised system that depended on Tito's personal power and charisma, the old-boy network of his Partisan officers, and the ubiquitous presence of the UDBa security police. Despite the fact that Yugoslavs and foreigners could generally come and go in what appeared to be a relaxed atmosphere, Yugoslavia was still very much a Communist country. Sympathetic Western observers often missed this point, so intent were some of them to portray Yugoslavia as a plausible "third way" between socialism and capitalism.

How did Yugoslavia plunge so deeply into horror, and what, if anything, can be done about it? The historical background of the tragedy merits a somewhat more detailed consideration than we gave it in earlier chapters.

THE ORIGINS OF SERBIAN NATIONALISM

Medieval Serbia, Eastern Orthodox in faith and centered in the Kosovo region (south of the present Serbian core area), was an impressive kingdom from the twelfth to fourteenth centuries, but the Ottoman Turkish victory at Kosovo Polje in 1389 crushed Serbia for nearly five centuries. Serbs never forgot their kingdom or forgave the Turkish occupiers. Embellished by legend, the figures of the *haiduk*, the anti-Turkish bandit, and the *chetnik*, the anti-Turkish guerrilla, commanded respect. To fight Turks was a noble task, no matter what the odds. Montenegrins, who are simply a branch of Serbs, still note proudly that the Turks never subdued them. Starting in the late seventeenth century, as Austria pushed back the Turks, Serbs fled Ottoman control for protection under the Habsburgs. They were welcome; land was not scarce since local populations had been decimated by the Ottomans, and the Serbs, who had been fighting the Turks for centuries, were tough settler-soldiers on the Military Frontier (*Vojna Krajina*, the precursor to the present Krajina region of Croatia), the long-standing buffer zone between the Habsburg and Ottoman Empires. This is the origin of the widespread Serbian communities deep in Croatia and Bosnia. The longstanding problem—the connecting link between Sarajevo in 1914, the chief recruits of the Partisans in World War II, and Sarajevo in 1992—has been Serbs living outside of Serbia.

In these mixed areas, Serbs generally got along with their Croatian Catholic and Bosnian Muslim neighbors. They spoke the same language, what came to be known as Serbo-Croatian, although Serbian is written in Cyrillic and Croatian in Latin, because the former were Christianized from Constantinople, the latter from Rome. The Bosnian Muslims, also known as Bosniaks, originated in a heretical Slavic sect, the Bogumil Christians, who were persecuted by both main Christian branches. Under the Turks, the Bogumils converted to Islam, giving rise to the blond, blue-eyed Muslims and Alpine mosques one finds in Bosnia today.

The three groups lived in relative peace under Ottomans and Habsburgs because sovereignty lay far away, either in Istanbul or Vienna. There was no quarrel over who was to be boss on a given piece of turf or who had the last word in law; laws came from afar, for some centuries in Turkish and then in German (or, in Croatia, in Hungarian). The difficulty came when these people had to rule themselves. As the Ottoman Empire weakened, the Serbs of Shumadiya revolted against the Turks in 1804 and by 1830 won autonomy as a principality within the Empire. The major Russian victory over the Turks in 1878 brought independence to most of the Balkans, including Serbia. The core of the new Serbian kingdom was much farther north than that of the old kingdom; the capital was now Belgrade, on the Danube right across from Hungarian territory. The 1878 Turkish defeat also gave Austria control of Bosnia, and there the trouble started, for Serbia claimed Bosnia as well.

Then, as now, an appreciable fraction (but never a majority) of the Bosnian population was Serb. At times Bosnia had been tied dynastically to the ancient kingdom of Serbia and later to Croatia, but neither constitutes a valid historical claim. The new Serbia was fired by the modern notion of nationalism and took its cues from the recent unification of Italy under Piedmont. Serbia was to be the Piedmont of the South Slavs, liberating them from foreign rule and gathering them under its own benevolent rule. Serbs saw themselves as entitled to this role as the preeminent anti-Turkish fighters. At this same time, pan-Slavism deepened ties between Serbia and Russia, a tie that exists to this day.

Austria's annexation of Bosnia in 1908 enraged Serbian nationalists both in Serbia and Bosnia. At the University of Belgrade, Serb students from Bosnia joined the underground nationalist society Unity or Death, which included Serbian officers. Much like modern terrorists quietly receive state sponsorship, Serbian officers gave Bosnian students revolvers and grenades. On June 28, 1914, they assassinated visiting Austrian Archduke Franz-Ferdinand and his wife in Sarajevo. The day was the hallowed anniversary of the Serbian defeat at Kosovo Polje (Field of Blackbirds) and the day of Serbia's patron saint, St. Vitus, *Vidovdan*.

THE FIRST FAILURE OF YUGOSLAVIA

Yugoslavia began falling apart almost as soon as it was born after World War I. When they lived under others, Serbs, Croats, and Bosniaks had little difficulty. Croats and Bosniaks did not especially like being ruled by, respectively, Hungarians and Austrians. With a certain amount of good will on all sides, the Serbian monarchy in 1918 pulled together the Kingdom of the Serbs, Croats and Slovenes. Croatia also had a specific fear: that without Serbian protection Italy would seize the Dalmatian coast (which Italy later did, in World War II). But within a few years Croats discovered that being ruled by Belgrade was no improvement over being ruled by Budapest. Croat politicians complained about biased and indifferent Serbian administration. Serbian nationalists saw them as disruptive ingrates; one fanatic Montenegrin gunman shot down Croatia's top representatives on the floor of parliament in 1928. Exasperated, King Alexander proclaimed a royal dictatorship in 1929, renamed the country Yugoslavia (Land of the South Slavs), and divided it into artificial administrative districts named after rivers (on the French revolutionary model).

By now, most of Yugoslavia's nationalities harbored extremist movements. Ante Pavelić, a Croat admirer of Mussolini, founded the Ustasha (Uprising), a Croatian fascist movement. The Internal Macedonian Revolutionary Organization (IMRO), with Bulgarian backing, practiced terrorism in an effort to recover a unified Macedonia from the Serbs and Greeks. Bulgarian Premier Stambuliski was an IMRO victim in 1923. Another IMRO gunman—with Ustasha, Hungarian, and Italian help—assassinated King Alexander in Marseille in 1934. The Serbs, however, continued to see Yugoslavia as simply the Greater Serbia, a monarchy ruled from Belgrade.

It took the Germans all of eleven days to conquer Yugoslavia in the spring of 1941; many Croats welcomed the Germans, who indeed set up Pavelić in a Croatian puppet state with greatly enlarged borders that included Bosnia and some of Serbia. Ustasha massacres of whole Serbian villages in Croatia and Bosnia along with a Croatian concentration camp killed at least 350,000 Serbs. (Some claim the true number is 750,000. The Partisans murdered some 100,000 Croats, alleged Ustashas, in revenge in 1945.) Serbs have never forgotten their holocaust and act in many ways like Israelis, determined to shoot first rather than let themselves be put at the mercy of their enemies. Some people suppose that the violent enmities that characterize today's Yugoslavia trace back to ancient hatreds. This is not quite accurate; for most of history the several nationalities got along. Current hatreds trace back only to the killings of World War II.

Neighboring states also had little regard for Yugoslavia, which they considered artificial and an intrusion on their former holdings. Hitler remembered that Slovenia had been part of Austria and ordered it returned to the Reich. Italy took the Dalmatian coast, which had long been under the Republic of Venice (except for Dubrovnik, renaissance Ragusa, an independent republic). Bulgaria harkened to its medieval kingdom and took Macedonia, where the language is very close to Bulgarian. Albania took the Albanian-inhabited part of Kosovo, and Hungary took the part of the Voivodina that was most heavily settled by Hungarians. All the neighbors except Greece and Romania took a piece of the Yugoslav pie.

Was Yugoslavia, then, simply not meant to be? The idea of uniting the small, Slavic-speaking nationalities of the region was not a bad one, for most were too small to stand on their own. What had killed it was Serbian domination. The Serbs, after all, were never a majority of the country's population, but all power was centralized in Serbia's capital of Belgrade. The Yugoslav Communists thought they had the cure: a federation in which no one group would dominate. This was the vision they sold to Yugoslavs of all nationalities and used to build their Partisan units. Their chief recruits were Serbs from Croatia and Bosnia, the victims of fascist extermination efforts, but Partisan units could be found in every part of the country. By the war's end, the Partisans had liberated roughly half of Yugoslavia; the Third Ukrainian Army swept the Germans out of the northernmost part of the country in 1945.

THE SECOND FAILURE OF YUGOSLAVIA

Why did Communist Yugoslavia appear to work for some decades? First, Tito was a genuinely charismatic figure whom even anti-Communists respected. With a Croat father and Slovene mother, Tito was above the nationalities quarrel and could assure the other nationalities that he would not restore Serbian hegemony. Second, Tito ruled with a network of Partisan veterans, the elite of the League of Communists of Yugoslavia (as the Party was called), inserted into all important positions. Third, Stalin's 1948 blunder in expelling Yugoslavia from the

Yugoslavia: A Fake State

Tito's Yugoslavia was no more stable or durable than interwar Yugoslavia. Tito, trained as a Stalinist, still carried the Stalinist conceit that you can set up any system you wish and force it on a population. The Titoist system was not only totally fake but constantly changed from above, never rooting itself into the hearts of the people. Some weaknesses:

1. A new constitution every decade. According to Titoist theory, the system was so innovative and evolving so fast that no fixed constitution could keep up with reality. A new constitution was needed about every decade. These flaky, experimental constitutions generated no sense of legitimacy. The 1946 constitution was a copy of the Soviet Union's 1936 Stalin constitution. The 1953 constitution then repudiated Stalinism. The 1963 constitution included a *five*-chamber legislature. The 1974 constitution set up an extreme form of federalism. They were working on a fifth one in the 1980s.

2. An extreme form of federalism. Especially with the 1974 constitution, Yugoslavia turned hyperfederal, even confederal. The republics owned much heavy industry. Both chambers of the Yugoslav parliament gave equal numbers of deputies to each republic regardless of population; it was like the U.S. Congress having two Senates. Politics focused on power in the republics.

3. A collegial presidency. Yugoslavia's nine-member collective presidency had one member from each republic and both autonomous provinces (Voivodina and Kosovo) plus the head of the Communist party. The acting president was to be elected by his peers for just one year, Swiss-style. While Tito lived, he was permanent president. After he died, the presidency got stuck. A quarrel among the republics over who was to be president was the last step in pulling Yugoslavia apart in 1991.

4. No opposition parties. There was one party, which took the name of League of Communists of Yugoslavia (organized at the republic level, so that one was a member of the League of Communists of Croatia, for example). A front organization, the Socialist Alliance, drew from a variety of "self-managing" organizations to nominate candidates, all controlled by the LCY. Thus elections were essentially fake. This in turn meant:

5. No cross-cutting cleavages. Keeping with Communist theory, every Yugoslav was a "worker." There was no middle class. As a result, no cross-cutting cleavages developed that connected workers to workers and middle class to middle class across republic lines. Parties based on cross-cutting cleavages help cement pluralistic countries together.

6. No capitalists. A little-noted advantage of capitalism is that it gives the ambitious something to pursue besides political power. Ambitious Yugoslavs under communism had only one outlet: control of republic-level economic and political structures, which they pursued greedily. Yugoslavia as a nation mattered not a bit, only power in the republics. Institutionally, Tito's Yugoslavia was poorly thought out and soon paid the price.

Communist camp—Stalin thought that Tito was not sufficiently obedient—rallied Yugoslavs of all nationalities against the Soviet threat. Fourth, as a result of this expulsion, Tito experimented with a "middle way" economic system that brought more freedom and economic improvement for some years. This created a sense of confidence and unity and brought in abundant foreign credits. And, fifth, Tito encouraged a federalism far deeper than the Soviet variety. Yugoslavia's six republics were staffed by local talent and made highly autonomous decisions.

Why then did Yugoslavia fall apart eleven years after Tito died? On closer examination, the above attributes were either short-lived or inherently flawed. Charismatic leaders do not groom charismatic successors. Yugoslavia's constitution named Tito president-for-life; a Swiss-style collegial presidency with a rotating chairman succeeded him. In effect, no one was in charge after Tito died in 1980. Further, by the late 1980s the Partisan network had largely been replaced by younger leaders—many of them nationalists at the republic level—and the cohesion forged in battle fell apart. Yugoslavia's "market socialist" economy, chronically unstable and constantly "reformed," careened back and forth between relatively free and centrally controlled. Inflation was endemic. Much depended on foreign loans, and Yugoslavia's debt climbed to dangerous levels.

Worst of all, Tito had not solved Yugoslavia's nationalities problems. There was, to be sure, federalism, too much of it. Each republic had its own steel mill, railway network, and jealous regard for its rights. Belgrade, however, attempted to retain fiscal and monetary control, including money supply and foreign exchange, and this is where tempers flared. Slovenia and Croatia, the most advanced and productive republics and the biggest earners of foreign currency, argued that they should keep their gains. The backward republics, led by Serbia, argued that they needed major capital investments to bring them up to standards. Croats and Slovenes argued that such investments were inefficient and wasteful. (Similar regional resentments now flourish in Italy, where the prosperous north dislikes being taxed to develop the poor south.) The break came when Zagreb and Ljubljana could no longer tolerate the profligate printing of money by the Serbian-controlled federal government in Belgrade, which produced hyperinflation in the early 1990s. The Titoist slogan, "Brotherhood and Unity," by then rang hollow.

In 1990 republic elections—there never were nationwide elections—Franjo Tudjman, a former Communist and general turned Croatian chauvinist, won in Croatia, and Slobodan Milošević, a former Communist and banker turned Serbian chauvinist, won in Serbia. By that point, with the two strongest and least flexible personalities of Yugoslavia's two leading republics whipping up their respective constituencies, breakup was nearly inevitable. The immediate cause of Milošević's victory was agitation by the ethnic Albanians of Kosovo for greater autonomy. These Kosovari, as the Albanians there are called, form some 90 percent of the population. Serbs hate them and fear they will eventually unite with neighboring Albania, which indeed happened during World War II. Milošević launched his political career in 1987 with an electrifying nationalist speech to Kosovo Serbs in

Searching for Blame

Who is the bad guy in ex-Yugoslavia? The media concentrated on the depredations of irregular Serbian forces in Bosnia. The truth is a little more complicated. First, all sides committed atrocities in the fighting (but the Bosnian Serbs more). There are few angels in the Balkans. Many Serbian families still remember losing a parent or other relative in the Ustasha massacres in Croatia and Bosnia during World War II. Serb fears were perhaps exaggerated, but the appearance of Croatian units in 1991 styling themselves and dressed in the uniforms of Ustashas was like waving a red flag in front of a bull. Besides, philosophically, if Croatia can withdraw from Yugoslavia, why cannot the Serbian areas of Croatia withdraw from Croatia? This, of course, is the flaw in "self-determination": it doesn't specify which *size* community can determine itself.

The 1971 book by Bosnian President Alija Izetbegović indicated that Bosnian Muslims ought to be the masters of Bosnia, where they were a plurality (44 percent) but not a majority. To Serbs, it sounded like an Islamic fundamentalist state that would persecute Bosnian Serbs. The initial government of independent Bosnia in 1992 welcomed all to participate, and some Serbs, especially intellectuals in cosmopolitan Sarajevo, felt completely at home with it. Some Serbs actually fought on the Bosnian side.

Outside observers were also appalled at the fact that Bosnian Serb militias seized about two-thirds of Bosnia's territory, although Serbs are only about a third of the population. Actually, the seizures largely reflected tracts of land owned by Serbian farmers. The Ottomans had favored the Bosnian Muslims, who tended to become town-dwelling artisans and functionaries, leaving land in the hills to poor Serbian peasants. Over the ages, Serbs ended up owning most of the land.

Serbs blame Germany. They argue that newly unified Germany still dreams of a Nazi-type march to the east; this is why Germany recognized Croatia and Slovenia in 1991 and Bosnia in 1992, thus pressuring other Western powers to do the same. It's true that Germany is rather pro-Croat and Slovene out of old historical connections, but Germany argued that international recognition would calm the fighting by giving the new countries legitimacy and the right to purchase arms to defend themselves. German recognition of Croatia came after fighting was well under way; it is not clear that it either calmed or deepened the struggle. It may have been a mistake, but a plot it's not.

Serbs held they were *defending* their people. They denied that massacres even took place, or, if they did, then Serbs were the victims. (The news media were anti-Serb and regularly mislabeled photos and videos, Serbs claim.) The maddening thing about the Balkans is that everyone is the aggrieved party, all entitled to justice against their unjust neighbors. If you must blame something, blame the unworkable mess Tito left behind.

which he vowed to keep Kosovo Serbian. In office, he erased Kosovo's and Voivodina's autonomous status in 1989 and put them under Belgrade's direct rule, an unconstitutional move. Dissent in both areas was crushed with a heavy hand, and most Serbs approved.

The final breaking point came in 1991, when the members of the Federal Presidency could not agree on who was to be the new executive president and what his powers were to be. One Serb resigned, complaining he had insufficient power to meet the crisis. Then a Croatian, the reform-minded Ante Marković, was in line for the position, but Serbia blocked the move. Yugoslavia's curious collegial presidency, meant to hold the country together, pulled it apart. Without Tito, Yugoslavia simply did not have sufficient central executive authority; it was too federal to survive. After the Federal Presidency briefly considered an even looser confederation—they were unable to agree—Slovenia and Croatia declared their independence in June 1991, and fighting began.

THE WARS OF YUGOSLAV SUCCESSION

At this same time, or even a little before, Serbian areas of Croatia (Slovenia has few non-Slovenes), which had been getting weapons and training from the regular Yugoslav army for some time, declared their self-rule and set up a "Serb Republic of Krajina." When Bosnian Muslims declared an independent Bosnia in 1992, local Serbs declared their separation from Bosnia in another mini-republic. Serbs simply refused to be ruled by non-Serbs, arguing that they would again be in mortal danger. In defining what is a Serbian community—and most such communities in Croatia and Bosnia had mixed populations—Serbs were generous to themselves. If an area was even partially Serbian, they claimed it. Said one Bosnian Serb militia commander: "Where there is one Serbian grave, there is Serbia."

Greater Serbia—a mythical entity that would place under Belgrade's rule all the far-flung Serbian communities—was not Belgrade's initial goal. Initially in 1991, the goal was to preserve Yugoslavia. The war began as a conservative (i.e., ex-Communists who renamed themselves Socialists) Serbian coalition led by Milošević and including the commanders of old Yugoslavia's army, decided to use all means fair and foul to keep Yugoslavia together and under Belgrade's tutelage. Serbia had always seen itself as the heroic molder and pillar of Yugoslavia, and most of Yugoslavia's civil and military officers were Serbs. Accordingly, a great many federal jobs were at stake. Events appeared to unroll spontaneously, but that was not quite true. Rather, with varying degrees of control and efficiency the general staff of the old *Jugoslovenska Narodna Armija* (JNA, Yugoslav Peoples Army) in Belgrade planned and executed the war. The JNA first tried to preserve Yugoslavia by force of arms, but this quickly became impossible, so the JNA lowered its aims to carving out a Greater Serbia. In this war local Serb militias would do much of the dirty work in "ethnically cleansing" all areas of Serbian settlement in Croatia and Bosnia. Amid totally unreal claims of impending genocide

Maximum Extent of Serbian Conquest, 1992-94

against the Serbian people, Serbs who did not like this policy were isolated as "enemies of Serbia." Outside news sources were cut off, and Serbs were fed nothing but propaganda.

Although the JNA deliberately cloaked its actions in the fog of war, it appears that most lines of authority led back to the general staff in Belgrade. With nothing more than a change in patches (conveniently attached by velcro), Serbian officers, specialists (intelligence, communications, radar, artillery, and so on), and even ordinary soldiers rotated in and out of the Krajina (western Croatian) and Bosnian Serb armies. The commander of the Bosnian Serb army, Ratko Mladić, for example, was a career JNA officer who was assigned to his current post in May 1992, after consolidating Serbian gains in Krajina.

The Bosnian Serb and Krajina armies tried to preserve the fiction that they were purely local militias defending their respective Serbian communities. But weapons, ammunition, and fuel flowed from Serbia. Heavy equipment was returned to Serbia for repair. Seriously wounded were evacuated to Serbia. Military conscription continued in Serbia, although ostensibly "Serbia" was uninvolved in the fighting. Milošević in 1994, when he decided his overextended situation was unsustainable, cut military supplies to Krajina and Bosnia, both of which suffered major military losses in 1995, a measure of their dependency on Belgrade and the JNA.

The first fighting flared in mid-1991 as Slovenia, the rich northwest corner of old Yugoslavia, declared its independence and moved to take over border posts. In a few days of fighting with a few dozen killed (only 14 of them Slovenes), the JNA decided to withdraw, at least for the moment. Once they had taken care of Croatia, which declared its independence at the same time, they'd arrange things in Slovenia. But Croatia put up unexpected resistance. The Croats were terribly outgunned, relying on the meager arsenals of the territorial defense forces that had been set up in the old Yugoslavia. These resembled the U.S. National Guard except they relied entirely on republic (i.e., state) funding with which to purchase weapons, mostly from the federal government in Belgrade. The richest republic, Slovenia, did buy arms, including non-Yugoslav weapons. Poorer republics, such as Macedonia in the extreme south of the country, could afford almost nothing. "When the war began, the Serbs had as many tanks as we had rifles," said Croatian officers, who also claim that a few hundred armed Croatian civilians held off two JNA brigades attacking Vukovar for weeks. At the end, only 137 Croats surrendered, to the Serbs' amazement. "Vukovar is our Alamo," intoned Croatian officers, who swore revenge.

Nonetheless, with plentiful manpower and munitions, Serbian forces took from Croatia what Belgrade decided were areas of Serb settlement: Eastern Slavonia (including Vukovar), a spur of Western Slavonia, and the large bulge of Krajina that curves around Bosnia and pushes toward the coast. Then in 1992 they resumed the process by taking some two-thirds of Bosnia, from which they expelled the non-Serb population by the most unpretty of means—indiscriminate shelling of cities, rape as a weapon of war, property seizures, forced emigration, and outright murder—that aroused the conscience of humankind. In searching for secure multiple outlets to the sea, Serbian forces thrust westward to the Adriatic coast at Zadar and southward to the coast at Ploče, both connected to the interior by rail lines. It looked like Serbian nationalists would get their Greater Serbia.

But they did not. In 1991 and 1992, Croatia lost 27 percent of its territory to Serbs but regained most of it in 1995. The Croats had little choice. Always a curious shape, with its long, thin Dalmatian coast, Croatia was hollowed out to resemble a horseshoe and was not economically viable. The major Croatian city of Karlovac was 12 miles from Serbian-held territory, within artillery range. Serbian lines neared the coast, but the Croats beat them back. Belgrade had its eye on the important port of Zadar; otherwise Serbia's only outlet to the sea is the port of Bar in Montenegro, which stayed with Serbia in the rump Yugoslavia.

The most serious loss to Croatia was the westernmost bulge of the Krajina republic, specifically the town of Knin, through which pass the only rail line and

Hyped Hatred

Contrary to what much of the media told us, the fighting in Yugoslavia did not trace back to ancient ethnic hatreds. The hatreds were relatively recent—World War II—and then hyped even more recently by manipulative politicians on all sides. Most of Krajina did have a Serbian majority stemming from at least the late seventeenth century. Under the Austro-Hungarian empire, Serbs and Croats in this region lived together for centuries without violence. There was, to be sure, some social distance and occasional private disparaging remarks. Ethnic relations in Titoist Yugoslavia were not bad. (To be sure, if you said otherwise, you could do jail time.) Many neighborhoods were mixed, and people got along quite well. One such Sarajevo suburb still remembers kindly Dr. Radovan Karadžić, who helped all his neighbors—until he became the murderous head of the Bosnian Serb government. Intermarriage increased—by the 1980s one Yugoslav in seven was from a family of mixed heritage—and growing numbers declared their nationality as "Yugoslav" (rather than Serb, Croat, Muslim, and so on).

Ethnic cleansing was not a spontaneous outpouring of hatred but part of centrally planned campaigns to produce a climate of extreme ethnic stereotyping on all sides. The Belgrade government told Serbs to regard Croats as natural-born fascists who strive pathetically to imitate Germans and Austrians. Serbs were instructed to see themselves as the historically aggrieved party, as brave and sturdy defenders of an authentic Slavic culture against Turks and Teutons alike. Croats were told to regard Serbs as non-European barbarians who lived so long under the Turks they became like them. The Zagreb government instructed Croats to see themselves as Central European rather than Balkan and heirs to centuries of Habsburg high culture and civilization. Croatian hatred for Serbs became virtually racist. Some Croatian officers proudly identified themselves with the Ustasha, who, they said, also fought for Croatia.

Ethnic relations in Yugoslavia were not foreordained to erupt. With the right leadership and political system, the murderous ethnic cleansing could have been avoided. It was opportunistic politicians playing their nationalist cards to put themselves into power that made this happen. The only thing that needs cleansing are ex-Yugoslavia's leading political figures.

main highway from Zagreb to Split, chief city of the Dalmatian coast. With these cut, one had to first go to Rijeka, tucked up under the Istrian peninsula, and then journey by road or boat down the coast. In effect, Dalmatia, home of an important regionalist movement in Croatian domestic politics, was semi-isolated from Zagreb. The tourists who flocked to the Dalmatian Coast, Croatia's big foreign-exchange earner, didn't come during the war years. Recovery of Knin was thus an urgent political, economic, and military vital interest for Croatia, and Croat officers swore they would not rest until all of Croatia was again under their control. Even Croatian antiwar pacifists wanted their territories recovered.

In 1992, the Serb-Croat front calmed. A United Nations Protection Force (UNPROFOR) patrolled ceasefire lines, observed by both sides because both wanted a respite, unlike the war in Bosnia, which continued at a low but hideous level. The media focused us too narrowly on Bosnia, as if that were the only problem in the region. The Serb-Croat fight was deemed more or less settled; after all, UNPROFOR was in place. This was seriously deceptive, for Croatia and Bosnia were simply different fronts of the same war. The U.S. Central Intelligence Agency and news media did not help matters when they published maps showing the extent of Serbian conquests in Bosnia alone or in Croatia alone, and on two different maps, as if to imply they were two wars. They were one war.

AND WHAT OF BOSNIA?

There may be a Bosnia, but it probably won't be as big as its traditional borders. Two forces conspire to carve out big chunks of Bosnia for themselves: Serbia and Croatia. This has happened before. In 1939, as the original (Serbian monarchist) Yugoslavia shuddered toward breakup, the leading politicians of Serbia and Croatia, Cvetković and Maček, respectively, did a deal on Bosnia, which both Serbia and Croatia claimed. They devised a line to split Bosnia, half to go to Serbia and the other half to Croatia. The Cvetković-Maček agreement was never implemented; World War II soon began, and in 1941 the Nazis set up a puppet Croatian fascist state that included all of Bosnia.

Visiting London in May 1995, Croat President Tudjman dined with Paddy Ashdown, leader of Britain's Liberal Democratic party, and had a bit to drink. A newsman asked Tudjman about the future Bosnia. On the back of a menu, he drew an S-shaped line that roughly divides Bosnia, the western portion for Croatia, the eastern for Serbia. He had probably already reached an agreement with Milošević to partition Bosnia along the lines of Cvetković-Maček.

Often neglected is the fact that Croats have claims on Bosnia as well. The full name of the republic is Bosnia-Herzegovina; Herzegovina is the southernmost fifth of the republic, triangular in shape, mostly Croat in ethnic makeup, with Mostar as its (once) beautiful chief city. Herzegovina is commonly described as the heartland of Croatian fascism, for it historically produced the fiercest Croatian nationalists. It was there that local Croats set up their mini-republic of "Herzeg-Bosna," much like Bosnian Serbs set up their "Republika Srpska." Croats do not like being ruled by Muslims any more than do Serbs. For the better part of a year, in 1993-94, Muslims and Croats fought each other in Herzegovina. The Croats were perfectly willing to knife the Muslims in the back for their mini-republic. Croats claim that historically they have never been anti-Muslim the way Serbs are; the Ottomans occupied only about half of Croatia, and for not nearly as long as they occupied Serbia. There may be some truth to the assertion, but one would never have known it from the ferocity of Croat-Muslim fighting. For a while, there was a three-sided war in Bosnia.

Three Balkan Wars and How They Ended

The war in ex-Yugoslavia in the early 1990s gains clarity if we look at it as the Third Balkan War—a purposeful, planned move to enlarge the power and territory of the Serbian state. The first two Balkan wars also offered some clues as to how the third would end. Alas, not many decision makers studied the Balkan wars in preparation for peacekeeping moves in ex-Yugoslavia.

The First Balkan War (1912-13) concerned how big Ottoman Turkey's holdings in Europe should be and ended when a military coalition pushed Turkey back to its present corner of Europe. The Second Balkan War (1913) concerned how big Bulgaria should be and ended when a military coalition forced Bulgaria to give up some of its recent conquests. The Third Balkan War concerned how big Serbia should be and ended when a military coalition forced Serbia to give up much of its conquests.

The first two Balkan Wars narrowly preceded World War I and were to some extent evidence of the breakdown of the great-power balance that had kept general peace in Europe, albeit with increasing difficulty, for a century. The Third Balkan War broke out in 1991 as Yugoslavia disintegrated, which to some degree reflected the end of the superpower duopoly that had kept Europe in peaceful though tense equilibrium for more than four decades.

The First Balkan War was a multilateral (Montenegro, Serbia, Greece, and Bulgaria) effort to erase the remaining belt of Turkish territory that stretched across the peninsula from Albania on the Adriatic to Thrace on the Black Sea. Bulgaria gained Western Thrace (giving Bulgaria direct access to the Mediterranean Sea) and claimed Macedonia, both of which had been part of the medieval Bulgarian kingdom.

This claim led immediately to the Second Balkan War. Serbia and Greece refused to evacuate Macedonia, and Bulgaria attacked its erstwhile allies. Meanwhile Romania struck Bulgaria from the north in order to obtain Southern Dobrudja (the wedge of land south of the mouth of the Danube). It is for such behavior that "Balkan war" connotes an opportunistic pile-on. Overextended Bulgaria lost, and Greece and Serbia divided Macedonia between them and ordered the local inhabitants to speak, respectively, only Greek and Serbian. (Not all complied.) After World War I, Greece took Western Thrace from Bulgaria. In World Wars I and II, Bulgaria, allied with Germany, occupied Macedonia and Western Thrace only to be thrown out as the wars neared their end.

The Third Balkan War (1991-95) ended when a military coalition (Croatia and Bosnia with the backing of the United States, Germany, and other powers) pushed Serb forces out of most of Croatia and much of Bosnia. There wasn't even much of a fight, for by then Milošević had decided to cut his losses and settle the war. Milošević was a great opportunist, intent on preserving his political power, rather than a great Serbian nationalist. All three Balkan Wars were about territory and power.

UNPROFOR Lousy, IFOR Excellent

The UN Protective Force, originally designed to supervise the Serb-Croat ceasefire of 1992, quickly found its mission expanded to Bosnia, where, without benefit of any ceasefire agreement, it was to get food and medicine to civilians and prevent civilian casualties. The wrong mission in the wrong place with the wrong rules quickly became not only a failure but a laughingstock—and not due to the abilities of the French, British, Spanish and other soldiers assigned to UNPROFOR.

The problem was weak and vague ROEs (rules of engagement), the rules that tell soldiers when and how they may shoot back. They were assigned strictly as peacekeepers—when there was no peace to keep—and allowed to shoot only if clearly attacked. They were under specific orders to not participate in any fighting—even to defend UN-designated "safe areas." As a result, Bosnian Serb forces laughed at them, ignored them, and sometimes arrested and handcuffed them before proceeding to massacre Muslim civilians, as in Srebrenica in 1995. The Dutch UNPROFOR unit, good soldiers all, just stood by. UNPROFOR's ROEs were inherently weak because the UN can be no stronger than its quarreling members, and they never wanted UNPROFOR to fight a war. The Serbs knew this and took full advantage of it.

IFOR (Implementation Force) took over in 1996 and was totally different. First, it wasn't UN; it was NATO, sometimes described as the world's most effective alliance, with an integrated command structure and lots of practice working together. This time the United States was there, contributing about a third of IFOR's 60,000 personnel. IFOR came only *after* the Dayton accord produced a ceasefire, the only way peacekeeping can possibly work. And IFOR arrived with heavy weapons, ready to fight a war, and with "robust ROEs" to shoot whenever necessary. The Serb forces did not laugh at IFOR. While IFOR was in place, the ceasefire held. The moral: peacekeeping is not for peace marchers; it's for warfighters.

Superficially, it looks like Bosnian Croats and Muslims patched things up with a U.S.-brokered agreement signed in Washington in March 1994. They agreed to both form a Croat-Muslim federation within Bosnia and then confederate this with Croatia proper. The pact solidified Croatian power in Herzegovina and provided Bosnian Muslims with much easier access to arms and munitions. The improved relations mean that Croatian airfields and ports serve as conduits for war materiel from sympathetic Islamic states. How well this agreement, which was pushed on Croatia and Bosnia by the U.S. ambassador to Zagreb, will last is highly questionable. By the time you read this, it could be a dead letter. Croatian currency, license plates, and police uniforms are standard in Herzeg-Bosna, as if it were already annexed to Croatia. Local Croats talk as if they are citizens of Croatia.

What Should We Do?

"It's none of our business," say many Americans. "If these people want to kill each other, stand back and let them." Things are not that simple. If the Balkans explode, many U.S. interests will be damaged. If fighting expands to Albania, Greece and Turkey would join the fray (against each other), collapsing NATO's eastern flank. NATO and the United States would stand revealed as powerless, something our adversaries around the world would carefully note. Remembering how both world wars began in East Europe, we should pay attention to stabilizing the region.

First, we are already in it up to our elbows. The United States, operating through our embassy in Zagreb, tilted us quietly but strongly toward Croatia. We devised the "confederation" of Croatia and Bosnia in March 1994 and made sure they got weapons from third countries (even Iran), desite the arms embargo we said we adhered to. We arranged to have retired U.S. Army officers, working for a private contractor, train the Croatian and Bosnian armies. Apparently they were advisors for the lighting takeovers of Western Slavonia and Krajina in 1995. (We should be proud of that.) Before you criticize such secretive moves, remember Croat military victories are what laid the basis for the Dayton peace effort.

What else can we do? First, a moderate U.S. military presence—first in Macedonia, then in Bosnia—serves notice on disruptive forces that we are on hand to stop them. But a massive U.S. presence is infeasible and even counterproductive. We want the countries of the region to band together to look out for their own security. Hungary (as well as Poland and the Czech Republic) wants to join NATO. Such an expansion would give us a highway into the Balkans. (Hungary already served as the jumping-off point for U.S. forces moving into Bosnia in 1996.)

Other countries may not be ready for NATO membership but could still participate in regional security. Poor, frightened Albania threw itself in America's arms to get protection from Serbia. We help equip the impoverished Albanian army and conduct joint exercises. In return, we get an Albanian airbase. Other Balkan countries are interested in forming similar relationships. By building a ring of political, economic, and military arrangements around obstreperous elements in the Balkans, we can promote (but not guarantee) stability, and at low cost. The ultimate question: does America wish to lead?

Within a few years, I suspect, the Serbian areas of Bosnia will become part of a Greater—well, somewhat enlarged—Serbia, the Croatian areas part of Croatia, and the leftover bits a Bosnian rump state. Bosnia, already "confederated" with Croatia, could become a Croatian protectorate in all but name. We can live with that, and so can the antagonists. What then was the purpose of the November 1995 Dayton agreement? To stop the killing, especially of civilians, that's all. Any grander aims—a unified Bosnian state, restoration of old republic boundaries, the

East Europe's Unsettled Borders?

Some people, including more than a few academics and journalists, suppose the borders of East Europe are uncertain and contested. This is not true; no European country has any border claims on another. The 1975 Helsinki Final Act affirmed all of Europe's boundaries and has been signed by every country of Europe. The touchiest situation—the Oder-Neise border between Poland and Germany—has been confirmed and reconfirmed. Even Hungary has no claims on any of its neighbors, all of whom have sizeable Magyar minorities; Budapest seeks only language rights for them.

Still, what's on paper today may be torn up tomorrow. There are a few spots that bear watching, aside from the problems discussed in this chapter between Serbs, Croats, and Bosnians. Another problem of ex-Yugoslavia is potentially dangerous: Macedonia. All four of its neighbors—Serbia, Bulgaria, Greece, and Albania—have occupied part of Macedonia's territory at one time or another and probably wouldn't mind doing so again. Ownership of Macedonia prompted the Second Balkan War (see earlier box). The oldest claim is Bulgaria's, for Macedonia was part of the Bulgarian kingdom before the Turkish conquest, and the languages are very close. Greece is still enraged that an upstart country could take the name of Alexander the Great's original homeland. The Serbian monarchy used to refer to Macedonia as South Serbia and called the language bad Serbian. About one-fourth of Macedonia's population is ethnic Albanian, and Albania seized good chunk of Macedonia during World War II. A small UN force in Macedonia, with some 500 U.S. soldiers participating, has calmed and stabilized the situation, so that no one has any claims on the table.

Romanian nationalists still hearken back to the Greater Romania of the interwar years. They want the ex-Soviet republic of Moldova back, along with a strip of territory along the Dnester River inhabited by a mixed population. And Poland and Lithuania have problems with their minorities on each other's territory. Still, at present East Europe could not be called a steaming caldron of conflicting land claims.

arrest of war criminals—is far beyond the abilities of IFOR, its smaller successor SFOR (Stabilization Force) or any other outsiders. The Bosnia-wide elections in 1996, provided for by Dayton, were rigged or boycotted by Bosnian Serbs and Croats and settled nothing. The elected Serb, Croat, and Bosnian leaders never even met to set up a joint presidency. Outside, chiefly U.S., pressure to make these elections part of a healing process were misguided and infeasible. It was much too late to heal anything. Those who wish to implement Dayton to the letter should understand that it would take a long and massive U.S. and NATO presence with the possibility of serious fighting. No outside powers have any national interest in the particular boundaries of Bosnia.

WHAT COULD BLOW UP

The region could still blow up. The likeliest place for a blowup is Kosovo, Serbia's southern province and, before the 1389 Turkish conquest, heartland of the Serbian kingdom and church. Now its population is some 90 percent ethnic Albanian, but Serbs swear they will never relinquish it and govern it under martial law. Some Serbian militiamen in Bosnia, such as the gangster-murderer Arkan, swore they would "cleanse" Kosovo after they finished with Bosnia. Tirana claims low-level ethnic cleansing and the creation of refugees has long been underway. Although the local (underground) Kosovar leadership urges self-restraint, the province could explode at any time.

The following scenario is thus possible. Fighting in Bosnia could flare up as newly equipped Bosnian forces probe for areas where the Serbs are stretched thin and lack heavy weapons. In the meantime, if Serbia has not returned Eastern Slavonia to Croatia, Croatia would attack to regain its lost territory. With classic Balkan opportunism, Bosnians and Croats could pile onto a weakened Serbia. Bosnian Muslims and Croats would, of course, then settle accounts with local Serbs. One might expect renewed ethnic cleansing, this time with Serbs as victims.

Meanwhile, the underground ethnic-Albanian leadership of Kosovo, possibly in consultation with Tirana, would sense that this is their chance and attempt to seize control of what it has already declared an independent state. Serbian resistance to this attempt would be savage, and refugees and fighting would spill over into neighboring Albania and Macedonia, thus internationalizing the war. One must include the possibility that Greece, an historic ally of Serbia, would move to secure its claims to southern Albania (Northern Epirus to the Greeks) and southern Macedonia, which, according to the Greeks, should not even exist. It is also conceivable that Hungary could take an interest in northern Voivodina, where 400,000 ethnic Magyars are virtual hostages under Serbian control and pressure. Hungary held this area during World War II. The Third Balkan War could be quite large. If the United States has no interest or presence in the region, the chances of a blowup are much greater. Only the United States can stabilize situations like this. If we don't lead, no one will.

SUGGESTED READINGS

AKHAVAN, PAYAM, AND ROBERT HOWSE, eds. *Yugoslavia, the Former and Future: Reflections by Scholars from the Region.* Washington, DC: Brookings, 1995.

BENNETT, CHRISTOPHER. *Yugoslavia's Bloody Collapse: Causes, Course and Consequences.* New York: New York University Press, 1995.

BUGAJSKI, JANUSZ. *Ethnic Politics in Eastern Europe: A Guide to Nationality Policies, Organizations, and Parties.* Armonk, NY: M. E. Sharpe, 1994.

CIGAR, NORMAN. *Genocide in Bosnia: The Policy of "Ethnic Cleansing."* College Station, TX: A&M University Press, 1995.

COHEN, LENARD J. *Broken Bonds: Yugoslavia's Disintegration and Balkan Politics in Transition*, 2d ed. Boulder, CO: Westview, 1995.

GAGNON, V.P., JR. "Serbia's Road to War," *Journal of Democracy* 5 (April 1994) 2:117-31.

GLENNY, MISHA. *The Fall of Yugoslavia: The Third Balkan War*. New York: Penguin, 1996.

LAMPE, JOHN R. *Yugoslavia as History: Twice There Was a Country*. New York: Cambridge University Press, 1996.

MALCOLM, NOEL. *Bosnia: A Short History*. New York: New York University Press, 1994.

MOJZES, PAUL. *Yugoslavian Inferno: Ethnoreligious Warfare in the Balkans*. New York: Continuum, 1995.

RAMET, SABRINA P. *Balkan Babel: The Disintegration of Yugoslavia from the Death of Tito to Ethnic War*, 2d ed. Boulder, CO:Westview, 1996.

WOODWARD, SUSAN L. *Balkan Tragedy: Chaos and Dissolution after the Cold War*. Washington, DC: Brookings, 1995.

CHAPTER TEN

Lessons, Hopes, Fears

SOME LESSONS

1. Socialist Economies Work Poorly

They don't collapse overnight; they simply slow down and fall behind capitalist economies. Let's get straight what is here meant by socialism: state ownership and control of the means of production. What is not meant by socialism is the welfare state, which is actually just a variation on capitalism. The welfare state, which is promoted under a variety of labels (social democracy, democratic socialism, social market, and American-style liberalism), taxes the better-off to pay for a welfare floor or social safety net for those lower down the economic ladder. It also supervises the macroeconomy by guiding interest rates, the money supply, and foreign trade.

All industrial societies are welfare states, some more than others. We can get a rough idea of the magnitude of a welfare state from the percent of gross national product that is absorbed by taxes each year. This figure ranges from 30 percent in the United States to 50 percent in Scandinavia. (However, much of this money does not go for "welfare" expenditures but for ordinary government expenses such as defense, police and fire departments, and administration.) In other words, there is only a 20 percentage point difference between the expenditures of the highly developed cradle-to-grave welfare states of Sweden, Norway, and Denmark and the relatively parsimonious expenditures of the United States. The expenditures of the rest of West Europe fall between these two extremes. The amount of welfare a country has is largely a matter of taste and political culture. Swedes want and like a big welfare state; Americans do not.

The economies of advanced industrialized countries are pretty much the same: they all have capitalism, markets, and competition. Swedish capitalists, for example, are among the world's fiercest. The "social market" model of Germany

Is Marxism Dead?

For most applied purposes, yes; but an honest thinker can still be a Marxist. One might at first suppose that the colossal failure of communism and its ouster in East Europe "proves" Marx was wrong. It certainly demonstrates that trying to apply a system based on Marx's ideas can easily lead to catastrophe. Clearly, Lenin's concentration of power led directly to Stalin's abuse of that power. But remember, Marx concentrated on criticizing capitalism and predicting its downfall; he had practically nothing to say about socialism except that it would be better than capitalism.

Various interesting and valid criticisms of capitalism are still around. Some of them might fit under the label of Marxist or Marxian. Just asking certain questions shows the continuing relevance of Marx. For example, does capitalism, unless regulated, increasingly concentrate wealth in the hands of a few? Does capitalism require massive amounts of debt—consumer, business, government—in order to keep running? Does big money influence elections in democracies?

When Marxism is simply a mode of inquiry, it is quite useful. It trains us to look below the surface, to ask who really benefits, and to view conflict as the norm. Where Marxist political systems are put into practice, Marxism becomes an excuse for tyranny. Marxist regimes resist probes below their bland surface lest they reveal sharp class differences and smoldering conflicts. If Marx returned to life, he'd get in trouble in Communist countries. One can and should split the theoretical from the applied. Unfortunately, politically committed Marxists emphasize the connection between theory and practice. (They often use the German word *Praxis* to make it sound more scientific.) But if they persist in arguing that practice determines theory, they in effect are refuting the whole Marxist package. One of the great challenges for modern Marxists will be to explain what went wrong in East Europe. After they find a valid explanation, many will no longer be Marxists.

is frequently discussed in East Europe. The *Sozialmarkt* of Ludwig Erhard in the 1950s certainly promoted economic growth, and the term has a nice ring to it, a combination of a market system with social concern. Examined more closely, Germany's social market is just plain capitalism with some state prodding to direct investment into recovering from war damage, such as encouraging apartment building construction and selling off East Germany's backward state industries.

In only a few West European countries does the government own much of the means of production. France, Austria, and Italy have considerable state ownership (Sweden does not), but these firms are run largely like capitalist enterprises. They compete on a world market, are expected to make money, and are not run by government. They may be able to get government loans and subsidies more easily than private industry, hence they may be less efficient than privately owned

What Is The Alternative to Capitalism?

Do you mean to say that there is no alternative to capitalism, the reader may ask. You mean this is it? The capitalist rat race: work hard, consume a lot, and never know quiet contentment. No, I think there is an alternative to capitalism, only it's not socialism. If you don't like the sometimes brutal forces of the market and of materialism, you can opt out by joining bohemia. Bohemianism is a rejection of the prevailing bourgeois culture of hard work and high consumption in favor of a laid-back ethic of beards, battered clothes, and individualism. Bohemia (mistakenly named after the Czech lands in earlier centuries that were the supposed homeland of the gypsies) has taken many forms over the years, but it always features a rejection of conventionality. Artists in garrets (as in the opera *La Bohème*), angry writers in blue jeans, or hippies with guitars, all show their contempt for the conventional or "square" life. They do not live to work and would rather have leisure time than material possessions. Bohemians and leftists overlap; both reject the bourgeoisie, the former culturally and the latter politically. Most bohemians have leftist political values, and leftists tend to bohemian lifestyles.

Individuals can opt into bohemia; society as a whole cannot. This was the great mistake of socialist thinkers, such as Marx, Engels, and Lenin, who themselves were bohemians in lifestyle. They supposed that their contempt for bourgeois culture could become dominant and serve to build a humane, just society where material output would be so high that people would cease being materialistic. It didn't work; the socialist economy never delivered the high material output. Nor did socialist teaching create a New Socialist Man, who would work for the sake of society. People generally need the motivation of material rewards to persuade them to work hard and produce a lot. And if one could devise a society composed entirely of bohemians, no one would do much work. Actually, bohemians need a square society to live off and make fun of. Bohemians define themselves in their opposition to a conventional lifestyle.

When I say, "Socialism works poorly," I am not urging everyone to become an eager capitalist or a conformist bourgeois. I am suggesting that the opposite of capitalism is not socialism but bohemianism. If you don't like capitalist society—and there are several good reasons why you might dislike it—you can make an individual choice to drop out, all the way or part way. But, please, do not try to inflict your individual choice on the rest of society.

companies. These state sectors grew haphazardly and piecemeal for a variety of reasons—to boost industry, develop poor regions, prevent bankruptcies and unemployment, and punish wartime collaborators—but not to usher in a socialist utopia. There is little element of socialist planning about these industries; they operate on the basis of supply and demand. Accordingly, do not confuse the welfare states of West Europe—even if they have some state-owned factories—with the socialist states of Communist East Europe. Neither are welfare states "middle ways" between capitalism and socialism. They are capitalist economies with some of the rough edges smoothed by government programs.

For the socialist systems, in which the state owns and runs virtually all the industry, the verdict is now in: they worked poorly. In absolute terms, they showed some growth. In relative terms, they were weak performers and fell behind the market economies. Their technologies, designs, workmanship, and quality control rendered their products uncompetitive on world markets. Did anyone buy Romanian stereos? Missing from their economies were the crucial ingredients of innovation, risk taking, and customer service, items Marx and the Marxists ignored. Without them, socialist economies fell behind.

This is not such a tragedy, some people say. So what if socialist economies underperform capitalist economies? Socialism, by promoting greater equality, is inherently fairer than capitalism. (Overall, incomes were more equally distributed in East Europe than in Western countries, but highly placed Communist party people gave themselves generous extra helpings. Some had lavish estates and secret Swiss bank accounts.) But is equality of income and of the standard of living a good thing? Should lazy workers be paid as much as energetic ones? If they are, motivation collapses and productivity declines.

Some defenders of socialism say material goods are not the be-all and end-all of human existence. Capitalism has brainwashed people to want more and more, they argue (and it may well be true). Socialism teaches people to move away from material pursuits and toward cultural and leisure activities. Perhaps such a shift would be a good idea, but it certainly didn't happen in socialist countries, where people were often more obsessed than Westerners with acquiring a bit of material comfort. One of the great lessons of East Europe is that people really are materialistic, and little but material incentives motivates them to work. As an American philosopher once said, we live in a material world.

2. Political Culture Is Not Very Malleable

The Communists had over 40 years to remold East European political culture, and they failed miserably. The basic Stalinist premise that attitudes can be molded is simply wrong. The Communists may have controlled the overt means of socialization, the mass media and school system, but these were vastly outweighed by the informal means of socialization found in family, friends, and the church. The biggest factor working against popular acceptance of communism was probably the direct and personal perceptions by people of the system's pervasive inequality, inefficiency, and corruption. The Communist media's constant spouting of propaganda in the face of a deficient reality simply turned people off. They became anti-Communist or cynical or both. Political culture has a considerable life of its own and is not easily changed by government edict.

3. Empires Are Expensive

Retaining East Europe cost the Soviets a bundle and economically netted them very little. Their imperial costs, plus the slow deterioration of the socialist economies, left them broke and behind the West. It is for reasons such as these that no empire lasts forever.

4. There Is No Middle Ground between a Communist and a Democratic System

The two cannot be blended. Communist regimes are so unpopular that permitting even a little criticism unleashes a torrent of protest. Then the regime must either crack down with repression or go all the way to democracy, thus putting itself out of business. Happily, the Communist regimes of East Europe consented to going out of business.

5. Likewise, There Is No Middle Ground between a Centrally Controlled and a Market Economy

Elements of the market, introduced experimentally into centrally controlled economies, subvert them. In Yugoslavia, Hungary, and China, such experiments produced initial growth, but they soon developed bottlenecks that could be relieved only by further marketizing the economy. After a while in such mixed systems, the state sector will be minor and the hold of Communist officials weak. Again the regime must decide whether to put itself out of business or revert to the controlled economy. China now faces this choice. Some Balkan regimes talked about "third ways" between capitalism and socialism. This is the sign of not-so-ex-Communists who do not wish to relinquish power. They should be warned that such paths have never worked for long. This brings us to the next point.

6. A Rapid Transition to a Free Economy is Best

This was and still is controversial. Many observers, both inside East Europe (and the former Soviet Union) and outside, blame "shock therapy," the sudden introduction of a market economy and private enterprise, for the poverty, dislocations, and extremist politics such countries have endured. Maybe, but a 1996 World Bank study of 26 East European and ex-Soviet economies concluded that the quick reformers recovered from their downturns sooner and enjoyed faster growth. No pain, no gain. The countries that stall on building a free market are wastefully subsidizing certain industries and the Communist fatcats who run them. Such systems are marked by high inflation, for the government is printing more money than there are goods to buy. Economists trained under the Communists sometimes have trouble grasping this basic element. Reasonable people may disagree over the precise means of making the transition; every country does it a bit differently. The Czech Republic under Prime Minister Klaus, for example, bought labor peace and low unemployment by generous government handouts.

Anti-Ifonlyism

As noted previously, I think honest Marxists can contribute to our understanding of the debacle of communism in East Europe. Dishonest Marxists (and other shallow thinkers) will try to dodge intellectual responsibility by advancing "if only" claims. They will pick out one or more specific problems and announce that things would have gone differently and better "if only" such and such a factor had been corrected. You may encounter such speculative arguments as the following:

1. If only Lenin had lived a few years longer, he would have been able to establish real socialism.
2. If only Lenin had been firmer and prevented Stalin from rising to power, the Soviet system and subsequently the East European systems would have been much better.
3. If only Stalin had had a nicer personality...
4. If only Poland had stuck to the Curzon Line as its eastern border...
5. If only Stalin hadn't signed the 1939 pact with Hitler...
6. If only Roosevelt hadn't signed the Yalta agreement...
7. If only Stalin hadn't selected such repulsive little puppets to set up the first Communist regimes in East Europe...
8. If only Truman hadn't overreacted and started the Cold War...
9. If only Moscow had permitted East European lands to take their own paths to socialism, as in Yugoslavia...
10. If only Communist officials had been more honest and energetic and had set a better example...
11. If only East Europeans had worked harder and been more enthusiastic about socialism...
12. If only Communist regimes had eased up a bit and offered major reforms much earlier...

You can go on and on with such philosophical junk food. The basic line is a tautology: If only things had been different, then they would not have been the same. A person who makes an "if only" claim doesn't want to come to grips with the fact that things happen for good and sufficient reason, not by accident. Indeed, the non-accidental nature of history is a basic point of Marxism, one Marx picked up from Hegel.

The structure of the Soviet system let the most ruthless power manipulator take it over. Stalin and his system were no accidents. The Stalinist straitjacket imposed on East Europe was required to make sure these lands stayed absolutely obedient. When the Stalinist controls were eased, a tidal wave of criticism and even hatred poured out. When the controls were abandoned, the regimes collapsed. There was nothing accidental or gratuitous about the East European police states. Their draconic controls flowed directly from the Soviet effort to establish alien, unpopular regimes. When the Soviets abandoned that effort, the police controls eased and then the regimes folded. An "if only" claim can be fun as a game of speculation, but nothing more.

SOME HOPES

1. East Europe Will Join the European Union

It will take some time and much adjustment, but East Europeans hardly have a choice in the matter. At first, only six West European countries (France, West Germany, Italy, Belgium, the Netherlands, and Luxembourg—Charlemagne's original Holy Roman Empire) signed the Treaty of Rome that founded the Common Market in 1957. Britain and Scandinavia turned up their noses at the Six and joined a looser grouping, the European Free Trade Association, dubbed the Outer Seven. The Common Market, though, produced such prosperity that by 1963 Britain too had applied to join. Although rebuffed by de Gaulle's "Non," Britain, along with Denmark and Ireland, did join the European Union, the EU (as the Common Market now calls itself), in 1973. Later Greece (1981) and Spain and Portugal (1986) were eager to join. At the end of 1994, Finland, Sweden, and Austria made it the EU of the Fifteen, encompassing nearly all of West Europe. EU membership means a gigantic market, efficiency, modernity, and prosperity. Goods, services, labor, and capital freely flow across members' borders.

A few countries with peculiar situations may decide to stay outside the EU. Norway with its oil and Switzerland with its neutrality and banking secrecy have so far rejected membership. But no East European country has the luxury of saying, "No, we won't join the EU. We'll become another Switzerland—rich and aloof. Or maybe we'll discover lots of oil and become another Norway." East Europeans look at the EU and ache to join a paradise of 370 million well-fed West Europeans with a combined 1995 GDP of $7.4 trillion. East Europeans see in the EU their only major market, investor, and employer of surplus labor. They simply have no choice about joining the EU, and the Central European lands have applied and already have associate status.

Full membership will take some years. Poland, the Czech Republic, and Hungary will be the first, probably early in the next century. Applicants must demonstrate that they have a market economy, political democracy, and a will to become Europeans. Brussels made Spain and Portugal wait several years and participate in difficult negotiations. The good news here is that stringent membership requirements will force the East European countries to shape up. They will not be considered for membership if they still have a state-run economy; it must be a free market economy. They will not be considered if they do not have a thorough and proven democracy; the Balkan lands flunk on this ground. Regimes that govern with riot police, abuse ethnic minorities, and mouth anti-Semitism will likely not be admitted. Remember, the EU is not eager to admit everyone. Furthermore, East Europe will have to clean up its pollution catastrophe and meet fairly demanding EU environmental standards. East European air may become breathable again. The necessity of joining the EU means the governments of East Europe have only a limited menu to choose from. They have got to come up to West European standards and cannot dawdle.

More "Fried Snowballs"? Is Market Socialism Possible?

No, at least not in a stable, long-term manner. Introducing elements of a market economy into a centrally run economy quickly brings new difficulties and bottlenecks that can be solved only by introducing more market elements. After a while, you have only a market economy left.

The question is an important one that has enticed thinkers for decades. The idea of a system that combines the theoretical best of socialism—its emphasis on equality and fairness—with the consumer plenty of the market has long been intriguing. Some socialists still think that such a combination is possible and desirable.

The evidence seems to be against it. Where tried, market socialist economies veer more and more toward the free market. The regime, worried that it is putting itself out of business, curbs and restricts the market elements and returns partway to the centrally run economy. The experiment of market-plus-socialism becomes a zigzag of looser and tighter state controls that never find a stable balance and often contribute to economic decline.

To be sure, one can, on paper, chart out which portions of an economy should be state controlled and which should be left to the marketplace's law of supply and demand. Typically, planners specify that major industries, such as steel manufacturing, stay state owned and run according to a central plan. Consumer-oriented industries, such as the making of refrigerators, on the other hand, should become private and competitive. It looks, on paper, like the best of both worlds: big industries for the state and small industries for private entrepreneurs who are better attuned to consumer needs.

Quickly problems appear, what economists call "distortions." The refrigerator manufacturers, operating competitively, try to make the best product in large numbers to obtain the lowest price. But they need steel, and the state-run steel mill will have no incentive to make the best steel in large quantities at the lowest price. Under the government plan, the mill produces only so much steel at a set price. What if not enough steel were produced to satisfy the consumer demand for refrigerators? What if the quality of the steel were wrong or the price too high? "Tough," says the state-owned steel mill, "take it or leave it." State ownership of the steel mill, therefore, produces distortions in the output of refrigerators. A market socialist economy would still have some of the rigidities of straight-out socialism, that is, an inability to respond to markets.

The cure in this case is to make the steel mill part of the market sector by selling it to private investors or its own workers. Competition would quickly appear. The steel mills, now seeking a profit and responding solely to market forces, make more steel of the right quality and price for refrigerator manufacturers. The economy is now a little less distorted. But the steel mills still depend on state-owned industries for their raw materials, the iron ore and coal. But these industries, still operating under a government plan, have little reason to boost their output to suit the now-private steel mills. The solution: Do to the iron and coal mines what you have earlier done to the steel mills. Privatize them into profit-seeking, competitive entities and thereby eliminate another market distortion.

As you can see, by the time you eliminate all the distortions of a market socialist economy, you have no socialist elements left. Like a little Pac-Man, the market sector eats up the socialist sector.

This is what happened to the two biggest experiments in market socialism, Yugoslavia and China. Communist authorities, trying to add the vigor of the market to the control and planning of socialism, permitted the market sector to expand in both these countries. But they choked when they saw that it would keep expanding until it subverted the entire socialist structure. So, when the process started picking up speed, they clamped down with new restrictions on the market sector, such as limits on profits and firm size. They subsidized money-losing state industries because they feared bankruptcy and unemployment. Massive distortions appeared. Inflation, inequality, and unemployment—long portrayed as evils of capitalism—shot up. Corruption grew worse than ever because there were now more ways to use public office for private gain.

The Yugoslavs, after decades of not wanting to admit that their highly touted market socialist economy was in decline, saw their country collapse as its most prosperous republics, Slovenia and Croatia, fled from having to pay for Belgrade's ruinous subsidies to state-owned industries and its limits on private capital. The Chinese face the decision of going all the way to a market economy. The Special Economic Zones of the south have recorded the fastest economic growth in history; their tax revenues virtually prop up the state-owned dinosaurs of socialist industry. To go all the way, however, means abandoning socialism, in deed if not in rhetoric. Sooner or later, it seems, a market socialist economy must choose one system or the other.

2. The Russians Don't Panic Over East Europe

With the departure of Soviet troops from Central Europe, the Cold War definitively ended. There are no Russian forces in the region any longer, aside from a handful assigned to Bosnian peacekeeping (under U.S. command). One reason they were not withdrawn more quickly is that there was no housing for them in Russia. Germany actually subsidized Russian troops in East Germany and built barracks for them back in Russia to facilitate their exit. The Warsaw Pact put itself out of business, and NATO isn't quite sure what to do with itself. Most European armies are small; many countries are ending or shortening conscription in favor of volunteer armies, as Britain has done for many years.

The happiest point about the rebirth of East Europe is that the Russians have demonstrated to themselves that the retention of East Europe really was not vital to their security. At long last Moscow has shaken off the argument posed by Stalin, Khrushchev, and Brezhnev, that East Europe is the Soviet Union's defensive shield that must never be given up. It was simply not true. In fact, Soviet control of East Europe made the Cold War happen and created the massive insecurity that plagued the Soviet Union and the world.

In fact with the breakup of the Soviet Union, Russia now barely borders East Europe (only where Poland meets Kaliningrad Oblast, the wedge of old Prussia now separated from Russia by Lithuania). Otherwise, Belarus and Ukraine now form a belt between Russia and East Europe.

In terms of their economies and politics, a democratic and prosperous East Europe is an important example and trading partner for Russia and the other Soviet successor states. As for NATO, Moscow need not worry. NATO has become totally unthreatening and is moving slowly in adding new members, although the Central Europeans are slated to join. Even if Poland, the Czech Republic, and Hungary join NATO, they are unlikely to have any foreign troops on their soil and will pose no threat to Russia. It would be a mistake to let Russia have a veto over their joining NATO, as it would show Western weakness. If NATO is to expand, let it happen when Russia is weak and cautious.

3. East Europe Turns Capitalist and Prosperous

This is happening rather rapidly but still takes some time and much pain. Within two years of the economic "shock therapy" that began at the start of 1990, the Polish economy began to turn around and show signs of vigorous growth. By now most of the Polish, Czech, and Hungarian economies are in the private sector. The Balkan countries lagged behind, but ultimately have little choice: get capitalist fast or fall even farther behind. Most East Europeans are frightened of the tremendous economic restructuring they must undergo in order to compete on world markets. As one worried Hungarian economist told the author in 1990: "Who will buy our [lousy] products?" (The actual word used was considerably stronger than "lousy.") This question could be heard throughout the region. But East European economies have a few things going for them and are learning fast.

First, their wage rates are lower, in some cases much lower, than West European wages. Polish, Czech, and Hungarian labor costs only a fraction of German labor. (Admittedly, German labor costs are the world's highest, about 30 percent higher than in the United States.) And much of the East European workforce is educated (at least through high school) and skilled, although they lack the high-tech knowledge of the advanced countries' labor forces. Most East Europeans want to work. They have glimpsed the good life in the West and want it. In contrast, some of the more prosperous West European lands are showing signs of taking things easy after several decades of hard work. East European productivity is weak, but the introduction of modern machines and newer methods produces major gains in productivity, the key to economic growth. General Electric, for example, bought a majority share of Hungary's Tungsram light bulb industry. With U.S. technology and marketing, General Electric now manufactures for the European market (going up against the Netherlands' Philips, for example).

At first it may seem that all the good products are made elsewhere in unbeatable quality and price. But no one knows what tomorrow's fast-growth areas will be. If you had predicted a quarter-century ago that people would be wearing fancy, mostly leather athletic shoes, selling for $50 and up, and made in Southeast Asia, you would have been dismissed as a nut. Who would pay that much for sneakers? Who knows what East Europe will make? They will probably start out by imitating the West, but soon they will develop their own designs and innovations.

West European, American, and Japanese investors will set up shop in East Europe to take advantage of the low wages plus the presumed access to the EU. Without such access, foreign investors will quickly lose interest. You're not going to manufacture light bulbs, cars, or cosmetics for the Czech market; you're going to manufacture them for the European market. Westinghouse didn't go into Spain in the 1970s just because the Spanish economy was growing and wages were low. It went in because Spain was likely to enter the Common Market, which it did. This is the great motivator for East Europe to join the EU. No EU membership, no major foreign investment.

Some critics on the left may object that foreign investment means exploitation. The foreigners are not investing out of the goodness of their hearts but to take advantage of the low wages and the fear of unemployment. They plan to sweat the maximum profit from helpless East Europeans. East Europe will become the poorly paid proletariat of the First World. The answer to this silly argument is that, if you don't want the exploitation, keep out the foreign investment and stay poor. Virtually all foreign investment flows into situations where investors think they can get the best returns. American industry was in large part founded in the nineteenth century by massive inflows of British and French capital seeking to "exploit" American workers. After World War II, U.S. capital flowed to West Europe for the same reason. Such workers do not stay exploited for long, however. After a while their productivity and wages catch up with those of the higher-cost nation. Playing on a famous quip of Oscar Wilde's, a 1990 British report noted: "There is only one thing worse than being exploited, and that is not being exploited."

The foreign investors provide badly needed management skills, technical know-how, and competitive designs. They are showing East Europeans how to market for export. Just as important, they are getting East European competitive juices flowing after four decades of socialist sloth. New service industries and subcontractors are springing up around the foreign investments. Soon the East Europeans will be showing the foreign capitalists a thing or two. Poland and the Czech Republic already run positive trade balances. Prague's budget surplus was the envy of West Europe and enough to make a U.S. Republican weep for joy. East Europe, especially if permitted into the European Union, could be a major economic growth area.

SOME FEARS

1. Authoritarian Regimes Take Over in East Europe

Only one regime could unquestionably be called authoritarian as of this writing: Yugoslavia (the rump state consisting of only Serbia and Montenegro). Elections were unfair, and Milošević rules as a strongman. Mečiar in Slovakia shows strong tendencies to one-man rule. Tudjman's death in Croatia may limit authoritarian tendencies there. Until the elections of 1996 Iliescu in Romania ruled with a party of ex-Communist apparatchiks intent on hanging on to their good positions. Authoritarian tendencies are present elsewhere in the region. Poland's Wałęsa was often exasperated with his fractious parliament and unstable cabinet and suggested a de Gaulle-type of strong presidency to solve Poland's problems. Wałęsa kept a portrait of Marshal Piłsudski on his office wall; Piłsudski came to the same conclusions about the tumult of democracy in the interwar years and took over as strong president in 1935. Wałęsa's electoral ouster in 1995 curbed the problem.

2. Extreme Nationalist Regimes Take Over in East Europe

Often coinciding with authoritarian regimes, extreme nationalism characterizes Romania and ex-Yugoslavia. Some observers suspect their respective strongmen of using nationalism to deflect discontent away from economic privation and onto neighboring states. Many politicians in the region, however, are playing the nationalist card, including Mečiar of Slovakia. At the mass level, many East Europeans still harbor prejudiced stereotypes against other nationalities. A 1993 survey by the U.S. Information Agency, for example, found that most Poles had markedly negative views of Ukrainians, Romanians, and Jews. The survey demonstrated that old prejudices linger a long time and offer demagogues a chance to build their own power by whipping up mass prejudices. Working against both authoritarianism and extreme nationalism is the desire to join the EU.

3. West Europe Fails to Open Its Markets to East Europe

The EU does not expand its membership easily and has a protectionist attitude toward outside producers. The way they see it, the EU already has too many poor members (Greece, Spain, Portugal, and Ireland), who constantly demand that Brussels transfer more funds from the rich members. Some West Europeans are cautious or even afraid of too much competition from low-cost producers. German workers have long complained that their factories were being shipped to Spain and Portugal. Now they do not like seeing them shipped to Poland and the Czech Republic to take advantage of the low labor costs. French farmers long protested over cheaper Spanish and Portuguese vegetables. Now they behold the beautiful vegetables of Bulgaria. Danish pork producers dislike competing with their Polish counterparts.

Is Germany a Menace?

No. Some people fear that a reunited Germany will become a Fourth Reich, an expansionist military power. This is improbable. German democracy is as firm as any in Europe. Only a fringe of Germans talk about the recovery of lost lands to the east. The Oder-Neisse border with Poland has been confirmed and reconfirmed. Germany has accomplished so much more with peace than with war that it is unlikely to return to militarism.

But let's imagine a worst-case scenario. Suppose an economic depression once again puts a right-wing extremist party in control of Germany. Berlin talks about altering the treaties that gave up the eastern territories and builds a large military machine. Does the rest of Europe worry? No, because three European powers have nuclear weapons, and Germany does not. Germany is bound by treaty to acquire no ABC (atomic, bacteriological, or chemical) weapons. The Soviet Union, Britain, and France, either alone or in concert, would be able to block German expansionism.

Let's take an even worse scenario. This rearmed Germany breaks its treaty commitment, acquires some nuclear weapons, and threatens to use them. Such a threat would not be credible. Even if Germany could fling a few dozen warheads at its neighbors, Germany would simply disappear into radioactive rubble under a rain of nuclear weapons from the other European nuclear powers. Crowded Germany—where, as the peace movement noted, the towns are only "two or three kilotons apart"—is extremely vulnerable to nuclear strikes.

Those who hate all nuclear weapons and would ban them worldwide might consider that they are the ultimate guarantee that Germany stays peaceful. Europe and the world simply do not have to worry about a militarily aggressive Germany. German dominance in trade, as we shall consider, is another matter.

Ungenerously, the EU locks out much East European production and allows in only a trickle. The East Europeans aren't asking for much, just for a a few-percent share of the big West European market. But trade blocs can be highly protectionist; the EU answers only to West Europeans, who have strong farm, labor, and manufacturing interest groups. Brussels feels no responsibility for East Europe. With their old Soviet market now gone, East Europeans look around in desperation for new customers. If they don't establish vigorous new trade ties, preferably with the industrialized democracies, they may turn bitterly inward and support authoritarian and/or extreme nationalist movements.

4. A United Europe Locks Out Foreign Goods

The hopeful notion that East Europe will join West Europe in an enlarged European Union has a dark side to it. The EU is already protectionist. They especially protect and subsidize their farmers, and this keeps out much U.S. agricultural production. We get mad. They severely limit the number of Japanese autos that can be imported. The Japanese get mad. The Europeans couldn't care less. Their attitude: "Our first and foremost responsibility is to European farmers and workers. The massive influx of foreign products will put them out of work, and this we will not allow."

The danger here is a series of retaliatory trade barriers. American farmers, who historically have always exported grain, are already angry at being excluded from free competition in Europe. A feeling grows that we buy European products freely while they buy few of ours. (Actually, in the 1990s the United States ran a small trade surplus with Europe.) The mood to retaliate by tariffs or quotas on European goods grows. Any U.S. retaliation will be met by European retaliation in the form of higher tariffs and lower quotas. World trade could then decline, harming everyone's economy. One major component of the Great Depression of the 1930s was fierce trade protectionism that only deepened and prolonged the economic downturn.

Americans look approvingly at a United States of Europe—imitation is the sincerest form of flattery—but must ask what kind of Europe will it be. Will it be one with few barriers to trade or many? Will a united Europe look inward or outward? We were happy to see East Europe escape from its poorly working Comecon bloc. Will they now become locked in another bloc? To be sure, the European Union is the kind of bloc they like. Even better would be a Europe that welcomes trade and competition with the world, not just among its members. A major American investment presence in East Europe would be one way to keep Europe relatively open to foreign trade. This, unfortunately, may not materialize.

5. Foreigners Fail to Invest in East Europe

It was assumed that Western firms would invest heavily in the region and lift it quickly up to world standards of productivity and prosperity. But Western investment was anemic, except (initially) for Hungary. The capitalists mostly held back in caution. Hungary, the favorite of Western investors, got some $5.5 billion from 1990 to 1994, but then new investments slowed to a trickle. The biggest investors in Hungary were the neighboring Austrians, followed by Germans, and then Americans. Poland got $3 billion, with Italian investors in first place (including Fiat), followed by Americans and then French. Czechoslovakia took in $2.3 billion, with Germans as the biggest investors, followed by French and Americans. (Volkswagen bought 31 percent of the Czech Škoda automobile plant.) The Balkan lands and Slovakia attracted only minor foreign investment, a measure of their political and economic uncertainty. Billions more are needed.

What had gone wrong? First, in many cases East European legislatures were slow off the mark in setting up legal frameworks for private ownership. Without assurances that their investments are safe, capitalists don't like to invest. Next, the industrialized world was just then going through a lingering recession and did not have much capital to spare. Furthermore, the costs of German unification were far higher than expected and kept German capitalists busy lifting up their own eastern regions. American firms, who after World War II plunged into West Europe, were slow and cautious about pursuing major investments in East Europe. From bold, expansion-minded risk takers, American capitalists turned into timid pensioners. Much of the problem is that America doesn't have much capital to export. For some years, America has been a major capital importer as foreign investments have poured in to cover soaring U.S. trade and federal budget deficits. The world's biggest debtor nation is the United States.

Without massive foreign investment, East Europe will continue to lag far behind West Europe. On average, East Europeans have only about one-quarter of the per capita GDP of citizens of EU countries. This gap tends to keep East Europe politically and culturally backward and a breeding ground for extremist politics. It was the implied promise of rapidly reaching West European economic standards that fired the imagination of many East Europeans; to cut off this hope could produce a potentially dangerous backlash.

6. Germany Takes Over East Europe

United Germany is already Europe's number-one nation. It has the biggest population (aside from Russia), the largest economy, the most skilled workforce, and the biggest trade surplus. East Europe is its natural area for investment and trade. Between the two world wars, Germany totally dominated trade with East Europe, in part by a deliberate foreign policy. It is likely to do so again, although not necessarily with any sinister designs. After bringing East Germany up to West German levels of productivity and prosperity, Germany will naturally turn its attention eastward, as it has done since the Middle Ages. The impulse for the *Drang nach Osten* (the "push to the east") continues in our day. To the west, as before, Germany faces strong and developed nations. To the east, as before, it faces weak and backward lands that exert an almost magnetic pull on the German imagination.

Would German dominance of East Europe be such a terrible thing? As long as it is purely economic, no. German capital and trade are likely the best and fastest ways for East Europe to rise economically. If it turns into something besides a free and fair economic relationship, though, the picture turns sinister. If Berlin in some future year starts talking about the recovery of lost lands, rigs trade deals, and uses East Europe for toxic waste disposal, we've got a problem. A thrifty, hard-working Germany could be a great benefit and example for East Europe. An arrogant and bossy Germany, however, could remind East Europeans of the Nazi vision of inferior and subservient East Europeans serving as Germany's slaves and victims.

This is why a U.S. presence in East Europe is important: It serves as a counterweight to German power. East Europe should not *belong* to anyone, not to Russians, Germans, or Americans. A moderate American presence—economic, political, and cultural—could serve to keep East Europe open and free. U.S. dominance, considering our present hesitation to get involved overseas, is impossible. Our goal should be to get East Europe out of the pattern it has been trapped in for several centuries: caught between empires.

SUGGESTED READINGS

DAHRENDORF, RALF. *Reflections on the Revolution in Europe.* New York: Random House, 1990.

GRAUBARD, STEPHEN R., ed. *Exit from Communism.* New Brunswick, NJ: Transaction, 1993.

HAVEL, VACLAV. *Summer Meditations.* New York: Knopf, 1992.

HYDE-PRICE, ADRIAN. *The International Politics of East Central Europe.* New York: Manchester University Press, 1996.

KOVÁCS, JÁNOS MÁTYÁS, ed. *Transition to Capitalism? The Communist Legacy in Eastern Europe.* New Brunswick, NJ: Transaction, 1994.

LAMPE, JOHN R., ed. *Creating Capital Markets in Eastern Europe.* Baltimore:Johns Hopkins University Press, 1992.

PRZEWORSKI, ADAM. *Democracy and the Market: Political and Economic Reforms in Eastern Europe and Latin America.* New York: Cambridge, 1991.

INDEX